MASTERING AGILITY

MASTERING AGILITY

SUCCESSFULLY NAVIGATING UNCERTAINTY

By Hans Amell and Kurt Larsson

Minerva Group Publishing

Copyright © 2016 Hans Amell and Kurt Larsson
All rights reserved.
ISBN-10:1522787844
ISBN-13:9781522787846

1. Executive Summary

Agility is the Key!

Batten down the hatches; great change is upon us!
Increasing excitement and uncertainty, in larger and more frequent doses, will define business from here on. To successfully navigate these uncertain waters, you and your corporate crew will need to understand *business agility* and practice *mastering its use,* if you want to survive and thrive in these mounting seas of change.

Colossal megatrends combined with a perfect storm of precarious economic, geopolitical and societal circumstances will make the choppy economic seas of the past look calm in comparison. No business will be safe using tools, methods and management styles developed for yesterday's *business as usual.* The pace of change is becoming frantic and to continue to cope will require a flexible, more agile state of mind, plus powerful tools to help you tackle what is soon to come. Success can no longer be maintained by measuring and *anal-eyes-ing* what has already occurred.

Get Agile Now!

Here is a book packed with simple, practical tools to prepare you and your crew for the ride of your life! It is designed as a light, easy read to open your eyes to a deadly serious topic. Whether you are running a small or medium enterprise, or grappling with the demands of a super large, multinational concern, being agile in thought, action and result is now a necessity. It is no longer only about making good decisions; it is about *mastering* powerful tools to implement changes *quickly, effectively and sustainably.*

It's about executing change with simple, decisive and engaging leadership skills and then powerfully communicating them *with everyone involved* to get each participant on board *fast,* so they can quickly create measurable results. The message may delivered in an enjoyable, easy to understand fashion, but by the time you put this down we hope your corporate cage is rattled enough to get into action decisively.

Prepare to cast off!

Contents

1. Executive Summary · v
2. Comments by those who have read "Mastering Agility" · · · · · · · · · · · · · ix
3. Acknowledgments · xiii
4. Prologue · xv
5. Make Change Work for You! · xvii
6. Introduction · xix
7. Get Agile or die? · xxiii

Section One *Current Megatrends & Opportunities* · 1
Current Megatrends and Opportunities · 3
    8. The Singularity · 5
    9. Abundance, especially lots of money · 15
    10. Disruptive technologies · 25
    11. Success accelerates · 39
    12. Societal Shifts · 45
    13. Environmental consciousness on the rise · 55
    14. Negotiating Megatrends Demands Agility · · · · · · · · · · · · · · · · · · · 57

Section Two *The "Perfect Storm"* · 59
The Perfect Storm · 61
    15. Economic Uncertainty Rising · 63
    16. Geopolitical Tensions Increasing · 91
    17. Environmental Damage Mounting · 97
    18. Societal Strains Reaching Their Limits · 107
    19. Does the Future always go to Agile Entrepreneurs? · · · · · · · · · · · 135

Section Three *Get Agile NOW!* · 137
Get Agile NOW! · 139

20. Get Agile or Die? · 145
21. Defining and distinguishing agility · 151
22. The Age of Agility is here! · 163
23. Incorporating Agility · 167

Section Four *Incorporating* Agility · 171
Incorporating Agility · 173
   24. Some tips when incorporating agility into your organization · · · · · · · · 175
   25. Overcoming the BIG inhibitors of change: · · · · · · · · · · · · · · · · · · 177
   26. Agility and what you can do · 217
   27. DNS Tools and Modules · 219
   28. The Agility Toolbox · 221
   29. Tool One: Understanding Transformation and Agility · · · · · · · · · · · 223
   30. Tool Two: Forward Decision Drivers: Constant Monitoring (FDDs) · · · 231
   31. Tool Three: The Seven S Framework · 237
   32. Tool Four: Inclusiveness Funnel (IFS) · 241
   33. Tool Five: The Rolling Budget System (RBS) · · · · · · · · · · · · · · · · 245
   34. Tool Six: Marketing Responsibility Assessment (MRA) · · · · · · · · · · 253
   35. Tool Seven: Overhead Value Analysis (OVA) · · · · · · · · · · · · · · · · 261
   36. Tool Eight: Simple, Effective Leadership Assessment · · · · · · · · · · · 267
   37. Tool Nine: Carve-Outsourcing Services (CORE)
       for specialized functions · 271
   38. Tool Ten: Injecting Entrepreneurship · 279
   39. Tool Eleven: DNS and the Strategic Triangle · · · · · · · · · · · · · · · · 293
   40. Tool Twelve: STA+R Training Analysis · 297
   41. Tool Thirteen: Setting up your virtual or physical DNC · · · · · · · · · 303
   42. E-Learning and Blended Learning and LMS · · · · · · · · · · · · · · · · 307

Conclusion · 309
Index · 313
Sources · 317
43. About the Authors · 321

2. Comments by those who have read "Mastering Agility"

The message is clear: listen to what's going on with all your senses. Get your business associates and partners to do the same. Pay attention. Get agile....

Bob Waterman, Co-Author; In Search of Excellence, Author; The Renewal Factor, Adhocracy – the Power to Change, What America Does Right

    Hans Amell has written a really important book. For a couple of decades now we have seen a lot of volatility. This is unlikely to change in the foreseeable future. This book provides the reader with a sound intellectual framework for how to cope in different volatile situations using agility as a headline for different activities. It also gives practical advice coming from the vast experience of the author's long life in the corporate sector. It is a book I really recommend for anyone entrusted with leading companies in the next volatile decade....

Leif Johansson; Chairman Ericsson & AstraZeneca

    Terrific opportunities! This book charts a clear course for your C-suite to consider for quickly and easily leading the business through the 'perfect storms' of uncertainty....

Hans Levenbach, President Delphus Inc. MS, MA, PhD, Co-Author; Forecasting, Practice and Process for Demand Management

    Hans is the wisest Person I know. This wisdom comes from thirty years of advising on leadership and agility. Hans has packed this book full of practical methods to improve on organizational agility. By making his valuable insight available to all, Hans created a lasting legacy...

Martin Wade III, CEO Broadcaster, BOD Professional, Head of Investment Banking in Price Waterhouse.

Reading the book "Mastering agility" you cannot help but feel at mercy against the forces changing the world in devastating directions, at an ever increasing pace. The quest for agility is made so clear that even a fifth grader would lay down his video game, which he or she has just learned to master with great agility. As CEO and majority owner I have transformed F.E.Bording, a Danish Plc, from printing on paper to IT and communication services over the last 10 years. The authors make it evident that we do not have that long to succeed in the next agile transformation of the business model for my company. To be agile, as the book excellently stresses, it is mandatory to stay vigilant and predict the magnitudes of the disruptions happening when you least expect it. Read the book and your perceptions change, forcing you to think about your pertinent concerns....

Hans Therp, CEO F.E.Bording, PhD Nuclear Physics Stanford

"Mastering agility" is a powerful book describing how excellence is no longer enough. Getting agile also must include how truly great leadership can and should create engagement, plus decisive execution by training in the mastering the senses, mindsets and relationships between people. Kurt Larsson and Hans Amell provide great insights and deliver simple effective tools to address that important and growing field. Enjoyable reading and learning!"

Remy Nilson, Senior Advisor and former CEO, ATG, Sweden

Mastering Agility has captured lightning in a bottle - the elusive understandings of dynamic leadership that is required for success in a world of tectonic global business and economic transformations....

Norman Friedland, JD, Non-Profit Attorney

Mastering Agility offers a timely look at some of the global political, economic, technological and social forces rocking today's corporate world and offers plenty of well-crafted advice for not only staying afloat but sailing ahead. It is a must read for current and future business leaders who want to navigate the sea of changes taking place...

Dr. John W. Graham, Ph.D, Professor of Economics, Rutgers, The State University of New Jersey

Today's problem is that change is speeding up. This book can help you better deal with that challenging fact....

G. Chris Andersen, Investment Banker

Anything that can save time and money and enhance quality for the healthcare system is mandatory. Mastering Agility with its suggestions can do just that. A must read for all leaders in healthcare and elsewhere. On a more personal note, I first met Hans some years ago feeding pigeons in "pigeon park" in San Juan, Puerto Rico. After a start like that, how could things go wrong? We discovered many common interests; family, friends, golf, and most of all our "love" of lawyers and politicians. My friendship with Hans and his family has been a rewarding element in my life through good times and bad. I congratulate both authors for this important, eye-opening and timely book ...

John Kirkpatrick; MD, MBA, FACS, Executive Director The Surgical Advisory Group, LLC

Mastering Agility is a very impressive guide to why Corporate Agility is an absolute required trait for corporations going forward. As important as a cup of coffee in the morning....

Henrik Perlmutter: MBA, M.Sc., Entrepreneur

Every time I've tried my hand in the commercial world it has been an absolute disaster. However as the leader of a successful and respected not for profit Company, DCTV, I've managed to build an organization - that survives and thrives on many of the principles detailed in Mr. Amell' s book. If I were setting sail in challenging waters I would feel more confident and better prepared if I had his book next to me as I cast off and chart my course....

Jon Alpert, Co-Founder DCTV and 16 time Emmy award winner

"Hans is the very definition of intellectual, emotional and physical agility. His vision and belief in Platinum Equity, when we were just starting out, made an indelible impact, and over the past two decades I have seen firsthand his power to think creatively, act decisively and inspire others to succeed."....

Tom Gores, Founder & Chairman/CEO, Platinum Equity Group

3. Acknowledgments

We would very much like to thank our families and our wives, Barbara and BrittMarie, for trusting us to pursue this latest adventure. We would also like to thank our friends at the Stockholm International Rotary Club, our recently departed friend Carl Wilson and his lovely wife Art Kosol for providing us the opportunity to meet. We would also like to thank the Minerva Team in both Stockholm and Gothenburg, Sweden for their help and support, friends and colleagues from McKinsey, Ari Kienänen, Bob Waterman and Remy Nilsson for their friendship and encouragement. Special thanks also to Erik Obermeyer and Barbara Amell for the final run-through regarding grammar and spelling, Well Done! A warm thank you to Veronica Gyllenstedt and especially Ricardo Acevedo for their patience and help on the graphics. Finally, a warm thank you to friends departed like Don McFarland, Patrick Collard, all the other wonderful people we have come to know through them and their guidance in re-learning what it means to be physically, consciously and financially agile. We are all connected!

Finally, a special thanks to Chalotta Bond for her great idea that ultimately became our agile book cover.

4. Prologue

I have known Hans for years. Long ago we both worked at McKinsey. During that time we both skied together, and due to a certain agility in our skiing ability and thinking, we survived an avalanche that could have killed us both. We had ventured into some terrain that looked beautiful, but our senses said "wrong." We gave the snow a kick and a slab of snow, a meter thick and hundred meters wide broke from below us, gained momentum, picked up more snow, and crashed into the valley below.

Most skiers I know wouldn't have survived that avalanche. Hans and I, with years of skiing experience, could employ this book's idea of listening with all our senses.[1] The snow "sounded" wrong. We immediately knew what to do. As this book explains quite clearly, leaders in business must be able to sense avalanche-size change in their markets and to react appropriately and quickly.

Throughout this book, the authors enumerate and elaborate the forces that could destabilize your business world or mine. Whether these forces or others combine to create the perfect storm for your business or mine, the authors don't pretend to know. But they do make a convincing case that the same or similar forces have, in recent years, decimated company after company and industry upon industry. The message is clear: listen to what's going on with all your senses. Get your business associates and partners to do the same. Pay attention. Get agile.

The last part of the book is full of suggestions on how to get agile. Full disclosure: one of the frameworks they use for ensuring agility is the 7S framework that Peters and I developed in our search for excellence. In my admittedly biased view this framework is still one of the best tools that's come along for recognizing the

---

[1] I'm told the Swedish word for this is *Lyhordhet*.

complexity of change, for changing in ways that reinforce rather than confuse, and for changing in ways that yield strategic advantage.

Bob Waterman, co-author *In Search of Excellence*
author *the Renewal Factor, Adhocracy – the Power to Change, What America Does Right*

5. Make Change Work for You!

In Search of Excellence (Waterman, 1982) is one of the most influential business books of all time. Written by two great McKinsey leaders, Thomas J. Peters and Robert H. Waterman, it was published in 1982. When written, it was a bit of an adventure in the same vein as the book you now hold in your hands. It captured the essence of the exciting times that were just then emerging. Their message was simple, "Why does one corporation do extraordinarily well, while another, similar company just wallow in mediocrity?" The 1980s and even the 1990s were focused on being bigger, better and faster than everyone else. That worked until it didn't. You could almost say that this book is responding to the excesses and turbulence of the mindset that book helped to create. As with any powerful trend, excellence finally peaked. Somewhere between 2001 and 2009, excellence morphed into something more uncertain. With human nature and the pursuit of power and pleasure being what it is, those who prospered from excellence and got used to riding that wave chose to "party on" using any means necessary. The focus switched to *keeping the good times rolling!*

Fast-forward to the beginning of 2016. After several market crashes and with the growing probability of another deep one on the horizon, you would have to have been asleep to miss that the trends of expansion have now been pushed far beyond excellence. With the help of record levels of debt, hypercompetitive development, much shorter product/service life-cycles and globalization, uncertainty is again *back in style*, but now *with a vengeance*. The consequences of these trends are a string of so-called "*dislocations*" that are now beginning to bite hard. Not only individuals, but now companies and increasingly *even countries* are suffering from the damage caused. An avalanche of debt, fiscal mismanagement, geopolitical and, social upheavals brought on by increasing greed, uncertainty and fear are causing even more turbulence. So, you may still consider yourself *excellent*, but if you get caught up in your own hubris and are not agile enough to avoid or tackle these uncertain economic seas, the chances of you and your excellent organization being swallowed whole by them grows daily.

Therefore, it's time to get on board; don your captain's hat, put on your rain slicker, batten down the hatches and prepare for the ride of your life! For you not only have to be aware of danger, but also be ready to embrace the ever larger, more juicy opportunities that are popping up more frequently as well! In this new era, *business agility* will be *The Key Trait* for survival and success. Finally, never forget:

Your customer still comes first, last and always!

6. Introduction

The deep ocean currents of societal and technological *megatrends* are so extremely potent that they can easily be perceived as both exciting and scary. Simultaneously, we seem to be experiencing a build up to a potentially *perfect storm* regarding geopolitical, financial and even social issues. These two major forces of megatrends and perfect storms contribute to one single BIG and unavoidable consequence. *Count on being bombarded with larger, newer opportunities and threats at a rapidly increasing pace*! This torrent of unforgiving change will **force** you to listen more closely and *consciously adjust* your way of doing business quickly, or you will perish. In short, it is high time to *get agile or die*.

As fellow stewards of and participants in our new brave new world, each of us needs to understand the nuances of these major friction points. We need to learn and practice to be exceptionally agile in our ability to respond decisively and measurably. Mastering the art and practice of agility will allow us to transform our companies while we simultaneously grow professionally and as responsible human beings. What if *from this point on,* **practicing agility in all you do** *will become the most important key factor in your bid for success?*

Bear with us a moment as we explain why sailing a yacht may be the perfect metaphor for comparing the running of a modern corporation in an increasingly uncertain world. As captain you MUST be assured that you and your crew can change direction quickly if you want to survive, much-less thrive. It is no longer remotely good enough to take a year to react when economic, legal and customer demands are changing daily. This book explains our reasoning about why *consciously understanding* powerful megatrends, anticipating the perfect storm and focusing on what's ahead, while avoiding to get bogged down with tradition and legacy, will determine your ability to be agile. Understand these traits, practice mastering the tools we offer and watch your path to success become increasingly certain!

So now, please sit down comfortably in the captain's chair on your own 85-foot Catamaran sailing yacht. Your friends call you "El Capitan" and your corporate yacht is called The CatAmar. Under your command is an eight-person crew of competent friends and trusted colleagues. The plan for your trip is to leave from the Connecticut, Indian Harbor Yacht Club in Greenwich and reach St. Thomas in the U.S. Virgin Islands via Bermuda. On a normal 85-foot single hull vessel, such a trip would take about twelve days. However, you can easily do it in nine days including a well-deserved 48-hour break in Bermuda. Whether it's your first trip or your twentieth, it promises to be quite an adventure. Although your destination is fixed, is it at all prudent to expect and prepare for just fair winds and easy sailing?

Figure 1 Smooth sailing, but for how long?

To avoid the worst of the hurricane season, you have decided to start the journey in mid-November. Even so, winds change; sails must be trimmed and adjusted *very quickly* for those shifting winds. Equipment will break, obstacles will appear and currents will change. Your crew must learn *in detail* about this particular yacht and its equipment. Mastering each role and responsibility will contribute to everyone's safety and success.

The engines and generators must work flawlessly; the yacht must be generously bunkered with fuel and provisions. Radar, sonar, weather fax and plotter must all be *perfectly calibrated* for an accurate view of what lies ahead, especially when your vision is limited and surprises appear, seemingly from nowhere. Do you get the picture?

EVERYTHING and everyone must be synchronized and all must trust each other as well as their own *keen sense* of what is going on around them at all times. Everyone on board must learn to sense and anticipate the opportunities and dangers, as well as be ready and able to change direction at a moment's notice. Finally, in order to respond effectively, you need to stay on top of the constantly changing situation. **This is agility**. If you think the oceans of research and development have changed society fast and hard in the past thirty years, then get ready. *You ain't seen nothin' yet!*

Hold on tight to your captain's hat. The next thirty years will bring numbing and totally explosive threats and opportunities, each one potentially dangerous and loaded with transformational power!

7. Get Agile or die?

Absolutely!

By the time you finish this book you will understand why this bold statement is truer than ever. You will also be much surer about what to do. Rapid and effective change as well as directional adjustment allows and encourages companies to shorten their reaction time, just like a sailboat on a stormy sea. Product and business life cycles are shortening drastically and continuously. At the same time, recent polls show that people feel more uncertain about their lives, jobs and the future than they have in generations. All of this spells both an increased threat to protect against and an opportunity for more and faster success than ever. Will you choose agility and success or die trying to avoid failure?

To increase a corporation's capacity to survive and thrive in a time of shortening business cycles offers both the challenge and opportunity for a more agile organization. The time frame for development, production, distribution sales and services is constantly shortening. Your organization has to quickly respond to an ever-increasing number of external and internal forces, both under and out of your control. Many of these forces are potentially lethal to your business, especially if you do not have the ability to respond or adjust quickly. Too much success or too much failure can be equally devastating. If this reality makes you feel a bit more challenged than usual, you are not alone. As all these issues converge, it becomes unavoidable that, without taking on *agility as a lifestyle,* your chances of being chewed up and spit out even by challenges you successfully navigated in the past, when business cycles were longer and more forgiving, increase.

Figure 2 The consequences of Business as Usual?

Turbulence, connection and transformation

Even if you don't fully sense it yet, you will soon notice and understand what quantum physics is proving. That is we are all connected in many ways and on many levels. Moreover, wherever there is a conscious connection, transformation can then take place. From the cellular level in each of us, right up to the corporate boardroom and to top levels of government, the need for recognizing these connections and for increased agility, cooperation and openness are growing. Continuing to *disregard this trend increasingly risks peril.*

Even though we are fundamentally creatures of habit, we have an incredible ability to adapt and overcome new obstacles. Each individual has a different understanding and threshold of agility that is not always in harmony with fellow workers and others. The more we become aware of these differences, the more we can navigate and overcome challenges we will inevitably face *together*. Practicing this is the way to ensure your form of transformation *sticks*.

Volatility increases everywhere. Everything from trusted leaders to ancient institutions are now being called into question and with good reason. Corruption has infected virtually every type of organization, from local football clubs to organized religion. The result is personal frustration and an increasing sense for many of us that major change is coming, whether we like it or not. Both business and society have become more volatile.

MASTERING AGILITY

Figure 3 Danger/opportunity

If you still haven't sensed the need to become more agile, you probably will soon.

As with anything that changes, both threats and opportunities will arise. The more agile you become, the more you will anticipate and handle what lurks just over the horizon. Just as this Chinese symbol represents both danger and opportunity, so do the times in which we live.

In our effort to try and explain and give you the tools to handle this epic situation that is approaching, we will divide this book into four sections:

- Megatrends
- The Perfect Storm
- Therefore, Get Agile or Die
- Incorporating agility into yourself and your business

Section one: The Megatrends
These are those deep, long-term, unavoidable, tectonic trends that are so large they can neither be easily seen nor controlled. They can often only be recognized afterwards and either avoided, dealt with or exploited *on their terms*. We will list some of the largest here, *but this is in no way meant to be a comprehensive list.* Our point is to increase your awareness to their existence, danger and the opportunity megatrends provide.

Section Two: The Perfect storm
This section describes some of the most potentially negative, often erratic trends that will sooner or later overwhelm and force change, *like it or not.* Just as unconsciously sailing into a hurricane, discovering another vessel on a collision course with your ship, or walking way out on fresh, new beach before a tsunami hits, ignoring or avoiding volatility is not a winning tactic. The more you can prepare for these outcomes, the more you increase your agility. Of course, where there is increased danger, there is also increased opportunity.

Section Three: Therefore, Get Agile or Die!
Just as success can overwhelm you as much as failure, your ability to remain *consciously agile* about what unfolds will increase your ability to survive and your chances to prosper. In increasingly turbulent times, it may not be as much a question of

being more successful as it is a question of survival. "*I am not so much interested in the return on my money as I am in the return of my money,*" explained Mark Twain.

Section Four: Incorporating agility into yourself and your business
This final section will help you with simple, practical tools to better weather the exciting and turbulent seas of change. It attempts to describe what makes us tick and how we can consciously choose to handle the above trends and storms. *It provides proven tools, methods and training tips* to become consciously agile and successful, thus benefitting you and everyone in your organization. *If you already recognize and understand the need for agility and are in a hurry to get agile, you can skip directly here.*

In short, we can either continue to react habitually, from years of training and conditioning, only to suffer a similar result as Captain Smith, skipper of the Titanic. Or…

We can instead increase our agility and consciously respond to the situation. We can practice using our expanded toolbox in the most appropriate and effective way, here and now. Which approach *do you* imagine offers the best chance to survive and thrive in these increasingly uncertain times?

Most of all, Wake up!
Start practicing to actively sense which way the economic and social winds are blowing. Marvel at our technological progress, yet increase your vigilance for what it is being used for and by whom. "*Follow the Money!*" Most of all remain curious and a bit skeptical. Consciously and tirelessly question everything and everyone!

Always strive to improve your position. However, we challenge and encourage you to do it in a way that benefits everyone else. Live like we are all connected, even if you don't yet feel it. What if your agility ultimately depends on the agility of all those around you? Remember that a "*smooth sea never made a skillful sailor.*" We only improve our skills through experiencing unpredictable and at times perilous situations. The exponential growth of new exciting technologies is occurring with increasing ferocity. Many of them will fundamentally change everything we do.

Welcome aboard and prepare to set sail!

SECTION ONE

Current Megatrends & Opportunities

Current Megatrends and Opportunities

Recognizing the corporate sea, climate, seasons and weather
Let's start this journey of discovery by discussing just some trends we have been following that are so deep and potent that no amount of adjusting or long-term manipulation can change them. Just like the Gulf Stream or the jet stream, they are constantly there, but you have to know what you are looking for to notice them.

Most megatrends start their development agonizingly slow, too slow to be noticed. Yet as they grow in size and importance, they begin moving quicker. If you are not prepared when they begin to matter, you may be in danger or you may miss out on the opportunities they provide. Just like knowing how to ride the currents, riding big trends will put the power of wind and water at your back.

No matter what we do, the few trends we list here and others are set to continue. So we had better learn to ride them well. You will probably understand, as you delve further into this book, that there are many other trends, which are not discussed in these pages, which are building and may appear at any time. Our point is not to scientifically catalogue and measure each trend, but to prove you will fare better if you train now to act with more agility. Whether or not you are aware of these trends, *or others not discussed here*, count on them affecting you, your crew and all you do. Being agile will help you to navigate these noticeable or hidden trends more effectively.

8. THE SINGULARITY

We are all connected. There is more evidence emerging every day that just about everything is starting to merge together. This idea that things are starting to come together is also known as the *Singularity*. The *Singularity* started out as the term first used by Vernor Vinge to describe the moment when computers with superhuman intelligence overtake our ability to control them...

Below are the opening comments from Vernor Vinge's famous 1993 Singularity Speech:[2]

Abstract
"*Within thirty years, we will have the technological means to create superhuman intelligence. Shortly after, the human era will be ended.*

Is such progress avoidable? If not to be avoided, can events be guided so that we may survive? These questions are investigated. Some possible answers (and some further dangers) are presented.

What is The Singularity?

The acceleration of technological progress has been the central feature of this century. I argue in this paper that we are on the edge of change comparable to the rise of human life on Earth. The precise cause of this change is the imminent creation by technology of entities with greater than human intelligence. There are several means by which science may

---

2 (c) 1993 by Vernor Vinge Verbatim copying/translation and distribution of this entire article is permitted in any medium, provided this notice is preserved.
This article was for the VISION-21 Symposium sponsored by NASA Lewis Research Center and the Ohio Aerospace Institute, March 30-31, 1993.
It is also retrievable from the NASA technical reports server as part of NASA CP-10129.

achieve this breakthrough (and this is another reason for having confidence that the event will occur):

The development of computers that are "awake" and superhumanly intelligent. (To date, most controversy in the area of AI relates to whether we can create human equivalence in a machine. But if the answer is "yes, we can," then there is little doubt that beings more intelligent can be constructed shortly thereafter.

Large computer networks (and their associated users) may "wake up" as a superhumanly intelligent entity.

Computer/human interfaces may become so intimate that users may reasonably be considered superhumanly intelligent.

Biological science may find ways to improve upon the natural human intellect."

Since this famous speech was presented, the term Singularity has been broadened to include many socioeconomic factors that are also merging in Vinge's original race towards artificial intelligence. Many argue that our future will develop into something dark like *Skynet* from the movie *Terminator*. Whereas others argue that the difference between intelligence (artificial or natural) and human feeling will naturally become more pronounced. They argue that computers are incapable of developing the capacity to become self-aware, especially in a destructive manner towards humans. It is worth noting that this rosy declaration excludes those psychopathic or evil individuals who can program such cold-blooded behavior into machines.

The trend of an explosion in computing power is now firmly in place. To paraphrase Peter Siljerud from his company, FutureWise[i], "Soon everything that can be done with muscle will be done with robotics, and everything we can calculate with our brain will be done by computer." So far though, machines have been incapable of developing a heart, morals or a conscience. Regardless, we seem to be rapidly approaching the point where computer power will eclipse our ability to keep up with how it's used. If you think you are stressed now, how this will the eclipse of our power over computers affect your health, well-being and prospects for successful future?

Convergence of Technologies
Anyone working in the IT and telecoms business recognizes that the technological differences between competing companies as well as their solutions decrease with each passing day. For instance, the distinction between telephones, computers and televisions becomes blurrier every day. These three distinct technologies are rapidly fusing into one.

There are also different flavors of current technologies. But, for instance, if you trade in your iPhone for the latest Android, you should be up and running in no time. Agile competitors recognize this trend and help the fusion process along (possibly slitting their own throats in the process) by focusing on extras such as easy transference from one platform to another.

Open sourcing, where anyone can contribute to a program or the development of an operating system, also blurs the need to purchase and be loyal to a proprietary standard. The Linux operating system is one prime example. A brand new industry is further developing out of this open software boom. Companies such as Red Hat certify, customize and support the Linux open source code, thus making it safe and secure for large companies to build their own infrastructures and thereby freeing themselves from what some now call the *Tyranny of Microsoft*.

A huge and unforeseen side effect that contributes greatly to this open source trend is the increasing amount of data being gathered by companies such as Microsoft, Apple, Google, Facebook and others. One of the most interesting and ironic effects of this data gathering process is that the more our lives are being revealed over the web, the less we seem to trust governments, companies and leaders who "promise" that our personal information is safe.

Convergence of Intelligence and machines
David Pogue's article, *Robots Rising* in Scientific American[ii], updates the discussion about how we will converge Singularity with intelligent robots. In an interview with Max Tegmark, MIT professor and co-founder of the Future of Life Institute, he mentioned that artificial intelligence is even less forgiving. Professor Tegmark points out, "*When we invented less powerful technology, like fire, we screwed up a bunch of times; then we invented the fire extinguisher. Done. But with more powerful technologies like* human-level artificial intelligence, we want to get things right the first time."

"*The worry,*" writes Pogue, "*is that once AI gets smart enough, it will be able to improve its own software, over and over again, every hour or minute. It will quickly become so much smarter than humans that- well, we don't actually know.*" Tegmark concludes, "*It could be wonderful or it could be pretty bad.*"

For instance, Pogue writes, "*Programming machines to obey us precisely can backfire in unexpected ways. If I tell your super AI-car to get to the airport as fast as possible, it'll get you there-but you'll arrive chased by helicopters and covered in vomit.*" This is rather benign on the scale when compared to what AI weaponry could do…

Pogue also contributes a new, interesting slant about Robotics replacing workers. He emphasizes, "So much of our sense of purpose comes from our jobs. We should think hard about the sort of jobs we would like to keep doing and getting our identity from." He concludes, "*The loss of jobs will also mean the loss of human fulfillment.*"

Convergence of Old Industries

Depending upon the source, in the year 1900 there were between 300 and 800 different automobile manufacturing companies in Detroit alone. By the end of the depression, there were only a handful of them left. In the 1980s, there were a myriad of personal computer manufacturers ranging from IBM, Compaq, Olivetti, Ericsson, Philips, HP, Apple etc. How many are still in the game? Right now how many online gambling sites can you choose from?

As industries mature, Charles Darwin's Law of the *Survival of the Fittest* (or is it the shrewdest?) becomes apparent in the marketplace. Through bankruptcy, mergers, friendly and hostile takeovers, companies consolidate and expand. There still is perceived safety in reaching a larger size. So far, *bigger* still seems to be *better* to the point that *Too Big To Fail or TBTF* seems to be the ultimate goal. How long do you think this trend can and will continue? This is at a time when even more international giants use lobbyists, legislators and the mainstream media plus an increasing array of underhanded tactics to accelerate growth. The larger and more unmanageable these behemoths become, the more unstable, uncontrollable and untrustworthy they seem to get. Just as a tree cannot grow to the moon, peak limits will appear. Those found extending past these limits will lose all agility and ultimately crash and burn.

At the same time different processes are merging and many products are merging into one. For instance, look at the trend that started with the Sperry Univac in 1947. Computers became smaller and more powerful just as cameras, televisions and telephones did. All these technologies have now merged into smartphones and smarter tablets. Multitasking has become all the rage. How many young people even wear a watch now for other than a fashion statement? What's the point when you can just check your phone for the time?

Rockefeller combined all the processes from the discovery of oil to its final destination in the tank of your automobile, into a company called Standard Oil. Big players understand that the more you control the entire process, the more you set the rules. Want more proof? Look at the rise of subscription services. Customers can subscribe to everything from software to tampons, thus locking the customer into a complete process rather than just selling a product. Yes you are promised and sometimes get full service, automatic ordering, etc, but then try extracting yourself from it...

Convergence of Economies

Not only do companies merge in their quest for survival and profit; so do regions and even countries. Look at what happened to the world's first manufacturing center. Manufacturing started in the English midlands at the end of the 17th century. The baton was then passed to the United States at the end of the 19th century. It was then handed off for a time to Japan, then to China at the end of the 20th century.

Manufacturing evolves from simpler products to more complex ones in waves. In a very simplified economic history, the first wave was textiles. England began importing cotton from Egypt and the U.S.A. They used this raw material in their textile mills in the Midlands. The manufacture of textiles is usually followed by the production of increasingly complex items such as steel, railroads and cars now followed by even more sophisticated electronics. The United States took over the textile trade in the mid-1850s followed successively by Japan, China, Asia and now South America. Producing textiles begins the industrial process that leads to increasingly complex products followed by a wave of services. Just reflect on developments in the U.S.A, Japan, Taiwan, Korea, China and Vietnam. Consider IT. Most computers were once built in the U.S.A. Hardly any are built there now. Instead, more and more sophisticated software applications have replaced the once American dominated hardware trade.

The latest iteration is that China has cornered the market on production while India is dominating the market on software and services. These markets were won based on quantity, price and *hunger for success.* It will be interesting to see how this develops. Which countries will dominate which markets next?

This phenomenon was not just limited to one company or area. Often, a whole country or region was galvanized into action for a specific purpose. Think about the Glory Days of the (recently re-named) Rust Belt, Detroit or Silicon Valley. Wherever a production center locates to a specific place, financing is never far behind. Consider such places as New York's *Wall Street,* London's *The City or Hong Kong.*

As local economies grew so did the opportunity for education. When a certain population becomes more educated, skilled and wealthy, it develops industries faster and produces increasingly complex products. As the ability to transport products develops, so does the opportunity to produce and sell them all over the world. This global interconnectedness of products, people and economies even affects how we value economies. In agrarian societies the amount of land and resources owned was often the gauge of personal wealth and power. As the power of industry grew, this perception shifted to the value of what you produce. Now it is often measured by what you know and how you apply that knowledge.

Among others, Martin Armstrong of Princeton Economics International points out through his studies of wave cycles that natural resources and land do not alone determine the value of a national economy. Entrepreneurs, workers and others also generate products and services. This is what creates value.

Armstrong's poster child is Japan during the 80s and 90s. This island nation with few natural resources produced enough products to generate the World's second largest GDP. How did they do it? Japan became agile. It took the best ideas from around the world and tweaked their industries to make them more efficient. Look no further than the American automobile industry to see the effects of the Rising Sun's venture into the 1980s version of agility.

The book "*40 years and 20 million ideas*"[iii] is the story of Toyota's rise to become one of the world's biggest automobile manufacturers. Toyota embraced the idea of the suggestion box and listened seriously to each employee, encouraging him/her to contribute even simple and inexpensive ideas in order for the company to be the best. The genius of this concept was further demonstrated by focusing on the quality of the whole production process instead of only on the end result (a quality car). Toyota rewarded even those suggesting minor improvements in the process of manufacturing cars.

In a related example, David Habersham's book *The Reckoning*[iv], describes how Nissan (Datsun during 1960s and 70s) executives traveled to Detroit to learn about and improve upon the processes that Detroit was employing. While their American hosts were openly making fun of them, their Japanese guests took copious notes. Then they went back home, implemented those ideas into their production lines, and tweaked them further.

One look at what is now left of the market share of automobiles still produced in Detroit[v] compared to those by Japanese auto companies says it all. It is also rather humbling to note that Detroit, which once boasted to have the highest average income in the United States, now has trouble keeping the public water and electricity systems running. Some of those United Auto Worker hosts must be turning over in their graves as arrivals and departures in Detroit's Municipal Airport are now routinely announced in Japanese. Can arrogance inhibit agility?

Finally, according to IMP in Switzerland, Japan's focus on the process even threatened Mercedes lock on the luxury car market in the late 1980s. As referenced above, Toyota and Nissan had been focusing on how to create a better quality *process*. Mercedes had been focusing on creating better quality cars. When it came time to ramp up production to satisfy the burgeoning market of quality luxury cars, the Japanese could do it quickly without sacrificing quality. Mercedes, whose focus had been on each car and not the process, quickly overloaded its capacity. Its customers began experiencing increased quality problems. Eventually Mercedes resolved this hiccup, but not before severe impact was felt in both reputation and profit.

The story does not end here. It is of major importance that thirty years later Toyota has been suffering from lower margins and quality control scandals just as its Detroit counterparts did a generation ago. It seems that its entrenched leaders also chose *business as usual* and job security instead of maintaining and improving agility. In short, they lost their edge. The hazard of TBTF thus reveals itself in the auto business. This process still clears the way for hungrier, lower cost and more agile producers such as Dongfeng and Chery in China and Tata in India. The process continues as even such quality brands such as Volvo Cars and Saab have recently been taken over by Chinese automobile manufacturers.

Convergence of Thought
When two planes crashed into the World Trade Center towers in New York, it was instant news around the world. That is now fifteen years ago! Information travels even faster now. Just ask the "Flash Boys" in Michael Lewis' Book of the same name. These traders now make millions of dollars by being a few millionths of a second closer to the stock market computers than the rest of us *muppets*, thereby making faster, more lucrative *and increasingly suspect* financial trades. Fortunes can be made and lost in just milliseconds.

Just as the 100th monkey seems to learn a behavior without direct instructions, so can thoughts spread quickly and manifest in the rest of us. With the help of the World Wide Web, ideas and information are spreading faster than ever. Competing views and different opinions are just as available to anyone if he or she cares to look. Ideas can now incubate into products and services literally overnight, then quickly spread to the four corners of the world.

With the increasing availability of travel and emigration, world cultures are blending into each other at a more rapid pace than ever. Even whole languages are being lost at an increasing pace as more of us are assimilated into the same (usually English) world mix that can be found on the Internet. For better or worse, our thoughts, words and deeds are all becoming one.

Convergence forces commodification
The faster contact we have with each other, the less location matters. If you want to sell a lunchbox at Amazon.com, you can produce it in China just as well as in the U.S.A, usually at a cheaper price. Need a fancy box to package it in? Log on to Fiverr.com and find someone in Indonesia or Sri Lanka to design it for five dollars. They send a high quality pdf of the carton design to the Chinese factory of your choice. There it can be printed and matched to your product. The whole package can then be boxed and shipped by plane to the Amazon warehouse in the U.S.A. The total time from the idea to online sales is less than two months. The total cost is less than $1000. We know people who are making fortunes using this process on a daily basis.

If you create this product, you could make thousands of dollars per month. That gravy train will continue until someone more agile than you improves on your product or marketing process. Suddenly, another innovator begins outselling you and the process begins anew.

Congratulations, your creation has just become another commodity.

Regardless of whether you sell lumber, oil, milk, electronic components, clothes, legal or financial services, chances are that your product or service is now or shortly will be a commodity. Becoming a commodity means that price is now the most important decision factor for your customers. Check this effectively by observing how quickly the discussion of price comes up during your sales call. The quicker you start haggling, the more evidence you have that your product and/or company is now a commodity *for your customer*.

The lower the price, the more you sell, but the less you get to know about your customer. As even more products and services become commodities, it becomes more important to add value in every other way possible. Otherwise, your customer base will decrease as soon as the new lower, more efficient producer of an improved version goes viral on the Net.

There are two paths that must be taken to stay in business and both concern agility. One is to continue to offer more value for the same amount of money, *or less*. The other is to distinguish yourself and your fellow employees from the competition with more service. This means not only better, more personal level of service, but also an attractive, friendly and memorable way of doing business. If you forget or ignore these important aspects, expect your customers' loyalty to change with the wind. Continually doing both well is a powerful step in maintaining and/or increasing your agility and profits.

Convergence equals globalization
Globalization means the growing interconnectedness and interdependence of everyone on the planet. The world continues to get smaller. Going through this process, those of us who are paying attention are becoming more aware of how much our action *and inaction* influences others.

For instance, globalization is a wonderful development for the consumer. The consumer can now easily choose from a selection of products, services and prices from all over the globe. This creates a growing challenge for each producer as there are now competitors from all corners of the world competing for your business. Lobbying to enact stricter laws in your country to protect businesses often results in products being outsourced and produced elsewhere and/or just assembled in your country. When your business is affected, you must remain vigilant and be prepared to respond often in ways you haven't yet imagined.

As we become more aware of just how connected we are, it will become dangerously apparent that we can no longer afford the luxury of excluding others. With instant access to what happens everywhere at any time, secrets and personal behavior will quickly be discovered and dealt with, often by people from places you have never heard of. In short, it is becoming critical to our common survival that we include everyone in our plans and treat each other with respect. Otherwise, we could easily end up in a *Mad Max* type of future. The old "*Business is War*" axiom has consequences.

Convergence means increasing speed and intensity
All of the above trends point towards an incessantly faster pace of development and connectivity. The more these trends converge the quicker you will need to be to negotiate them and the more agility will be required.

9. Abundance, especially lots of money

Throughout history, man's struggle for success has been based upon the collective belief of scarcity. All the way up to through the Industrial Age scarcity has been a root cause of man's behavior. We will argue later that scarcity is the basis of the entire idea of business management. Yet something unique has occurred especially during the last few generations. A feeling of abundance has made its presence known.

Up until World War One, civilized society had always been somewhat governed by the belief that money had to be anchored in something of value. Different anchors had been used over the years, but between the Napoleonic wars and the First World War, international trade had been based on a gold standard. The late 1800s is still referred to as The Golden Age of Commerce. Look at most historical inflation charts. Notice that if you bought a house right after Waterloo in 1815, its price would have stayed relatively stable until the outbreak of violence in 1914. Interestingly, something unique happened while millions died in the trenches of Belgium and France.

As the costs of waging war mounted, one belligerent country after another left the gold standard and began to borrow and print money to finance their war. Had England, Germany, France and others held themselves to this prewar standard, they would have been bankrupt after the first year of fighting. Instead they threw fiscal responsibility to the wind and borrowed and printed their way through the rest of the war, causing untold hardship and suffering. To make a long and complex story short, once the so called "Great War" ended, the countries involved wouldn't or couldn't return to their prewar gold standard that backed most nations' printed currency with gold. The United Kingdom tried, but was forced to revalue (i.e. weaken) the pound in the beginning of the 1930s. Due to the debt forced upon them by losing the war, Germany couldn't comply. It suffered hyperinflation during 1923-4 in its vain attempt to repay those debts. The last holdout was the United

States of America, where President Roosevelt unconstitutionally banned private ownership of gold in 1933. This was publicly justified as a way to *revalue* the dollar and end the Great Depression. Something else interesting also happened on the way to all of these *revaluations*.

During this brutal process of *revaluing* currencies, those in charge of their nation's money learned something important. They discovered that the average citizen did not react or even notice whether those in charge printed and/or borrowed more. The so-called Bretton Woods Agreement of 1944 made the U.S. Dollar, which was then still backed by gold bullion, the world's reserve currency. This agreement permitted a few decades of relative monetary stability, but what began happening behind the scenes? In many cases, war debts were paid. In the 1960s, with the American war on poverty simultaneously being waged with the war in Vietnam, American borrowing began to increase drastically and affect the value of the dollar and its gold backing. By 1971 American gold reserves were reportedly down by almost two thirds. In response, President Nixon closed the so-called *gold window* and severed the connection between the U.S. Dollar and its *good as gold* backing. This was, in reality, a national default and its consequences lead to a rapid increase in the money supply, thus reducing purchasing power. By the end of the 1970s, with many more printed dollars flowing into the global economic system, inflation became a household word all over the Western World. Debts also began to rise first geometrically, then exponentially.

With every economic slowdown from the late 1960s forward, it became standard practice for central banks to print or borrow more money and inject it into the national economy. Like magic, every economic dip was followed by even better times. More money also meant more development and better technology. By the end of the Twentieth century though, the world began to develop more capacity than it could use. Just like a junkie needing a bigger hit as his/her body gets used to the drug, world economies began to require more *monetary stimulus* to sense the same *high* of prosperity. At the dawn of the twentyfirst century, this extra money had driven manufacturing capacity rapidly into overcapacity all over the world.

We are now coming to grips with this enormous amount of overcapacity. Standard economic theory tells us that when supply increases more than demand, prices drop. The deeper we get into this *twilight zone* of easy money, the less this fundamental rule seems to work. This is becoming more evident, especially when it comes to asset values compared to prices. A house that was built in the 1960s, which may have cost $20,000 can, more often than not, no longer be purchased for less than $300,000 to $400,000. Black has become the new white.

Source: U.S. Census Bureau, 2010

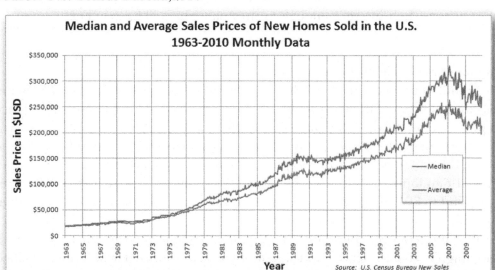

Figure 4 The Median Price of U.S. Homes

In attractive areas such as the east and west coasts of the U.S.A. and in and around most West European capitals, prices are a few times more than even these extravagant figures. This is the major question: *Has the value of your home increased so much or has the value of your money decreased?* Could this be due to the increase in your nation's money supply? At the same time the price of money, energy and technology has drastically decreased! Has this situation caused you to feel more uncertain?

This trend in uncertainty seems to be gaining speed as it is now estimated that the world money supply of Dollars, Euros, Yen, Yuan, Rubles, etc. has increased by the equivalent of upwards of 13 trillion Dollars since what is now being called the 2008-9 *Great Recession*. With interest rates now at unprecedented lows, large sums of money are easy as they have ever been to get, *if you have the right connections.*

The point here is not to provide a detailed economic history of the last 100 years, but rather to highlight that there is an enormous and increasing amount of money sloshing around, desperately seeking a low risk and high return home. This is causing financial uncertainty as economic fundamentals no longer work as they have since this discipline was born. The result is a much more volatile and fragile economic climate. This climate is one where the so-called *hot money* can accumulate in a sector or industry quickly and then suddenly dissipate to other places, virtually overnight. With most of this money now being in digital form over fiber optic cable, this process has literally progressed to the speed of light. This interplay between current abundance and historical scarcity has major and uncertain implications going forward, especially when it comes to being agile enough to anticipate what will happen next.

Five times more scientific developments
My grandfather was born in 1883. This was when horsepower *from real horses* and sails were still two of the most popular ways to move goods and people from place to place. Before he died, he witnessed the birth of the airplane and ultimately saw humans land on the moon. As Neil Armstrong remarked when he set foot on the moon, this truly was "*One giant leap for mankind.*" Less than fifty years later that rapid pace of development is looking increasingly like an even smaller step. Estimates now point to FIVE times more scientific developments over the next 100 years than have taken place *so far in human history!*

Our interconnectedness and sharing ideas over the Internet means the previously high costs of research and development can now be farmed out to skilled workers in much lower-cost countries, *immediately*. Just this development alone may end up making this estimate of five times more inventions and innovations a shameful underestimate.

Another telltale hint of the acceleration of development came from a recent conversation with a good friend from Red Hat. For agile players in the IT/Telecoms business, the luxury of separating research and development from operations is now ancient history. This *traditional* separate, *but equal(?)* configuration has given way to what is now known as *DevOps*. Thus, two former rivals for the same budget are now forced to work together as *one team* to increase the speed and effectiveness of beginning to sell and implement new products while still developing and innovating them. This forces new projects to be:

- More reality based
- Have more realistic time and budget plans
- Contribute something measureable, quicker
- Reduce the number of decision makers involved

The time to market from good ideas to saleable products can now be reduced to a fraction of the time it used to take the more development seamlessly merges into operations.

With each new development and *disruptive technology* comes both the threat and opportunity of more creative destruction. Need proof? Just look again at what Uber is doing to the taxi profession or the competition Airbnb is posing to the hotel business. How about Spotify or Apple's iTunes and the carnage they have caused in the music industry?

Up the down R&D Escalator
The best metaphor for the disruption caused by this rapid rate of development is walking up a *down* escalator. Picture today's rate of Research and Development as the current speed of the down escalator you are trying to climb. To reach the top of this down escalator your rate of climb must be faster than the speed of the escalator itself. If you just keep up with the escalator's current speed, you will make no upward progress. Even worse, the moment you slow down or stop climbing the momentum of the escalator will immediately carry you back down to where you started. Now, what happens when:

- The escalator starts gaining more speed?
- Even more people get on that you have to navigate or avoid?

If you are beginning to sense a bit of frustration, welcome to today's research challenge.

More competitors than ever from all over the world have the money and resources to bring even more ideas to the market place QUICKER. Is it any wonder that your job of navigating this sea of increasing change is getting tougher?

How long can you afford to rest before you miss the next wave of technology in your market niche? Sooner or later, without a healthy and continuous dose of World-class DevOps agility, you will lose your edge.

Cheap energy, for the moment, again
For approximately the past 150 years, energy has followed its own interpretation of Moore's Law applied to processing power. The amount of BTUs of useable energy available has risen while the corresponding costs have fallen, sometimes drastically. Wood, coal, whale oil, kerosene, gasoline, and nuclear energy prices decreased while the energy potential produced increased. Interestingly, this drastic increase in cheap energy has been mirrored by an equivalent rise in population. How long can this exponential climb towards the sky continue? That is an important question.

Until this trend does change, increased energy efficiency keeps exploding our boundaries of development. Abundant, cheap and powerful energy gives us cheap electricity, cheap fertilizer, cheap food and cheap building materials to fulfill our wildest dreams. Cheap energy has provided abundant power to produce abundant choices. Yet nature has a habit of shaking things up when we least expect it. Considering how much of our current Western standard of living depends upon cheap energy, any disruption to this supply could quickly cascade through our economy and society, causing massive dislocations and hardships. Although Hubbert's "Peak Oil" scenario has been avoided once again, remember the "Peak" refers to the relationship of availability and power to price. Right now, the cheaper the cost per barrel gets, the more rigs are taken offline. Putting them back online takes an enormous reinvestment.

Competitive global expansion in all industries
Look at Alibaba following ever closer on the heels of Amazon. Look at the growth of the automobile industry in China. Heck, Chinese investors even bought Volvo Cars and SAAB cars. Both companies, until recently, were icons of Swedish quality and engineering! As this trend of interconnectedness and cheap financing continues to develop, companies can quickly start and/or relocate to lower cost locations. Hungrier workforces, who are willing to do a quality job at a fraction of the cost will get the call.

As of this writing, the cost of finance, resources and transportation are all still sinking. This makes it easy to produce and market products all over the world, profiting from wherever the best conditions for your particular business happen to be located. Shifting production, sales and service from one place to the next can be done relatively efficiently, putting pressure on price and on those looking for a job in the wrong place or with the wrong training. This is creating a whole new class of workers with uncertain futures now being referred to as *The Precariat*. As Professor Guy Standing points out in his book *The Precariat, the dangerous new class* (Standing, 2011), "Job insecurity is a defining feature" of this new class.

The above trends show no sign of abating and, like so many other issues discussed in these pages, they all seem to be speeding up and intensifying. There is now an abundance of products and services in most industries with more choices coming online every day.

There is an old proverb in the sales profession that states, *"you are only as good as your last month."* With the trends that are now accelerating, we may want to update that to *"you are only as good as your next month."* Why? Except for checking if a competitor is gaining on you, looking backward now only distracts you from preparing for your next challenge. Looking backwards you are less likely to spot the next opportunity or threat ahead. Still not convinced? Keep reading.

Disintermediation

Disintermediation simply means eliminating the middleman. Although this is by no means a new trend, it is now also beginning to accelerate. What is the cause for this rapid acceleration? Economics.

With the focus on getting more stuff that costs less, many have intensified their search for ways to eliminate the middleman. Everyone likes going directly to the source. Direct access saves both time and money. Fewer moving parts means less to go wrong. The agile amongst us love inventing new business models to serve us in our search. In the IT business, disintermediation is commonly referred to as *peer-to-peer transactions*. Yes, it's another sailing metaphor that describes going straight to our destination without any stops along the way. This is efficiency; and in a world where efficiency is becoming the primary measurement, disintermediation is the natural response to getting the best product or service at the lowest cost.

Like life itself, disintermediation has its advantages and disadvantages. Here is an incomplete list with the aim of getting you thinking more in these terms:

Advantages:

- *Lower cost and faster delivery*
  As less hands are involved
- *Greater access and more control*
  Easier to see the whole delivery chain
- *More choices*
  Lower costs means easier entry for competition
- *More security*
  Decreased chance of points of failure due to fewer links in the chain

Disadvantages:

- *Increased responsibility and greater burden*
  You need to be able to respond more quickly and comprehensively yourself. There are fewer involved whom you can either praise or blame regarding the consequences of *your choices* and actions.
- *Time consuming*
  You are now in charge, which also means you need more time to do your homework and find what you are looking for. Not only that, but you need to find it from a trustworthy source.
- *Greater chance for bigger mistakes*
  Less links in the chain often means bigger failures when things do fail.

This trend is also showing up in other places too, such as our access to information. It is now possible to get a live video-feed direct online from an important event or disaster. The need (and trust) we have for our information handlers, now collectively known as the *Main Stream Media* or MSM is now eroding just as quickly.

E-commerce
After a slow and cautious start, doing business online has become generally accepted. The figures are growing exponentially. During the Christmas Rush of 2014, it was estimated that for the first time, the value of presents bought online either equaled or exceeded over the counter sales in so-called *brick and mortar* stores. This trend seems destined to continue and flourish. What does this trend mean for you and how you market and sell your product or service?

First it was the disappearance of the Main or High Street family-run shops. Due to the growth of suburban shopping malls, then later the *Big Box* stores, the small family-run shops and boutiques were no longer able to compete. Now we are experiencing the next step in this process as even shopping malls and strip centers are closing down. The reason is *e-commerce*. Why pay more at a store when you can buy something through your smart phone anytime, from virtually anywhere and get it delivered for the same or often a lower price? Many customers now visit their mall or a few stores, gather the necessary information and then order by phone or computer. This is obviously not profitable buying behavior for your local store owner's long-term survival. How often do we now end up saving a few bucks and then become surprised that our favorite store is no longer there to serve us? The latest retail innovation is showrooms that are now popping up in malls where you look at the product, (then stand in line to) ask a question, but then instead of taking your purchase home directly, you have to order via the net.

Factor in the realization that e-commerce can be initiated virtually (literally!) anywhere in the world. Products can now be purchased and consumed anywhere. Thus, your ability to agily respond to changing market conditions needs to be sharper and quicker than ever.

Customer capture to permission marketing
Voting with your wallet is turning passive customers into passionate, active ones who *expect* great service. Unfortunately, some chains don't get this trend is the natural reaction to being forced rather than invited to transact business. To retain

customers some chains have forgone creating customer loyalty and morphed into what is called *customer capture*. All kinds of traps, clauses and internet labyrinths have been devised to keep you *chained* to their business model. Some of this consumer frustration is surely caused by too much rapid growth for company back-office systems to effectively keep up, but much seems like it is caused on purpose. Regardless, word travels fast! If consumers get wind of a company or product that forces a purchase or (intentionally or not) *captures your business*, it will become increasingly tough to generate new or retain loyal customers.

The following recently occurred in a showroom in Stockholm. A gentleman was ready to sign for a brand new Mercedes for almost $100,000. Everything was complete. The sale was down to the last line in the agreement. Literally, *on the last line* was an unexpected title transfer fee of approximately $80. The customer, surprised and annoyed by this last minute development, politely stood up and walked out of the showroom.

It is currently estimated that in the online world of shopping, up to fifty percent of filled shopping carts are left at the website checkout because of some small shipping charge or handling fee that suddenly appears at the last minute. Take that irritating sum away or *bury it in the expected price* and the conversion rate increases drastically.

People are finally getting tired of being manipulated and increasing their sophistication. With the overabundance of products, services and places to buy them, customers are increasingly flocking to outlets they can trust and where they feel they are given the most respect.

The current Internet marketing model often starts with offering free stuff, followed by a gradual increase in value of what you receive and a corresponding increase in price for that value. Get this balance wrong and expect *at a minimum* to never see that buyer again. Place an email address on a mailing list without the owner's permission and expect your mail to be marked as SPAM. All of this means you have to listen more often and more closely to what your market and each potential customer needs, wants and wishes. Also remember that even if do you get the right balance, most people will only mention you and your product *when something goes wrong*.

From volume discounts to free

Digitalization has also ushered in an entirely new *cost of production* relationship. The industrial age was based on economies of scale i.e. the greater the production volume, the greater the savings. The new information age model brings the cost of duplicating a digital product down roughly to zero. Once you design and produce the product, set up the necessary systems for each new unit you sell and deliver, the cost for each new sale drops to nearly zero. Here are just a few examples:

- An extra subscription on a telephone network costs little or nothing to implement once the network is up and running.
- The cost of an extra e-book is virtually zero once the book has been written, formatted and the file produced.
- The cost of an extra song or film file also is close to zero once it has been produced.
- Adding one or one hundred more students to a virtual course costs nothing extra.
- The financial risks of adding another borrower to your portfolio, once you have your risk parameters in place, costs virtually nothing.

In each of these examples, the marginal cost for each new unit, once the investment costs to produce it are recaptured, is virtually nothing. Thus, if you create or find a winner, it can be a Megawinner! If you produce a product traditionally and a digital competitor enters your market, you could also be out of business in no time. The margin for error in this process continues to decrease.

10. Disruptive technologies

Given current and future technology trends, Gary Smith, the co-founder of U.K. MSP Prism warns:

> *"Technology is moving so quickly, and in so many directions, that it (becomes) challenging to even pay attention before we become victims of the 'next new thing' fatigue.*[vi]*"*

Technology advancement continues unforgivingly, driving economic growth and, in many cases, unleashing disruptive change. Economically disruptive technologies - like the semiconductor, microchip, the Internet, or good old steam power in the Industrial Revolution—radically transform the way we live and work, enable new business models, and provide openings for new players to upset the established order. The McKinsey whitepaper (James Manyika, 2015) explains:

> *"Business leaders and policy makers need to identify these potentially disruptive technologies (and services) and carefully consider their potential, before these technologies begin to exert their disruptive powers in the economy and society."*

Yes, new technologies are continually destroying *business as usual* and creating new opportunities simultaneously. Just look at what:

- *Uber* is doing to the taxi industry.
- *Bitcoin, BitGold, OneCoin* and other Blockchain monetary equivalents are doing not only to banking, but to long held ideas of money itself.
- *Spotify and Pandora* are doing to the music industry.
- *Airbnb* is doing to the Hotel Industry. Now you can put an extra room or your house up for rentals quickly, effectively and relatively safely.

- ***Fiverr*** is doing to task work. You can get SEO optimization, a referral, a logo for your company, a jingle for your sales campaign or a short video to promote your product for just five dollars.
- ***Kahn Academy and EDX are*** doing to the justification and sanity of paying taxes for schools and tuitions to attend college.

All of these opportunities and many more like them are forcing us to rethink what *business as usual* looks like. This trend of *unrecognizable change* is now accelerating.

Again from friends at McKinsey, "*Whether it's an old or established systems perspective or an institutionalized technological habit of getting business done, the ever increasing and now almost hyper-speed of technological change may indeed be perceived as a disruptive force, at first. But it needn't be. Change is always, and only disruptive as long as there is resistance. Resistance in the form of thought-patterns, practices, systems, and ultimately institutions, that are different or opposed to what is emerging. Once you open up to the possibility of the receiving and perceiving the underlying potency inherent in all change, you may find yourself gazing upon hugely broadened horizons.*[vii]"

How willing are you *personally* to opening your mind, discovering your points of resistance and relaxing your body from those learned or conditioned defenses? Your answer to this uncomfortable question will be crucial to developing your personal ability to address if and when you are ready, willing and able to become more agile. By becoming open and willing to entertain and incorporate disruptive technologies into your organization *and your life,* you increase your chances for success. For the duration of this exciting journey, you are invited and encouraged to test your curiosity and openness. Now is the time to discover and learn what is necessary to master the rolling seas of uncertainty and to increase your ability to change course with ease and grace.

The Blockchain

A trend that is just appearing on the horizon, but is definitely worth monitoring, is the rise of what is called *Blockchain technology*. You may not have even heard of it yet, but it may ring a distant bell if you know that it is the technology that drives Bitcoin and other so-called *crypto-currencies*. Remember, the PC and Internet started life almost as a joke, quickly growing to engulf society as we knew it. The *Blockchain* trend might even surpass those "jokes" with its impact. The reason this technology can be so groundbreaking is that it literally redefines what we define and use for money.

What if the difference between currency and money is that one is a freely agreed upon, borderless vehicle of exchange between free market players, while the other is dictated by legal "fiat" and then forced upon the market as "legal tender"? A problem arises when people lose confidence in the value of their money to purchase products. Whether it's tobacco leaves or dollar bills, this can happen to both money and currency. Confidence in currency has occurred in such places as Germany in the 1920s, Zimbabwe in 2010, and too often in Argentina. It even happened way back in Roman times as silver was "clipped" and cheaper metals substituted as Rome ran out of money. Gresham's Law states that, "*Bad Money Drives out Good Money.*"

Human behavior changes until another agreement is reached freely or is forced upon us by using the threat of violence or incarceration. Look no further than John Law and his printing of Livres and how it collapsed the French economy at the end of the 18th century[3]. Therefore, in a closed or fiat market, you are usually stuck with monetary decisions that you are helpless to control. Wondering why we are still finding buried caches of Roman Silver Coins? If the powers that control *your* money decide to print more of it, without your consent, your purchasing power decreases, since there is now more of it to chase after the goods you desire. Yet you still risk jail should you choose to use something else. In other words, *you're stuck!*

Since the crisis of 2008, it is estimated that central banks, worldwide, have printed a total exceeding the equivalent of more than $13 trillion in leading world currencies to shore up an increasingly uncertain system. This has sometimes been referred to as *quantitative easing*. If you or I did this, it would be called counterfeiting. The question then becomes, *whose money do you have in your pocket or on your bank card chip, really?*

Some very sharp people are now waking up to this challenge. Bitcoin, StartCoin, BitGold, OneCoin and other crypto currencies have now been developed based upon a technology that supposedly limits the amount of units that can be created. These payment methods work above our national borders and therefore cannot be controlled by any certain government. This is the genius behind Blockchain Technology. This thereby limits and possibly even neutralizes the control the Banking System and local lawmakers have over *your* money.

In short, crypto-currencies have been created as a *decentralized* and supranational agreement to offer the opportunity to take back private ownership of your buying power (and your corner of cyberspace). This new form of disintermediation could signal the beginning of an epic battle on what form our future money will take. As money currently "*makes the world go 'round,*" this struggle could highlight the issue of what *you choose or are forced to use for money*. In the short run at least, it will contribute further towards economic, governmental and societal uncertainty.

---

3 John Law and the Mississippi Bubble: http://mshistory.k12.ms.us/articles/70/john-law-and-the-mississippi-bubble-1718-1720

For instance:

- What would happen to foreign exchange rates?
- How would taxes be levied or collected?
- What effect would it have on run-away government spending?
- Is this technology scarier or safer than the current *fractional reserve system* we have in place today?
- How will crypto-currencies affect the way you do business?
- This same technology is said to allow for secure, direct voting. This could also eliminate the need for representative government and those increasingly expensive, full time career-politicians, many of whom masquerade as our "*public servants.*"

This year, a "Reinvent Money Conference[viii]" was held at Erasmus University in Rotterdam. The Netherlands seem to be shaping up to be a new *silicon valley* for crypto-currency development. Large banks have recently poured big money into Blockchain technology R&D. They understand that the security, portability and anonymity that crypto-currencies offer are beginning to threaten their fundamental reason for existing and they realize financial agility is now priority one. The fundamental question of what *your* money will look like in the future is far from over.

Fractional Reserve Banking means that only a *fraction* of the physical money we have in our *bank* accounts actually exists on *reserve*. The rest of your hard earned cash is just an accounting entry guaranteed by the statistical probability that you and everyone else will not withdraw your money all at the same time, causing what is known as a *bank run*. This system works *only as long as there is public trust* in the current banking system. What happens if or possibly when that trust erodes? Blockchain supporters suggest that this trust problem will be eliminated using crypto-currency, as there is no physical currency any longer. They suggest your currency will be available for peer-to-peer transactions as long as you have access to electricity and the Internet. Thus, according to crypto-currency advocates, this new system can function completely separate from the traditional banking system, *as long as there is electricity*. Do you feel certain now?

Big Data

According to a documentary program of the same name (BBC Horizon The Age of Big Data, 2013), the Era of "Big Data" was launched on the day we first got a search button on our browsers. Suddenly the prospect of accessing information anywhere, anytime became a reality. Since then, there has been a rapid dumping of all information, from dusty and all but inaccessible books into instantly accessible bits and bytes stored on the Internet. Yet according to Big Data experts, this is only the opening salvo of an incredible informational and societal shift.

Figure 5 Big Data Word Cloud

More and more information is coming online daily. This data deluge is incredible! Now with the use of algorithms, we are able to discover and chart hidden data patterns as well as reveal personal and societal behavior *in a completely new way*. These algorithms have the ability to transform raw data into useable information, *instantly*. As more and more sensors and RFID chips are planted in more and more products *and even in and on people*, more data becomes available to analyze. This so-called "Internet of Things" opens up a whole new way of looking at our environment and ourselves. This too is only just beginning!

For instance, a poignant anecdote was offered in this Big Data program. Target, a well-known American retail chain began a project to collect data on the shopping behavior of expectant mothers. The goal was to identify those mothers-to-be (based upon what they had been buying) in order to better market the specific products they would need as their pregnancy progressed. One irate father called his local Target store to complain that his 18-year-old daughter was being bombarded with such advertisements. Unaware of this internal marketing project, the Target manager, who took the father's call, apologized profusely for the *mistake* and promised to get to the bottom of it. A few days later he called the father back to inform him of the internal marketing project and to apologize again for the mistake. But now, it was now the father who apologized. He had since learned that his daughter was indeed pregnant. *Of course, Dad was the last to know...*

This type of surgical marketing is both very controversial *and growing exponentially*. With this marketing power and potential available, are you still wondering why:

- Your grocery store often sends you ads for your favorite cereal?
- Your favorite bookmarked sites offer ads you have recently Googled?
- Facebook posts ads on your timeline regarding something you mentioned in a chat?
- You receive invitations to book a place for your next big birthday party before you even realize you will be having one?

Some estimates are that Amazon has up to 100 various data mining projects going on at any one time. As a plus, these methods are much more effective at reaching particular prospects, saving the uninterested from these intrusive ads. As a minus, any sense of privacy you may have entertained is now part of a comfortable, isolated and distant past. It is going to take time for people to get used to software that tells complete strangers so much about their behavior, but like it or not, that is our current and future reality.

Another important point the BBC documentary makes concerns Facebook and other social networks. *A free service always implies some kind of trade-off.* For those of you who still think you are getting a free, no strings attached social platform that permits you to keep up with what your friends ate for dessert, think again. Facebook is constantly improving the data mining of your behavior and then packaging this information to sell as market analysis to companies with products *directly aimed at you and your wallet*. We mention Facebook as only one visible example, but this opportunistic behavior can readily be extrapolated to not only all other social media sites but to many other sites as well. So-called "Data Mining" is getting more sophisticated and intrusive.

Even if you haven't noticed it yet, you are starting to get fewer ads of which you have little or no interest. On the other hand, get ready to become the target for even more ads specifically tailored for you, your situation and with even more convincing arguments (which address your specific behavior and comments) to buy what you need NOW!

Big Data will also open up countless opportunities in just about every other conceivable niche of society. For instance, soon you will be able to access real time information about all sorts of currently frustrating rapid transit situations. Think Uber and your ability to know where and when the next driver will reach you. Then multiply this *at a minimum* by every train, bus and plane. The days of knowing if it's on time or not are soon over.

Also, the amount of medical information being gathered on you and others even now is immense. The state of your health and well-being will be known by, and probably marketed to, many other people, organizations and companies. Based upon your behavior and whether you care enough to act or not, the probability you personally have of coming down with anything from a common cold to heart disease, stroke or cancer will be available to not only to you, but insurance companies, employers and others. Issues of defending privacy will be challenged from all sides. In the name of progress and profit, count on most of these challenges to ultimately fail.

Finally, don't forget about the recent scandal regarding the hacking and exposing of *Ashley Madison's* database of 37 million *married people* who were looking for love in all the wrong places! Talk about a divorce lawyer's wet dream... Let this be a warning! For better or worse you now leave a signature on every site, transaction and on all forms of digital communication in which you consciously *or unconsciously* participate. Those so-called Internet "*Cookies*" are much more than just tasty snacks.

Add to this another mention of the the very real trend of interconnection. Data is being increasingly shared, *often whether it is legal or not.* Most government databases are now being hooked up into one seamless sea of instant accessible information. Although this can be a boon to, for instance, honest peace officers actively trying to track down a known criminal, it can quickly become a very powerful tool for oppression when put in the hands of less than honorable "*public servants*". What if, as a wise Hollywood monk who once said in the movie "*7 years in Tibet,*" "*There is no honor in politics*" is becoming increasingly correct?

Look no further than the U.S.A's National Security Agency and its giant database facility that is now online in Utah. Every phone call, bankcard transaction, text message and email you make is now catalogued, "*for your protection.*" Conservatively, as many as 40,000 new local, municipal, county, state and federal laws are passed each year. How long will it be before you and everyone else you know will have broken some statute somewhere in the Land of the Free? Step out of line and...

Whether you like it or not, Big Data is here to stay and it will now be up to us to figure out how to deal with it. As with any tool, Big Data can be used to enhance society, expand our individual freedoms and quality of life, or alternatively intrude on society, your personal freedom and your quality of life. The line between sharing information and intrusive surveillance gets greyer every day. Sooner or later we may even solve this problem. Until we do, increased awareness, vigilance and agility should be prized.

World-class information and education everywhere

With the help of Big Data, the latest generation is experiencing a profound educational shift. The Internet has destroyed the traditional relationship between money, privilege and higher learning. Starting now, everyone can learn from the best!

Ever since formal learning became important, access to quality education has been both a privilege of the rich and powerful, as well as an obstacle to upgrading your class or status in society. The relationship between money, power and status to education has helped to keep the ruling class ruling. This relationship has now been fundamentally changed. Inexpensive computing and the World Wide Web allow people from all over the world direct and instant access to the entire world's store of knowledge.

Figure 6 Gutenberg Press, France

With the introduction of (definition Wikipedia) *Massive Open Online Courses or MOOCs*, this trend of education anywhere, anytime is now accelerating faster. Prestigious citadels of learning such as Harvard, MIT and USC Berkley now offer their courses online, often for free (edx.com)![ix] What were once guarded secrets to the offspring of the privileged elite are now equally available to the determined son of a fisherman on a deserted beach in Sri Lanka. All that is needed is a laptop or a smartphone with an Internet connection to get world-class learning here and now. Inventiveness and curiosity have been proven NOT to be God's gift to the rich alone. Keep in mind that this trend is only a few years old. We have *not yet begun* to see *or feel* the enormous potential and implications of MOOCs. You are welcome and encouraged to ponder what this exciting development means for our collective future! What if estimating how determined and hungry for knowledge this metaphoric Sri Lankan fisherman's son is, may be a sign of *how agile you* ultimately choose to be?

For those willing to look deeper, it is now common knowledge that it wasn't just Martin Luther who was responsible for the Reformation. He had the winds of change at his back primarily due to Gutenberg's invention of the Printing Press, which was the Internet of its time.

Just as the Lotus 1-2-3 (Ringstrom, 2015) Spreadsheet ensured the success of the personal computer, the printing and distributing of the Bible in the local vernacular, such as Luther's and Gutenberg's own German, suddenly lifted the veil off the well-guarded Catholic Church secrets of what the Bible really said. All of a sudden, by translating the Bible into the local language of the people, the Catholic Church lost its monopoly on how God's word was to be interpreted. Consequently, the power and synthetic superstition that came with the Church's interpretation (while keeping them in power) were all gone. It became apparent to any who were willing to look how limiting access to the Bible had been the secret behind the power of the Medieval Catholic Church. Church officials had amassed large sums of wealth, literally in "the Name of God," by annointing themselves as the Only Way to Heaven and by charging the faithful indulgences[4] to gain personal access. Five hundred years later on, what if the history of increased information access and its effect on power is now repeating itself, only on a much broader and grander scale?

Now many other long-kept secrets of how our world actually works (and who is really in charge of what) are now being discovered and revealed to anyone with the patience and gumption to search for the correct information. Will this sudden and massive shift of well-guarded secrets to public knowledge cause initial uncertainty? Is the Pope Catholic?

Additionally, everyone who wishes to contribute his/her own personal knowledge and findings to the rest of us can now do so instantly. Personal blogs, informal networks, institutional and professional organizations are expanding rapidly. It's easier than ever to quickly find like-minded people online, *from all over the world.* We will shortly see faster developments and new patent requests coming from even the most remote places on earth! Instant access means that critical mass can now be reached overnight, such as on the implications of a significant scientific breakthrough, a burning political or financial issue, a *previously easy to manage* scandal or a well-kept secret. If you haven't yet been exposed to some sort of information leak that affects your trust in a leader or organization you currently hold in high esteem, it is probably just a question of time.

Professional networks such as *LinkedIn* and others like *Innovation Global Network* are also contributing to and building upon each other's work. Sift through all the recipes and selfie photos on Facebook, Twitter, etc. and you will also find a wealth of knowledge spreading here too. This trend to selflessly share knowledge is catching on and spreading like wildfire. Again, it is crucial to understand that we haven't even begun to feel the tremendous power and acceleration of this global megatrend of information dissemination. How fast will today's information blossom into tomorrow's inventions? Who knows? Still, two things are fairly certain. The rate of change will increase further and the more agile you and your organization

---

[4] Indulgences were sums of money paid by worshipers to the Catholic Church to ensure their safe passage to Heaven when they died.

become, the quicker you will be able to shift your energy and resources to invent or at least capitalize on the next big thing!

Enablers of world-class information
Have you started your blog yet?
> Have you Tweeted today?
> Called someone on Skype, Viber, WhatsApp, etc.?
> Posted an article on LinkedIn?
> "Liked" a post on Facebook?

Some genius has estimated that the amount of documented information, from the beginning of time until now, has doubled during *just the last two years.* This may or may not be true, but perform any Google search you can think of. Notice how many hits you get. Each one references anything from an article to a full manuscript. More people than ever are expressing themselves online. Be it via blogs, Vivo/YouTube clips, Instagram, Tweets or whatever, more people than ever are finding their e-voice and using it. What's causing this avalanche of information? It is the explosion of information enablers that are increasingly facilitating online communication.

Innovation, development and totally new businesses now appear overnight. Globalization, as we know it, is getting another shot of adrenalin. What will the next thirty years bring when we begin to see the effects of MOOCs? From the MOOCs providing education for free, to Big Data analytics and data mining services, information has become increasingly cheaper and we are now only scratching the surface of what this means for our development as a society.

A textbook case of the explosion of an established institution of information and knowledge is what *Khan Academy*[x] is doing to traditional education. Without formal educational credentials and with very little money, Salman Khan started his online education crusade in 2006. Since then his company has grown to 26 million REGISTERED and unique course participants. What is most interesting is teachers in their traditional educational settings are now beginning to use Khan Academy's course material, often piping it directly into their classrooms. How does this affect thousands of years of educational tradition? Tradition holds that a teacher in the classroom is the only proven method to deliver quality education. How can that still be true when traditional teachers are now using Khan Academy Material? What does it do to a school's business model?

As blogger Gary North points out, *"He (Khan) has turned the entire teaching establishment into the equivalent of teacher's aides."*[xi] To paraphrase Mr. North further, if one person with no formal teaching background can teach 26 million students, why should any person *with common sense* spend time and money to get an "official" certificate that permits him/her to teach a class of thirty? How will this realization affect the established *and expensive* path of formal teacher training as well as the costly educational apparatus that has been built to accommodate it? What will happen during the next inevitable downturn when public education budgets and university teaching programs land under the economic microscope? If you have taken a stand to make the world a better place by teaching as many people as possible in an effective manner, which path would you choose?"

Even today, there is so much information available that it easily overwhelms even the most determined researcher. More and more enablers are becoming necessary to sift through all this information, to find out what is relevant and also what is true and *from a reliable source*. Making matters more challenging is that much of this information is free. The problem is, even when the information is literally sitting at your fingertips, you must find it, verify its value, then be able to understand and use it. We are noticing a trend that we can best sum up by saying that, "*Information is free, understanding costs.*"

Other disruptive technologies
Emerging technologies such as 3D printing are slowly turning areas as diverse as traditional manufacturing to medical practices upside down. Already today you can print anything from body parts to guns on a 3D printer *in your own home*.

The medical profession is also being expanded with the use of digital and biotechnologies. Growing body parts in laboratories, laser surgery, and long distance surgery help people to live better and longer lives. The spread of information also allows laymen to not only understand health issues better, but also shop for the best medical deal.

Crowdfunding platforms such as *KickStarter* and others are not the only challenges to traditional banking. Transaction platforms from PayPal to Bitcoin challenge our beliefs as well as our behaviors about financial transactions and investment opportunities.

All this and did we mention that we're just getting started?

Increased misinformation and propaganda

"*Whatever you think it is, it's not.*" Ancient Chinese proverb

With the advent of emails and search engines, the likelihood of receiving *massive amounts* of incorrect, massaged or deceptive information has increased, dramatically! The use of so-called Internet *Trolls* is increasing. These are people who are often paid sizeable sums to misinform or cause doubt. This makes your job of finding the truth that much harder. We will discuss the subject of climate change again in the "Perfect Storm" section of this book. For now, it is enough to mention the controversy over climate change and whether the most touted evidence is real or doctored.

The only thing that most of us can absolutely agree on is that the climate continues to change all the time. The area where Sweden sits, for example, has had about 20 ice ages so far, each lasting up to 100,000 years. Every one of these cold spells produced an ice sheet on top of the countryside estimated to be about two miles or three kilometers thick. This is enough weight to compress the ground so that even today, it is still rising a few millimeters each year. Thus, water levels and climate continue to be influenced by changes and trends that started thousands of years ago.

Did you know that in this same Scandinavian area there have been an equal number of warm periods with sub-tropical temperatures of about 40,000 years each? Many scientists now agree that Scandinavia is again nearing the end of such a warm period; *but not all of them.* Statistically, Scandinavia can "soon" (meaning within the next 500-2000 years) expect another 100,000-year frigid era probably rendering the area uninhabitable, *again!* So much for the current global warming threat when you live in the land of the Vikings. Yet dig deep enough and you can find people and data making a convincing case towards the contrary. Uncertainty is still King.

If you are a decision maker, making the right decision *within the appropriate time frame* is at least as daunting as admitting that a decision you made was based upon false or misleading information. This of course, *takes into account some the technology you now have at your fingertips.* In such a case, you may have to reverse course completely and take a massive hit on both the time frame and your original budget estimate.

What if the more you base your decisions on pertinent factors using your experience, gut feeling and ability to communicate, while continuing to *display a strong sense of curiosity,* the quicker and more effectively you can act to *actually solve* problems?

"*I fear the day when technology will surpass our human interaction. The world will have a generation of idiots.*" Albert Einstein

Information saturation

There is now so much information bombarding us at an increasing pace that it becomes harder every day to digest it. Just as a glass of water once full cannot accept any more, so are we becoming so saturated, with so much information that we can no longer effectively handle it. This causes increased stress from the sheer amount of it, as well as that "*guilty feeling*" knowing we probably overlooked or forgot something important. This of course, increases our uncertainty and our tendency to postpone or avoid important decisions. It takes more time now to feel comfortable that we have uncovered all the necessary information. Only now, *when is that?* The result is increasingly prolonged decision and execution cycles, causing a pronounced decrease in overall agility.

"Creative destruction"

The Economist Joseph Schumpeter coined this phrase to describe the continuing procession of new game changing inventions that replace or destroy established industries and business models. For instance, buggy whips were no longer needed when the automobile took over as the popular means of transportation. The postal system is now suffering mightily from the advent of email and pdf documents. 3-D printing, nanotechnology and biotechnology are just some of the many game changers just coming over the horizon. Many decision makers miss or laugh off these game changers and end up paying the ultimate price of irrelevancy, followed by bankruptcy. Then there are the agile leaders who can sense change. Bill Gates once reportedly said, "*How come there are no railroad companies that now own an airline?*" This was his reply to justify why Microsoft would take the next huge step in their bid to respond to the challenge of the Internet. That fateful, agile decision not only kept Microsoft in the game; it allowed them to expand and prosper further.

If you are not agile enough to handle game changers and megatrends, then you are as vulnerable as you can be. *Regardless* of your past success, if you are caught expanding into another great depression it's game over. Being agile means also being vigilant.

11. SUCCESS ACCELERATES

To "get rich quick" has never been easier!
Matt Callen and his group at *Amazing Selling Machine*[xii] has produced incredible results for people who want to start an online businesses selling products online, such as on Amazon.com. They have helped hundreds of people to make *$10,000 and more per month* by following their ASM system. Recently, they held a webinar to announce the fourth round of their successful eight week course. Five thousand people signed up, for almost $5,000 per person, during this hour long webinar. This hour long extravaganza generated 25,000,000.00 Dollars from excited participants from all over the world!

This type of efficient and effective sales and marketing is increasingly common on the web. Success like this still takes preparation, but when it finally arrives, riches can go viral immediately. This new model offers you globally compounded results, instantly. This is, of course, providing you have prepared a system robust enough to handle the mega-rush of traffic.

When debt becomes an asset...
This creative destruction process even calls into question what money and debt have now become. Now that money can be printed with the push of a button, allowing governments to monetize their debt, it begs the question of what functioning definitions of money and debt really are? With interest rates currently sliding towards "negative," this literally means that you can get paid for borrowing money. Does this mean that debt has become an asset?

A little known fact is that although the dollar became the dominant world currency after it was finally cut loose from its gold backing by President Nixon in 1971, there was an equally important decision taken at the same time. This other decision was that U.S. Treasuries could now be used as collateral for borrowing money. Sovereign debt could now be used to finance more debt. The use of dollars as the *World's Reserve Currency* began increasing drastically all over the world, as people, companies and even governments could now invest in U.S. Treasury Bonds (government debt) to *loan against* and thereby, *put their "savings" to work.* The Debt Market increased exponentially and Dollars and Treasuries were used all over the world; and why not? Wasn't the U.S. Dollar and the treasury market "*backed by the full faith and credit of the United States Government?*" Was it still as good as gold? We may soon see…

In other words as of 1971, this strangely named *debt instrument* (still referred to as a treasury or *savings* bond) had now been magically transformed into an *asset with which you could borrow even more money against.* Black had indeed become white. Some governments tried to object to this, but the genie would not go back into the bottle, especially by the government that caused it. As Nixon's Secretary of the Treasury, John Connally, quipped to a visiting and upset dignitary, "*It's our dollar, but it's your problem.*" This may ultimately cease to remain true and that time may be approaching.

Repackaging different forms of debt, especially Government and so called Mortgage Backed Securities or MBS as assets worked brilliantly for quite a while. It helped fuel our massive and unprecedented world-wide economic boom. It worked at least up until 2007.

Yet something different seems to have happened that fateful year. The world economy began contracting. First, came the collapse of American MBS market, due to too many questionable house loans, followed by the collapse in value of pretty much everything else. This collapse in asset value was further excaberated by the loss of confidence investors began to feel. Investors sold and prices collapsed from October 2008 until March 2009. Our world economic system was only saved by a massive world-wide effort (interestingly, sponsored by the same people who caused the crisis) to borrow and print more money. Massive amounts of freshly printed and borrowed money flowed into the system while interest rates were forced to historical lows. Even so, the demand for more debt slowly began to weaken. Looking behind the headlines it is becoming a fair question to ask who is actually still buying all the new Governmental debt? Who in their right mind would pay for the right to own a debt instrument, expecting little or a negative return? Also, how is this colossal and historic infusion of new money affecting the market's (your) ability to accurately price things? How is not knowing the fair price of an asset, consciously or not, affecting your market confidence?

It just may turn out to be the 2007 collapse of United States' *housing bubble* and all the borrowed money supporting was the signal of the end of this current and unprecedented phase of global growth. Now, even the safety of the U.S. Treasury market and the policies of the U.S. Federal Reserve Bank are increasingly being called into question by the rest of the world. Will debt continue to be treated as an asset or will it go back to its more traditional role, meaning reverting to being a claim upon something else? Could the timing and impact of this "*reversion to the mean*" cause even greater volatility?

As with most issues in this book, the answer is currently, and at best, uncertain. Even so, there are a number of signs on the financial horizon pointing towards an uncomfortable answer. Desperate measures such as so-called "*Quantitative Easing*", "*Negative Interest Rates*" and the continual and deliberate erosion of the metrics used to measure employment and GDP all point to the use of increasingly unconventional methods *to minimize or postpone* another financial catastrophe. *Is this the same as solving it?*

What if printing money, debasing the money supply and tempting people to borrow even more, with negative interest rates, only further hollow out the value of our currencies? Regardless of how this is packaged, mathematically it still cannot work. Finally, how long can these constant *emergency measures* continue to further erode the trust people have in the current system *and those running it?* What happens next?

These stop-gap measures also put an enormous strain on the traditional source of funds for business expansion: *savings*. Traditionally, borrowing from middle class savings and retirement funds were the source of capital used to expand your business. Negative returns currently offer little or no incentive to save. Therefore, the savings of the middle class are now being spent on the good life or are seeking higher returns in *much riskier* investments such as: junk bonds, real estate, derivatives and overpriced stocks, to name a few. As an entrepreneur, your source of expansion funds becomes harder to find. Uncertainty increases.

Shorter life cycles on all products and services
You hardly have time to purchase a new smartphone before another smarter, better and cheaper one is released. The research and development cycle is shortening on a constant basis. How does this impact your organization's propensity for change?

When your authors started their careers, the Internet and the Web were unknown. Not until the personal computer revolution, starting in earnest with IBM's PC entry in 1982, did personal computing become a reality. It took another ten years to make these devices into what we would now recognize as *user-friendly*. Then it took about another ten years before true mobility and connectivity became possible. We who were in the computer business back in the 1980s used to joke *even then* that a common calculator had more computing power than the first Sperry Univac. Moore's law was already demonstrating its power

As a reminder, Moore's Law[xiii] States:

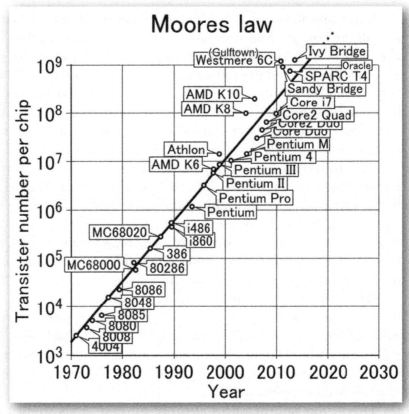

Figure 7 Moore's Law timeline

> "*The complexity for minimum component costs has increased at a rate of roughly a factor of two per year. Certainly over the short-term this rate can be expected to continue, if not to increase. Over the longer term, the rate of increase is a bit more uncertain, although there is no reason to believe it will not remain nearly constant for at least another ten years.*" G. Moore, 1965

The quoted year is not a misprint. If the pace of development seemed fast then, *fifty years later* it is downright blinding. Still, most people in the IT business agree that our current growth rate is still increasing in line or even faster than Mr. Moore predicted!

MASTERING AGILITY

Look at the following graph of what is being called "The Internet of Things." This depicts the connecting of all the *stuff* we use, to computer-based systems. Even now you can hook your room lights, your coffee machine, your security system and your thermostat to your cell phone. This graph points to the continuing explosion of this IT trend while also pointing to a *drastic increase in our interconnectedness,* not only with each other but even with all of our stuff!

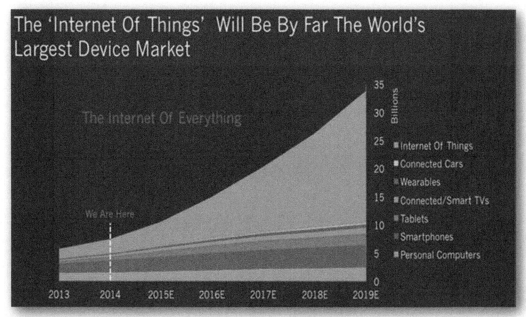

Figure 8 The Internet of things, Time Magazine, January 2015

This chart from Time Magazine clearly demonstrates that we are just getting started. Do you think this will increase or decrease each of the trends we have or will mention?

12. Societal Shifts

Let's take a quick look at just some of the megatrends that will be influencing society going forward.

Population explosion
By definition, overpopulation occurs when the number of people exceeds the carrying capacity of the region occupied by them. Overpopulation can result from an increase in births, a decline in mortality rates, an increase in immigration or a decrease in the resources necessary to sustain the people in the area. The idea of too many people in one area is nothing new. In fact the first real mention of it occurred in 1798 by Thomas Malthus in his work, "*An Essay on the Principle of Population.*"[xiv]

The human population has been growing since we began as a species. According to Wikipedia and others, the most significant increase has occurred within the last fifty. This is mainly due to agricultural, medical and sanitation advancements. As of January 1, 2014, the world's population is estimated to be 7.134 billion by the United States Census Bureau. This exponential population increase is again raising concern, since it seems that we are again getting close to the new and improved limits of "peak population." Challenges associated with overpopulation include the increased demand for fresh water and food and consumption of natural resources, which can create deterioration in our living conditions.

So far, every time we have reached our perceived limits, some new invention or technology has saved the day. Malthusian fears of mass starvation due to the lack of food have been postponed since 1798 by the development of better energy sources, mechanization and fertilization. The crop yield from one acre of arable land has increased drastically over the past 100 years. Many believe that technology will continue to save us from a tragic reckoning. This remains to be seen. Until then, one thing is for sure, our population will keep increasing, creating even more mouths to feed, along with even more creative ideas being launched daily. These conditions will most likely continue to contribute to your need for greater agility.

A major shift in corporate power

From McKinsey again, "*If you think the world's largest companies will remain in the West, think again. Research points to that the emerging economies' share of Fortune 500 companies will be more than 45 percent by 2025. This is compared to just a five percent share in 2000.*"[xv] What if the main reason for this dynamic shift is the agility of emerging economies?

With a younger, hungrier workforce, fewer laws, regulations, bureaucracy and legacy costs, these start-ups are quickly running circles around established competitors in the "developed" world. Going forward would you rather remain "developed" or become more agile? Ask yourself if development is more path or goal?

X-Box Generation, not bound by time/space-mindset

GenX and GenY are beginning to make their marks. Today's younger people have grown up in a time of abundance, entitlements and often raised by so-called "curling"[5] parents who doted over their every need. Many have never experienced want or accountability. In fact, many have been conditioned to expect everything to be solved and delivered *by someone else,* instantly. From blockbuster movies, to food, to finance, it can seem like nothing exists, especially for those born in the 90s and later, unless it is *immediately available.* Like interest rates, attention spans for them have decreased to almost negative rates. Many friends of ours, trying to relate the lessons of history to their children, often experience that their advice is met with either boredom or complete disinterest. What did George Santayana say about "*those who fail to learn the lessons from history…?*" More importantly, how will this type of behavior affect the way your future business is done?

Restlessness or boredom, seldom in the middle

Instant gratification, as in Freddy Mercury's, "*We want it all and we want it now,*" seems to be the motto for the current era. Although meditation and spiritual practices are slowly catching on, most still crave that "rush" of excitement, *just to feel*

---

5 "Curling" comes from the winter sport of the same name where you make the path of the curling stone free of any problems or debris by frantically brushing it all aside.

alive. Whether it is jumping out of a perfectly good airplane, free running or any other type of dare-devil experience, the underlying motivation is, more often than not, to feel less like a *human doing* and more like a *human being*.

Today's food and drink are now so loaded with sugar and other stimulants that a natural alternative usually tastes boring. We have become so addicted to outside input that we often do not know what to do when we find ourselves *offline*. Regardless, we are still faced with the GIGO principle of garbage in, garbage out. When was the last time you took a conscious look at what you typically feed your mind and body? What if we have unconsciously allowed ourselves to become more easily "programmable"? We allow ourselves to be constantly bombarded with information, usually without even noticing it. How much time do you spend reflecting over the underlying message or quality in the information you are currently digesting? We have known at least since Freud's nephew, Edward Bernays wrote *Propaganda* way back in 1928, that it is very easy to manipulate public opinion:

"*Universal literacy was supposed to educate the common man to control his environment. Once he could read and write he would have a mind fit to rule. So ran the democratic doctrine. But instead of a mind, universal literacy has given him rubber stamps, rubber stamps linked with advertising slogans, with editorials, with published scientific data, with the trivialities of the tabloids and the platitudes of history, but quite innocent of original thought. Each man's rubber stamps are the duplicates of millions of others, so that when those millions are exposed to the same stimuli, all receive identical imprints*[xvi]." Edward Bernays, Propaganda, 1928.

There still is a difference between *education* and *memorization*. Royalty and Politicians have known this for centuries. With this in mind, is it any wonder why it is so easy to become bored, restless or just collapse in a heap when things go silent? What if we are trained to want a constant stream of repetitive information? In this information rich, content poor environment, how easy is it to get your message across in a way that moves others to act? Creating agreement and action in a typical conversation become much more challenging when you compare it to the shock, awe and excitement found instantly on TV and the Internet.

Alternative education, both online and offline is gaining a foothold as the cost of traditional education channels, such as college, become too expensive and the quality deteriorates. Lately with the job market for younger people stagnating, the focus is beginning to shift towards educational tools students can monetize directly. Upstart companies such as Isaac Morehouse's learning-startup *Praxis*[xvii] offer one-year training programs where you study along with working for a prospective employer. The company gets your services by paying your modest tuition and you get practical on the job training plus an education by volunteering your time and energy. You directly enhance your future employment opportunities in real time and just about everyone gets hired directly after graduation. What will *Praxis*[xvii] and other less expensive online and blended learning upstarts do to what he calls traditional and boring "*conveyor belt learning*"?

More importantly, how will the skills of these hungry, ambitious and freer thinking individuals affect the job market for those who choose to follow more traditional routes? How will these new young managers (soon to become CEO's) lead and manage? Well, *we believe they will be more determined to accept agility as an important trait* of both people and organizations. They will probably train to become allergic to any change inhibitors they encounter and thus *become more restless*, bored or angry with any delays they experience.

Global family consciousness

The younger generation is dropping (or not being taught) many of the traditions that older generations were forced to learn and respect. No longer bound by social, hierarchical, class, religious and sexual limitations, they are free to form new, cross-border social platforms that often encourage expanded humanitarian and environmental ideas.

With the help of the Internet and social media, it is no longer a problem to connect with like-minded people anywhere on the planet. The subsequent exchange of ideas and friendships can greatly contribute to a more homogenized, and hopefully a more forgiving, world view for anyone with a computer and Internet access.

Even on a biological cellular level it is increasingly evident that we are all connected. Studies from the University of Michigan have shown, for example, that even when a group hidden behind a one-way mirror focuses on a subject's right thumb or left shoulder, sensors on the subject detect a temperature rise in the particular tissue or body part in focus. Somehow, even through a one-way mirror, we humans can sense the presence of others twenty feet away and connect. Count on even these soft-skills to be practiced to advantage in our brave, new and uncertain world.

At the other end of the spectrum, studies by Princeton Economics and others show convincingly that world financial flows are ultimately connected and will influence each other even more profoundly going forward.

Core family values dissolving

Although there is much debate regarding its cause, the idea of one husband, one wife and a few children living happily under the same roof is becoming rare. Yet the evidence states that statistically, these lucky children still consistently get better grades and adjust better to adulthood when raised in such *antiquated* environments. Unfortunately, today's trend seems to be for parents to choose a lifestyle that suits them first, then let their children adjust while everyone *hopes for the best*. For instance, there are many parents that after years of encouraging their children to get entertained by the computer or TV screen (so they can work just a little bit more) become shocked when they can't pry them away from it.

Not surprisingly, respect for authority, even in the home, is plummeting. This trend is tragically evidenced by stories such as the following. One of your authors has heard from two principals/rectors from two different schools that they have been scolded by parents because "it is the school's job," *not theirs*, to raise their children! We will leave for another time the issue of what, if anything, parental responsibility still means.

One look at how people currently dress, talk to each other and take care of themselves confirms that the result is pointing towards a more chaotic society rather than an organized one. Indeed, comparing a picture of a crowd today to one fifty years ago and it would appear that the more antisocial you look, the *cooler* your status will be perceived. Just look at any fashion magazine. It seems that the more you look like you *just don't friggin care*, the more attractive and successful you will become. Yet is this textbook *mixed message* actually true? But wait! Before you answer that, isn't it high time for a *selfie*?

Questioning authority 2.0
Many of us are trying to avoid *feeling* the true extent of the complexities *and stress* in our lives. Many others are questioning beliefs and even institutions that probably should have been questioned long ago. The Internet now provides us access and information to many more facts as well as different viewpoints and opinions. Not all of them comfortably support the status quo. Here's a small taste:

- How can you solve today's public or private debt problems with even more debt?
- Why do many spend money they don't have on items they don't need?
- Is it healthy or wise to eat genetically modified foods or use seeds that, among other very non-natural traits, can no longer reproduce?
- How long can we continue to use up resources faster than we can replace them?
- Is it right to kill others *in the name of peace* just because your leader says it is?

- What gives our public servants the right to expect to be treated like infallible and unapproachable royalty? Why do our *public servants* need bulletproof cars?
- Why should questionable job performance in corporations be rewarded with large incomes and perks?
- Why should some reporters, actors, entertainers, sport figures and other celebrities earn sometimes more than the average Fortune 500 CEO?
- Won't using antibacterial products sooner or later increase our susceptibility to diseases that our bodies don't recognize or are no longer prepared to handle?
- What is the wisdom or health ramifications in vaccinating yourself this year against last year's virus strain?
- Is there really *no harm* to the water table (and our health) when the chemicals commonly used in *fracking* have caused kitchen tap water to burn?
- Why does the "Federal *Open Market* Committee" meet behind closed doors?

With instant access to information, many of us are waking up and beginning to "follow the money." Some are realizing that not everything told to us by opinion makers on what is now known as the *Main Stream Media* or MSM may be in our best interest. Founding Father Thomas Jefferson's famous quote "*The price of freedom is vigilance,*" may be more appropriate today than when he said it. What if falling asleep while guarding the responsibility of remaining free eventually ensures the loss of that freedom?

At the same time, there is a diminishing need for young people to gain the approval of others. One of the most interesting traits of many young people is their fearlessness to being published or to instigate an instant public response about an issue via social media. This quality will make it much harder for these new generations to be controlled by those who wish to maintain their stubborn grip on public opinion. This in turn will encourage even more social and market turbulence. A real split seems to be festering between our ambitious, articulate and increasingly media savvy youth and the masses of so-called "*sheeple*"[6] who have actively or passively chosen to sacrifice their freedom for a (*false?*) perception of security. "*Don't rock the boat*" seems to be giving way to "*No guts, no glory!*"

In our experience, most people we know who have *hit the wall*, burned out or suffered a nervous breakdown did so due to being incapable of sacrificing their integrity any more for their *perceived* sense of security. If for no other reason than health, they begin to say "*no*" more often and thus began to develop

---

6 "Sheeple" a term denoting a cross between sheep and people commonly used on the Internet to signal people who have given up their personal sovereignty and the right to govern or think for themselves.

an ability to see through many falsehoods that they used to politely overlook. Also, it seems that many children react to a parent's burnout by resolving to never wind up in the same situation. They begin early to question assumptions and refuse to sacrifice their integrity for a paycheck. Questioning authority is beginning to make a comeback. How will this trend contribute to our world going forward?

Health, longevity and adaptability
Research now points with some certainty towards every other child being born today in Sweden (and other countries) will live to reach his or her 100th birthday. If someone reached that age two generations ago, it was front-page news! It is also becoming more likely that this new generation will remain relatively healthy and active longer. What are the ramifications of increased longevity for our society? How will we conduct business?

Focusing on just the OECD countries, the healthcare and leisure industries that cater to older people are already racing to keep up with the exploding demand. Given the recent economic boom, many retirees are really enjoying their golden years, due to their fat pensions and retirement accounts. As each economic earthquake gets bigger and more frequent, regal retiree lifestyles could rapidly change and probably will. Until then, many pensioners will continue having a ball, often at the expense of their younger colleagues who are still working to support them. This situation will increase friction as their own retirement prospects dim. The prospects for these two trends to continue are still getting stronger.

Retirement, more work or both?
By no means does every retiree experience this "*Golden age.*" Many workers realize too late that they did not save enough or that circumstances have limited or destroyed their retirement plans. Others see a chance to add to their retirement income and also do something productive in their spare time. This realization is causing shifts in the labor market as older (often perceived as more reliable) workers are postponing their retirements, *often for financial reasons* and taking jobs traditionally held by young entrants into the labor market.

A global retirement crisis is brewing and will play out for decades to come. Experts predict its consequences will be far reaching. Many workers will be forced to work well beyond the traditional retirement age of sixtyfive. Living standards will fall while the chance of poverty rises for the elderly, especially as they continue to stretch already over-stretched actuarial tables. This will be especially true in wealthy countries that built comprehensive and expensive safety nets while simultaneously raising retirement expectations.

In developing countries, the tradition of children caring for aging parents is still very common. Yet people's rising expectations may be dashed (and they may move) if their government cannot afford to finance a retirement system to replace this social tradition. These problems are now growing exponentially in the U.S.A. as the baby boom generation moves into retirement. Not only that, many of their children are beginning to realize that the luxurious level of their parents' retirement is quickly fading for them. In fact, many are now forced to live in their parents' basement to save money.

The baby boomers' certainty of a retirement era that some still refer to as "*golden years*" is now predicted come to a *surprising* (?) and abrupt halt all over the Western world. This is due to the mathematical certainty that boomers are retiring faster than their pension funds can afford. Pension payments, contributed by boomers for most of their working lives, have not kept pace with the underlying funds needed for future redemption. Many funds are moving slowly or quickly towards bankruptcy, especially those covering government and municipal workers. Cities like Detroit have already given up. So, if you have all your money and trust tied up in this increasingly fragile system, you may soon discover that your retirement expectations and hard earned funds have been misused, speculated with or outright stolen from you. Mastering agility, even as a retiree, may be wise.

Already, many persons aged sixty five and older are struggling to live on their retirement checks. Emily Brandon wrote this in an article for US News and World Report[xviii]:

"*The oldest baby boomers have already turned 65, and those in the oldest population brackets of the U.S.A. are beginning to swell. The age-65-and-older population grew 18 percent between 2000 and 2011 to 41.4 million senior citizens, according to a recent Administration on Aging report. America's first wave of baby boomers is now retiring at a rate of 10,000 per day. And these numbers are expected to further balloon over the coming decade.*" As baby boomers continue to reach retirement age, the traditional retirement age of sixty-five years old is being called into question. It is often stretched beyond the original retirement promise.

Ken Dychtwald, president of the consulting firm Age Wave and author of "*A New Purpose: Redefining Money, Family, Work, Retirement, and Success*"[xix] states, "*The boomers will be the first generation to overwhelmingly not receive some sort of guaranteed benefits from employers.*" He also says, "*We now live in a 401(k) world where people are responsible for their own savings, and baby boomers have not done a very good job. It's a generation that is going to struggle in old age in the absence of reliable anchors and support systems."*

This shift sometimes occurs with heart wrenching results. In a Dunkin' Donuts store in Northern Maine, one of your authors witnessed a sweet little old lady, who looked to be at least 70, taking our order from behind the counter. We saw her get yelled at by her twenty-something boss for being too slow. The tension and frustration of the situation was evident from both of them. It was plain to see that they both wished this sweet, but inefficient lady was somewhere else. From the look of the situation though, this was not an option. The way she sheepishly took her manager's abuse could easily have been due to the unexpected destruction of, or the lack of a viable retirement plan.

Baby boomers have also begun retiring in Europe. This marks a demographic shift that will reshape European labor markets over the next twenty years. It will also widen the skills gap many companies are trying to fill. Europe's aging population is now forcing them to rethink traditional retirement plans. The recent financial crisis has highlighted the fact that many aging Europeans, raised in socialism, will be forced to work into their later years mainly (surprise again) for economical reasons.

For companies in all countries, this precarious lengthening of the job market presents both opportunities and challenges. On the plus side, mature workers tend to have valuable and practical experience. Therefore, they can be wiser and more efficient than their younger counterparts. In entitlement heavy countries such as those in Western Europe, employers are learning that they can also avoid major disruptions caused by long maternity/paternity leaves by using older workers. This also lowers extravagant consulting and mentorship expenses AND older workers are less likely to change jobs. This saves employers lots of extra recruiting and training costs.

On the other hand, workplace friction can increase. Often, older workers with behavior patterns formed in another age, are forced to report to younger managers. They also are more apt to want to do things "*their way*." Older workers have historically demanded and gotten higher salaries and health care benefits, but even that is changing. They also may have minor disabilities and need special rules or treatments. These issues can require a large, *forced* dose of understanding from younger colleagues, who already feel irritated. With people getting older and either willing or forced to work, how will this situation impact your market, products and employees?

Staying put

Again from Emily Brandon's US News and World Report article from May 13, 2013[xx]:

> *"While many people fantasize about moving someplace sunnier or more interesting, most people retire where they spent the final years of their career. Between 2011 and 2012, only 3 percent of people age 65 and older moved, compared to 14 percent of people under 65. And older movers stayed in the same state (83 percent) and the same county (61 percent). Only 16 percent of people who traded spaces after age 65 relocated out of state or abroad."*

Health and disabilities overcome, for now

Health coverage is less of a problem for the current batch of retirees. This may soon change. It is absolutely going to change for future generations. Currently, Medicare, Medicaid and now "Obamacare," plus supplemental retirement packages mean that many can still afford the increasing cost of medical care. Even now most people who reach the age of sixtyfive can look forward to a relatively long active period before old age, and the common ailments it brings, catches up with them. Living longer and healthier lives also permits them to remain active in the workforce. Regardless of whether this is by choice or necessity, the fact that they remain on the job longer, or choose to find a new one impacts negatively on the chances of new job market entrants. This precarious situation will only increase friction between the older generation of *perceived haves* and the younger *have-nots*. Plan on your ability and your agility to respond powerfully regarding these issues to be tested.

Currently, *"about 13% of Europeans have some sort of disability,"* according to Luk Zelderloo, secretary general for the European Association of Service Providers for Persons with Disabilities. He has also said that, *"Another 25 million Europeans will be added to those ranks by 2025. This increase will mostly be due to age related problems."*

Still, according to these experts there remains an optimism that technology will develop and permit many of these people to actively contribute to society in their own way. How that will look?

Only time will tell, but recently one of your authors saw a 23 year-old war refugee working his smartphone, with what remained of his left wrist, faster than your author could feverishly work with all ten of his functioning fingers.

13. ENVIRONMENTAL CONSCIOUSNESS ON THE RISE

Talk to any child in school today about the environment and you will usually get a passionate and fairly educated (or is it memorized?) argument as to why we need to care more about it. This trend is a far cry from the collective apathy and ignorant denial that was present on the first Earth Day in April, 1970.

Sustainability and the green movement
What started out as a fringe movement is becoming a major trend. Many seem to finally be waking up to the fact that we can no longer ignore the consequences of treating our earth as a garbage dump. Although some large, multinational corporations will probably be the last to admit that this trend has to be taken seriously, this grassroots movement to get greener, buy local and save the planet *is impacting profits NOW.* This so-called *"voting with your wallet"* movement has started to catch fire.

More municipalities than ever are legislating the sorting of your trash to encourage recycling. Think about all those email signatures that urge you to *"think before you print"* and save trees by minimizing paper use. Buying local produce at farmers' markets is becoming both a marketing trend as well as a social event where neighbors meet. This trend is being fueled by the increasing distrust of the prepackaged, newly-termed *manufactured food* being sold in large chain stores. It is evident now that nearly everything sold in a box, can or bag has questionable additives that include salt, sweeteners, all kinds of preservatives and additives ranging from unhealthy to downright sinister. *"Better living through chemistry,"* once the proud motto of a large chemical conglomerate has now morphed into a sarcastic poke at chemical additives that range from a slight untruth to a negligent or fraudulent lie.

Most city air is now cleaner than it has been for generations. Even Beijing recently experienced blue skies for the first time in decades. The efforts of Greenpeace, the Sierra Club and organizations such as the Swedish eco-labeling company *Swan* now have the wind at their backs. Helped in large part by the availability of instant information from the Internet, consumers are voting with their wallets to purchase more ecologically friendly products and services. Even legislation is being enacted that protects the environment. All these steps contribute to making the world a little better for us all. Keeping up with this requires more flexibility to respond quickly to these *wallet voters*.

14. Negotiating Megatrends Demands Agility

Hopefully, these few megatrends listed here will offer you a taste of what we see on the horizon and will encourage you to think about the opportunities and consequences they can provide. Again, our purpose is *not to document in detail, or argue for or against* each trend, but to provide an *in-your-face experience* and encourage you to wonder how you will be affected by *or how you choose to affect* these trends *and others* going forward.

If not already, soon one and probably more of the following will powerfully affect you and your organization:

- Information Overload
- Increased globalization
- Increased competition
- Exponential Development

The increasing pace of faster, better and cheaper solutions is unstoppable. This means shorter, more intense cycles. Trying to suppress or avoid them will, at best, buy you a bit of time. *Learning to navigate them nimbly is a much wiser investment.* When facing major changes, shocks and surprises, the more agility and resilience you can muster and master, the better you can handle what comes your way. We will be using the metaphor of sailing a yacht to help us all better understand how to navigate safely through the threats and boldly towards the opportunities that lie ahead. Whether you are the Captain or a distinguished member of your crew, knowing what to do and being agile enough to do it, even in the roughest waters, gives you and your entire crew a better chance of success. This is not only true in sailing, but in business and life as well.

Agility also means knowing *when not to act.*

Understanding and distinguishing this important difference increases your level of responsibility. When you increase your *ability-to-respond,* navigating a big sailing yacht *or company* becomes simpler, easier and safer. As Peter Senge mentions in his excellent business book "The Fifth Discipline (Senge, 1990)." There is a major difference between reacting and responding. *Reacting* is automatic. It comes from Latin and literally means to "act again." *Responding* is a more conscious act. This word comes from Old French and literally means to "answer back," after consciously reflecting over your different options.

As life and business get more complex and turbulent, simplicity, ease and certainty become more important. The more you learn to conscientiously practice the tools, methods and processes we present in this book, the better you will get at *responding* instead of *reacting;* and the easier and calmer your path to success will become.

SECTION TWO

THE "PERFECT STORM"

The Perfect Storm

> "So far so good…" Heard from a jumper three
> floors before hitting the pavement…

Figure 9 The Perfect Storm[xxi]

Ever since the year 2000 movie with the same name, *the Perfect Storm* has come to mean a storm combining several sizeable storms together, where each one could be very deadly in its own right. This weather analogy is very much in line with the situation we look to be currently facing in the world today. A number of seemingly unrelated factors, each of which could be an economy killer in its own right, look to be coming to a boil at the same time. Should they combine, we would face an even greater perfect storm, like none we've seen before. Some, but not all of these factors are:

- Economic uncertainty rising
- Environmental damage mounting
- Geopolitical tensions increasing
- Societal strains reaching their limits

Like the Four Horsemen of the Apocalypse, these rather broad issues are beginning to integrate with each other while gaining further momentum and speed. Underlying this entire storm is the diminishing trust and, in some cases, growing contempt that more and more people seem to be feeling for those who declare themselves in charge.

As with the first part of this book, the points we present here and others are much more comprehensively documented in other places than here. *The point we are striving to make* is that ANY ONE of these forces could upset the global economy and your business all by itself, but when taken together, a new level of agility will be required to navigate through them for any hope of survival, much less success. Being able to handle them in the manner of a nimble samurai or agile sea captain will take both training and special equipment to be effective. That's the point of this book.

15. Economic Uncertainty Rising

Turbulence and market uncertainty seem to be cyclical and their cycles appear to go hand in hand with progress. With each new round of development, a feeling of excitement ensues; things then reach a boil and finally collapse to start again, fresh.

Economics, a seasonal comparison
Economic historians (*and occasionally distinguished economists*) have long understood that economic cycles can be likened to the four seasons. Some economists have predicted these cycles with such certainty that they have been persecuted, locked up or killed for their prescience. Kondratieff of the former Soviet Union was so clear about his work on cyclical patterns and what it said about the Soviet Union that Stalin chose to send him to his death in the Gulag rather than listen. Recently, Martin Armstrong seems to have been sent to prison on trumped up charges, due to his programming skills, which in part enabled him to program a computer to accurately predict upcoming economic events. He later beat the charges and was released to continue his research into the history of economic cycles. What do these men have in common? The similar *and predictable* comparisons they find in economic patterns and recurring cycles.
Simply described, the growing season works like this: after a winter of collapse and retrenchment, the growing cycle starts anew. Dormant seeds begin sprouting again in the sun. Summer comes with favorable growing conditions and the crops begin to reach their peak growth. The cooler breezes and clouds of autumn follow and wise farmers begin harvesting their work in preparation for the colder months ahead. Winter inevitably follows with its harsh environment, damaging and harming anything or anyone unprepared. Then the cycle starts afresh, once again.

In the economic sphere, a cold winter of debt and investment collapses and paves the way for fresh and optimistic entrepreneurs to begin *springing* into action. Their ideas sprout so-called *green shoots* and capital is raised to help them cultivate these start-ups. More and more monetary fertilizer is poured on them to make full use of summertime sun and rain. Sooner or later, the market starts to wane, as the economic days become shorter and colder. The wise entrepreneurs harvest their gains then by selling out. Resisting these natural cycles, others yearn to and do whatever they can to keep the economic growing season going.

They borrow more and continue expanding right into the colder and darker months of autumn. Inevitably, many of these optimists become overextended and their dreams collapse along with their credit ratings and company stock prices, as the harsh reality of winter sets in. They cause hardship for others and they disappear right into their own (and their shareholder's) *winter of discontent.* Everyone hunkers down in this harsh economic environment while non-performing debt and other claims are washed clean from the cycle. The whole process then starts afresh with the warming and fresh, new ideas of spring. This full cycle of business can be easily tracked a number of times, just since the early 1800s. Each cycle is often connected to leaps in communication or transportation technology, for instance:

- **The Canal Boom of the 1830s.**
  This lasted until overinvestment created an overabundance of canals and shipping prices collapsed.
- **The Railroad Boom of the 1870s.**
  Once the collapse of the Canal Boom was complete and the debt was washed clean, a new boom in railroads took hold. Tracks were laid all over the Western world until overcapacity and cheap finance crushed the transportation pricing mechanism once again.
- **The Automobile Boom of the 1900s**
  At the turn of the last century it is estimated that there were anywhere from 300 to 800 automobile manufacturers in the city of Detroit alone. By the end of the Great Depression, only a handful remained.
- **The Mass Communication Boom of the 1930s**
  The stock of Radio Corporation of America, better known as RCA, reached a height of about 400.00 U.S.D. per share right on the cusp of the 1929 stock market crash. It reached a low of approximately four bucks a few years later. The products were the same, yet overcapacity, deflation and a collapse of demand directly affected its value.
- **The Air Travel Boom of the 1960s**

What a great time to fly and to invest in the rapidly expanding airline industry. High service and high margins made this one of the darling industries until hijackings and increased fuel costs of the 1970's dampened all the fun.
- **The PC and Internet Boom of the 1980s and 90s**
  Ask anyone who was fully invested in the peak year 2000 how this ended
- **The Real Estate/Mortgage Boom of the 2000s**
  We are still feeling the effects of this cycle.
- **The Global Debt (bond) Market** is next, *according to the experts who profess to know.* These debt markets are estimated to be at least *ten times* bigger than the world's stock markets.
- And now… The ***Transformation Boom;*** where *agility* will be the key to sustainable and enjoyable success; as we describe in this book.

In each of the above examples, the momentum of what *"Sir"* Alan Greenspan famously called, *"irrational exuberance"* got the better of even the most conservative business people. Investment turned into speculation and increased credit transformed into overwhelming debt. Keep in mind that in each cycle, even prudent business people were finally *forced* to participate. They were often well aware of what they recognized to be a very uncertain play, but they ultimately *had to participate* just to remain competitive and keep their clients happy. Why? Among other things, it has now been proven that the *high* created by riches influences the same parts of the brain, as do stimulants like cocaine. You could say that we are "programmed" to get so involved in our excitement that we become addicted and easily throw prudence to the wind.

Charlatans and con-artists, who smell the potential of making a quick buck, also encourage this process to ultimately exceed all rational or prudent behavior. In all of the above examples, technological change is fueled by the availability of finance and even favorable legislation until such time that there becomes an overabundance of both. The whole process collapses upon itself and then begins anew.

Although we are capable of being conscious of this process and agile enough to leap from an old trend to a new one, *most have yet to master this dance.* Below are some symptoms that suggest that, for the agile amongst us, new opportunities to demonstrate this capability for agility are arriving as we write.

Black swans

Nassim Taleb's best seller, "The Black Swan" (Taleb, 2010), possibly sums up the challenge we face better than our following description of a perfect storm, especially with regards to uncertainty. As Taleb has now stated in different ways, the idea of predicting a black swan is preposterous! "*The very nature of a black swan is that it cannot be predicted.*" Even so they happen.

This is why the whole idea of agility is becoming more important. He makes clear in his book that the probability of one or more economic black swans is increasing. Although they are impossible to predict, just by their nature, to stay in the game we need to increase our vigilance and be agile enough to handle them.

Abundance equals overcapacity and commodification
With such easy access to financing and billions of new workers from the east entering the market, it has recently become very easy to set up a plant to produce just about anything. As the current business cycle nears its next economic winter, it is becoming clear that there is overcapacity in just about every industry. Latecomers such as Indonesia, Vietnam and Cambodia are now challenging even China and its ability to produce cheap products in excess. Yet the question so eloquently posed by writer and publisher Bill Bonner[xxii] remains, "*How long will Americans (and other westerners) continue to buy stuff they do not need with money they do not have?*"

Increasing everything
Along with this abundance trend there is a growing realization that we are finally reaching boundaries that have so far been theoretical. You have no doubt heard of Peak Oil but what does peak actually mean and what can it teach us about the big picture?

Peak oil does not mean we will run out of oil anytime soon. On the contrary with its recent drop in price there is more available than can currently be used! The peak refers to the economical peak where the finding, harvesting and refining of oil uses more energy, resources and actually costs more than the revenues generated by energy produced from it. Producing oil over Peak Production is uneconomical and the more that is produced, the more money is lost. The active ongoing debate as to whether we have already reached this point seems to have been postponed for the moment, but not really. For example it is currently estimated that it costs approximately seventy U.S.D. per barrel to produce shale oil from the Bakken fields in mid-western U.S.A. The current price is drifting between thirty and fifty U.S.D. per barrel with some analysts expecting oil to go down to the twenties! Money is being lost on almost every barrel produced. What will be the long-term consequences of that? What will happen to all the creditors and banks that loaned billions on business models based upon oil at 70.00 U.S.D. per barrel? Could this same phenomenon be currently playing out in virtually every other commodity and industry?

Overcapacity in production
Since China became the world's go-to place for manufacturing, the price of producing goods has decreased virtually every year. With the rest of Southeast Asia and South America now coming online, more and more producers are entering the market. With financing so cheap, making factories easy to build, this further distorts the market and pricing.

Has the balance of power clearly shifted from suppliers to buyers?

Shorter cycles, greater competition and deflationary prices naturally tip the scales in favor of the buyer.

Another game changer that will add to this problem of overcapacity is the decreasing price and increasing sophistication of 3-D printing. Count on this making a large portion of the remaining industrial complex obsolete. Why order a small part *even from China* if you can produce it in your own home? The time of mass-individual home production is not far off.

Increasing litigation
The legal profession has expanded all over the world, yet nowhere has it expanded as dramatically as in the United States of America, where ethical standards have also declined significantly. Although there are still champions that use their legal skills to do good for individuals and our society, many more have been compelled to or consciously *chosen to* stoop to *ambulance chasing*, and worse. On a recent drive through a lower middle class neighborhood in the State of New Jersey, many billboards were observed. A surprising number were pasted with advertisements promoting divorce lawyers boasting that, "*Now only one consenting partner's signature was needed!*"

When it comes to corporate law and legal proceedings, the horror stories keep piling up. Whether to defend sinister products, services and questionable research or to challenge negligent or criminal products, services and research, bad law has gummed up the courts and cost untold fortunes. An unknown lawyer who commented, "*You only get to eat what you kill,*" seems to have sarcastically summed up the current legal situation.

When money is involved, people often become ruthless in pursuit of winning their case. In big tobacco, food, finance and oil cases, to name but a few, their pockets are so deep that they can literally exhaust a smaller challenger's resources by continually throwing money and lawyers at the problem. This is regardless of who is ultimately in the right. Evidence suggests that the *Spirit* of the Law is clearly now of inferior value to the *Letter* of the Law. Here again, the power of accessible information and forces such as *Wikileaks* and *Truthout* are slowly, but surely exposing more and more blatant abuses of power. As trends forecaster[xxiii] Gerald Celente has often said, "*Justice* is now spelled *Just us*" and honest business people are starting to wake up to this message.

Even though there still seem to be many more tactics at hand to hide, suppress and distort the real story, these less than forthright agendas are slowly but surely being revealed. This is resulting in an increased distrust for the darker practices of *business as usual* and its cozy use of questionable litigation. Just Google "special interests and corruption" and you currently get 86 million hits. To anticipate and deal with a growing legal minefield will require any serious decision maker to be extremely prepared and agile, especially when it comes to issues of the Law.

It is a big problem for society when litigiousness becomes a way of life and that problem is now expanding rapidly to the rest of the world. Below are excerpts from a white paper written by Hans Amell, on the US Legal System. Please ponder the following excerpts:

1/ **Is it true** that every OECD country apart from the U.S.A. has the rule that "*the loser pays?*"

   In all other western countries, if I sue you and lose, I risk having to pay for your defense. Here in the U.S.A, who pays for what *has to be negotiated*. Consequently, this makes initiating a case a viable business decision or option. For instance, this means that in the U.S.A. you can use litigation as a delaying tactic, *even if you know you are in the wrong.*

2/ **Is it true** that every OECD country except the U.S.A, has an established relationship between injury/damage and the penalty? This is to say, the greater the neglect or injury, the higher the financial penalty. This is the norm in all OECD countries, with one exception. In the U.S.A. the norm is: "How much punishment/greater sanction will it take to ensure that the culprit does not repeat the action?" If I lose my little finger in a door stop on IBM's premises due to a faulty installation, I can sue for millions of dollars to maybe get a couple of hundred thousand. Yet if I lose my finger in my neighbor's door I may only get five hundred bucks, if anything. The same situation, but different pockets.

3/ **Is it true** that every civilized country has some type of jury system, but only the U.S.A. strictly stipulates the need to have a "jury of your peers"?

It is these "peers" who eventually decide whether you are guilty or not. The problem is nowadays that many lawsuits are extremely complex and need the explanation and understanding of true experts. If it is a complicated biological, psychological, medical or financial issue, most normal "peers" neither have the training nor the experience to comprehend the level of detail necessary to reach a responsible decision. Only in the U.S.A. are experts called upon *only as witnesses* and even this has to be negotiated! Tragically, a jury, often without the necessary understanding of the pertinent hard facts, is charged with assigning guilt in complex cases. Often, their judgment ends up being *based upon their emotions.* Hire a good lawyer, one who has mastered playing upon people's feelings, and you directly increase your chances of winning, *regardless of who is telling the truth.*

4/ **Is it true** that all OECD countries except the U.S.A. prohibit lawyers from taking commissions? Their reasoning? It undermines the necessary level of trust. Therefore, *"Ambulance Chasers"* are an uniquely American phenomenon. What if this makes trying to teach personal responsibility to our children a real challenge? For instance, how hot should coffee be? The result is the U.S.A. is the most litigious society on the planet. Bizarre cases of assigning guilt happen regularly to others instead of the person who probably should have been more careful or responsible in the first place. Ethics often end up taking a back seat to greed.

5/ **Is it true** that the U.S.A. has about twenty times more lawyers per capita than the average OECD country? What about the fact that the U.S.A. has about one lawyer per engineer whereas all other OECD countries have fifteen to thirty engineers per lawyer?

6/ **Is it true** that the U.S.A. also has about twenty times more lawsuits per capita than the average OECD country?

7/ **Is it true** that the US healthcare and insurance systems are between two to seven times more expensive than an average OECD country? How much of this difference has to do with insurance costs due to more exposure to legal risk? It is interesting to see how even the current healthcare reform costs so much while avoiding the two areas most in need of reform, malpractice and cross-state competition for insurance plans. After all, insurance costs are based upon statistics. Wouldn't it be better to discover and address the root cause (the legal system?) instead of the victims i.e. people and livelihood (via exorbitant healthcare, insurance, etc., costs?) Maybe the reason is in the next point.

8/ **Is it true** that over eighty percent of all congressional delegates in the Democratic Party are lawyers?

Although it may be somewhat less in the Republican Party, this still means there are on average four to five times as many lawyers in government as in other OECD parliaments. We also enact something like 40,000 more laws each year from local to federal levels. This would give credence to the old saying, "*If you are a hammer, the whole world looks like a nail.*" How do these thoughts affect your need to be agile?

Although the above points are focused on the US, we clearly face a challenging dilemma as this trend is expanding globally. For instance, the U.K. is well on its way in the same direction. In the US, it will be an uphill struggle to have "lawyers" take any decisions whatsoever against their own profession, especially in view of the last point. Yet how much money could we save if we reformed the legal system before we tackled, for instance, healthcare? Do you think the Founding Fathers meant this to happen when they wrote about checks and balances between the three branches of government?

Being subject to the whims of the current legal system only creates more uncertainty. Agility is most effective when the risks are visible and known. Agility is of less use when employed against the whims of opinion, deception and manipulation. Maybe if more people took these concerns to heart, something more positive might come as a result of these observations…

Overcapacity of decisions?

With all the information we are bombarded with, is it any wonder our ability to make choices has been damaged? Not too long ago, most families had one phone bill, one bank, one or two favorite stores and one school system to deal with. When you went into a store you would have fewer choices when it came to what you would buy, but you could quickly respond with a rational purchase decision.

The word "*decide*" comes from the same Latin family of words as homicide, suicide, genocide etc. The suffix *-cide* means to end or kill and in the case of *de-cide*, it means to end or kill the other choices. Often, just like in the *Terminator,* the choices keep coming. How and when can you be sure you are making the right one? How do all these choices make you feel when you land in a decision-making position?

Go into a store and choose a loaf of bread and you will be faced with probably over thirty different and attractive choices. Multiply this by the type and brand of soap, the cat food and the shampoo you need and your choices expand exponentially. The same is true for all the different retirement plans, telephone/internet providers, banks, healthcare and school choices you are confronted with. A few can be avoided, some delegated or postponed, but most need to be addressed. There are so many choices now that some business models actually take this into account and *prey on your information overload.*

Whether the intention is helpful or not, many companies are going to a subscription type of service from which it is often hard to extricate yourself. This form of *customer capture* is becoming more prevalent as we drown in a rising tide of excess data and decisions while being drained of the time and energy to address them. *How does this feel?*

Colossal government and personal consequences
In the interest of maintaining an image of control, those who govern us have recently been more active than ever in passing laws. More and more of these laws seem to have less and less to do with serving the public and more and more to do with serving special interests, getting re-elected and maintaining or grabbing even more control. Just a quick look at recent headlines will reveal that the term *Public Service* has lost its shine.

- What does the monitoring and cataloguing of every electronic communication and transaction have to do with freedom of speech?
- How does the militarization of the police contribute to their image as "peace officers"?
- Why do *Public Servants* sense the need for expensive bulletproof cars and bodyguard details *and then use your taxes to pay for them?*

What if we have too many laws as it is? Ask yourself when was the last time you heard about a spring-cleaning of obsolete, irrelevant or ridiculous laws? Laws that slow down our ability to do business or cause resistance to new harmless societal trends. Just like cleaning out a large closet and getting rid of two pairs of shoes for every new pair you buy, wouldn't it be healthy *and popular* for legislators to install a self-rinsing mechanism e.g. along the lines of "for every new rule, you have to retire at least two old ones"? Right now, certain watchdog groups estimate that average law-abiding citizens in many countries break an average of three laws per day, most of which they are not even aware. Off duty police have been sheepishly heard to admit that they often remain silent about their profession in social gatherings. According to them, guests often avoid talking with them once their profession is revealed, for fear of, consciously or not, saying something incriminating.

Keeping the economic party going

Most of us would love an endless summer; hardly anyone likes a good party to end. Just as with parties and the seasons, the business cycle seems to consist of waves. Much like wanting to continue to enjoy a great, late August beach party, most of us long for just a little more warm and sunny weather. We humans are physiologically wired to seek pleasure and avoid pain. Metaphorically for the past thirty five years, most of the developed and developing world has enjoyed a long, endless summer party, especially when it comes to economics and societal development. For anyone interested, evidence now points to that the continuation of the good times now increasingly relies upon financial shenanigans such as: cooking the books, larger debt burdens and currency printing, rather than upon solid, organic business growth, less rules and lower taxes. These disturbing trends increasingly beg the question, "*What if you don't need government negotiated trade deals as much as you do the freedom to do business with whom you freely choose*"?

Since the first real taste of an economic winter during the so-called *Great Recession* of 2008-9, estimates are that the world's central banks have printed 14 trillion *extra* dollars' worth of their currencies (Rubles, Dollars, Euros, Yen, Yuan, etc.) collectively. One unofficial, but provocative reason given for this behavior is, *to shore up growing uncertainty in debt markets*. Record levels of both governmental and corporate debt are now being reached or once again exceeded. Small business owners (the recognized backbone of a solid economy) all over the world are being forced to close while the big multi-national firms are growing. The difference is mainly due to the access that big business enjoys to this *easy money*, plus new, favorable legislation allowing higher volume with lower costs. High quality jobs are being replaced with low quality ones and low quality jobs are being replaced by robotics. Profits are larger, but questions are beginning to surface as to how much longer this unstable model can continue or how much longer already debt burdend consumers will be able to afford to buy more?

Measuring inflation and deflation is much like taking a temperature. As it grows colder it takes more energy and fuel to keep warm. Since the 1930s, when an economy cools or deflates, Keynesian economics has preached fueling the fire by borrowing and spending more money to revive it. The idea of borrowing our way to prosperity has worked flawlessly since John Maynard Keynes first suggested it during the Great Depression of the 1930s. Could something now have happened to suggest a sea change in the perceived sanity of borrowing even more? Recently, people, corporations and even governments seem to be reaching the limits of their borrowing capacity. Although currently very unpopular, there's even talk of austerity, of actually cutting back on expenses, instead of borrowing more. Since our current monetary system is now fully based upon increasing debt, talk of austerity puts the whole financial system in jeopardy. Due to the system's current structure of charging interest on every Dollar, Euro, Yen, Yuan, Ruble etc. printed, there is not enough money in the system to pay all the accumulated debt, plus interest back. The act of paying of interest on this newly issued money requires the issuance of ever more new notes. Since each of those new notes will also be subject to even more interest payments, it doesn't take a "quant"[7] to realize our system has a large *black hole* right in the middle of all this money printing. Just like a black hole, sooner or later our whole current monetary and financial system *must inevitably collapse into itself.* Many now point to the Great Recession of 2008-9 as the start of this volatile, dangerous process.

Too Big To Fail?
Safety in numbers has never been more popular. There has been an increasing rush towards *bigger is better* in companies and in government. Through acquisition, attrition and easy money-fueled growth, some large organizations have increased in size to the point of being untenable. What became very clear in the Great Recession of 2008-9 is that some organizations were seen, *at least by those in charge and their friends making laws*, to be "Too Big to Fail." The story sold to the public was that certain financial and industrial behemoths, such as Goldman Sachs, Citibank and even General Motors, to name a few, were given a special status that in effect denoted that if they went bust, it would be catastrophic for the American and possibly the world economy. Therefore, they were bailed-out with public tax money and given special super-legal rights to allow them to keep operating beyond the point where most sane accountants would have declared them bankrupt.

A most interesting issue arises here with regard to the discussion of agility. This is that these monster companies ended up needing these special favors due to their being *everything, but agile!* Now, almost 10 years later, most have grown even bigger and in the process, have become *even less agile!* Moreover, they have, by many headline accounts, become even better at throwing their increasing financial and legal weight around to protect their very profitable, but increasingly non-agile way of doing *business as usual...* and why not? Judging by all the profits being harvested by the banking industry, would you want to change if you were in their shoes? It may be worthwhile wondering what will become of them *and us* when the next inevitable downturn starts in earnest?

"*Too Big To Fail*" is both a symptom of and a threat to the current *business as usual* system that, like a cancerous growth, is slowly killing its host. The bigger these giants become and the more they protect their way of doing business over a freer

---

[7] Quant is financial slang for a financial analyst specializing in Quantitative Analysis.

and more agile market, the bigger the repercussions will be when *TBTF* is finally recognized as untenable.

Already there are signs that the leaders of these behemoths cannot and do not know, in manageable detail, what is happening inside their companies. Look no further than all the documented cases of price fixing and market rigging that have been exposed, *to which no Financial CEO has yet been charged or held responsible.* Can this mean anything more important than either the CEO is totally incompetent for not being aware of crimes being committed on his/her watch, or that he/she is blatantly disregarding the law? When the Law is bent or disregarded uncertainty surely increases.

The more you and your business are forced to play in rigged markets, the more your behavior will have to adjust to accommodate and anticipate the capricious market changes *that may or may not take place.* Like it or not, as long as this untenable situation keeps morphing into new uncharted waters, these highly uncertain variables will need to be dealt with. Using an increasingly outdated and inadequate set of traditional tools is a recipe for business suicide. This increasingly uncertain situation will eventually require a superhuman level of agility and a lot of luck. Feeling safer?

Financial repression

Another storm warning that is also a direct threat to any plans you may have to save for a better future is called *Financial Repression.* It is a financial tool used by governments and central banks to keep their borrowing costs manageable. It is a legislative slight-of-hand that has dire consequences for business and investing. It is the practice of forcing interest rates below the rate of inflation. This increases the law maker's ability to borrow even more money without significantly raising the total amount of the payments. Although it can (and should) be used to help pay down existing debt at a quicker pace, it is often used to borrow more. Unfortunately, the flip side of this is that anyone trying to maintain their savings or possibly get ahead is faced with serious financial and legal headwinds. As long as the interest rate on savings is below the inflation rate, any money being saved for a rainy day is losing purchasing power. This allows your elected (and increasingly unelected) officials to borrow even more.

The result is that even wise investors are forced to chase greater risk *just to break even.* This also screws up the market's ability to correctly price financial instruments causing increased volatility. This of course, increases the amount of "hot money" sloshing around in the system. This is money that quickly hops from one investment to another in order to increase return. Can you guess what happens to your ability to judge or price risk in this situation? The longer the financial repression, the bigger the waves of uncertainty have to become. We are now in the longest wave yet of interest rates below inflation rates ever and that is before considering the soundness of the reported figures. How will this end?

When credit becomes debt
As long as a company, government, you or I have the means to repay a loan and clearly see the possibility to make a profit on the money we borrow, then the money borrowed can be considered credit. When the money borrowed exceeds our ability to repay it, and/or the possibility to make more money by borrowing more ceases, this amount of optimistic credit suddenly converts to a pessimistic burden of debt. This may be oversimplified, but just try saying these two words: *credit* and *debt*. Then allow yourself to get a sense of which feels better to say...

Most economists, be they Keynesian, Austrian, Chicago School "Supply Siders" or whatever, now finally agree that most current governmental debt *can never and will never be paid back*. Further increasing amounts of corporate and private debt are also now openly being questioned. In fact, many "solvent" banks are only *still* solvent due to very favorable and questionable legislative changes *that govern how their solvency is now defined*. In short, a strong case can be built that *we are now collectively broke*. It increasingly seems that it is just a matter of time before ordinary people wake up to this nightmarish situation. Until that mass revelation, you still have time to prepare and get agile!

The Bond Market:
"*Gentlemen prefer bonds.*" - J. P. Morgan

Yes! The debt market is what currently makes our world go around. It is estimated to be at least ten times bigger than all the world's stock markets. Bonds have traditionally been the safest place to park Big Money for a low, but safe return. Recently, with the advent of ZIRP (Zero Interest Rate Policy) and now NIRP (Negative Interest Rate Policy) this is no longer true. Now many fund managers are either forced to chase yield in riskier markets, forced to receive no interest or increasingly *even pay for the privilege of saving!* Even in the case of traditionally rock solid Swiss Bonds, you now pay for the privilege of owning them. Retirees and others who were planning on living off interest income are now forced to seek greater returns and more risk in so called "junk bonds" or the stock market. Or, they just spend it.

The effect this downward manipulation is fourfold.

1. Risk can no longer be effectively valued or priced, increasing the risk of a major *financial dislocation* (a fancy term for financial ruin).
2. The pool of savings where businesses and corporations traditionally went for money to grow their companies has now been hollowed out.
3. As long as the inflation rate remains higher than what you can earn in interest, you are penalized for saving and encouraged to spend.
4. Funds for investing in future expansion and development is strangled.

These historically low rates have contributed to, and some even say created, the necessity to print more money in the form of what is now called *Quantitative Easing*. This freshly created money has been used to support (buy) this ever-increasing worldwide debt load. So far this practice has resulted in a low reading on the so-called VIX or *Volatility Index*. Recent gyrations though may indicate a coming rise in uncertainty and that is not all…

An average interest rate cycle in the sovereign bond market has historically been about 35 years from one interest rate low until the next. Our current interest rate cycle has now been going down for almost thirty five years while increasing yield. Interest rates are not only continuing to go lower but are going negative, *meaning you pay*! A negative interest rate literally means it is actually more profitable to put your cash under your mattress or buy something riskier that produces a return (and a commission for your bank/broker). *Could this be the real reason behind both the inexplicable rise in stock prices and the latest trend to suggest a cashless financial system?* What do you think will happen when this extremely tightly coiled spring of artificially repressed interest rates finally ends? Can you say, "no bid?"

Loan sharking made legal
Not even this is the whole story. It has now become profitable to again lend to more questionable debtors. Stories now abound about the so-called *NINJA* loans made at the height of the housing bubble to people with *No Income, No Job or Assets*. Recently, variations of these irresponsible forms of finance have begun appearing again. The victims always seem to be the least educated, lowest paid and unsurprisingly, the least *agile* amongst us. The trend has now caught on for NINJA auto loans. Loans to people with questionable credit histories can now be found with terms from six to even eight years! Although the monthly payment is

temptingly low, by the time you are finished making payments on such a loan, you have paid for your car a few times over. These loans also have a habit of defaulting more easily *long before* that lofty goal is ever reached. This tendency to default increases rapidly when the economy begins to sour. In this topsy-turvy market, even this type of business is somehow still profitable, *but for how long*, and what will any long-term consequences be?

Micro-loans are also controversial, as they allow small business in third world areas to borrow money to start businesses and contribute to the local economy. Now take a closer look at Muhammad Yunus, a Bangledeshi social entrepreneur. Many question the Nobel Peace prize committee's decision when it comes to giving a prize to this Banker. He did introduce micro-loans to help local poor people, yet it was later revealed his generous largesse came with *very high interest rates*. Loaning money to people with good ideas, but few options, at high interest rates, made him enormous amounts money. Was it unfairly off the backs of the poor people he was supposedly trying to help? One thing is now certain; in the process he became Bangladesh's first billionaire.

American student loan debt has recently reached 1.4 trillion USD. With a change in the law a few years ago most of this new debt can no longer be written off, *even in the event of personal bankruptcy*. This has effectively turned many often-unsuspecting students into debt slaves. With the downturn in the job market and increased competition from retirees who no longer want to retire, many graduates are choosing to remain unemployed. Their choice stems from avoiding having to begin repaying their massive debts. It seems that even getting a low paying entry-level job often triggers the start of their loan repayment responsibility, usually resulting in them owing more per month than they earn. As job prospects become more challenging, this situation becomes more precarious. The other danger is, the longer they remain unemployed, the rustier their skills are and the less employable they become.

Finally, governments have continually proven that they will support the banks before they support voters. *Bail-out* legislation (where tax payer money is used to make private banks solvent) has now given way to *Bail-ins* (such as Cyprus). This is where customer deposits are forcibly taken from innocent savers to make the banks solvent for their failed investments. Whether or not your tax money is used for private purposes or your bank savings are forcibly "bailed-in," you ultimately have no say in the matter. Someone else is deciding what to do with your money, *for your own good*. What suffers in this situation most is our trust in both the current *business as usual* practices and in our leaders. Uncertainty and risk increase again.

Safety in government paper?

Buying Government Bonds from most western countries has been considered a safe play for most of the last few generations. For over the last thirty years it has been a very profitable investment also. Since interest rates reached dizzying heights in the early 1980s, the price of bonds rose with each interest rate cut for anyone who kept their bonds. From the early 1980s long-term bonds have had an excellent run. Since then, different bond markets have had different fates, but with the growth of transnational investing, many interesting situations have arisen in the world of national and corporate finance.

It started with the so-called Yen-Carry-Trade and has extended to and developed in other countries since. This is where financial institutions see much less risk in borrowing money in one currency, at a low rate of interest and investing in another country/currency for a greater return. For instance, the Japanese Yen has been used for many years due to its extremely low borrowing costs. Yen are borrowed in order to invest it in another government's or corporation's debt, which return a presumably safer, but still higher yield. It makes sense! Why would you risk lending money to a private company in a turbulent market when you know governments hardly ever dare risk a default? Although this is true superficially, there are lots of things that can happen behind the scenes. Such as:

- The borrowing of more and more money
- Rating agencies forced to rate a country's ability to service debt higher than it really is.
- Printing of more money to repay maturing debt.
- Shifting of expensive long-term debt into cheaper short-term debt.
- Increasing long-term certainty of ultimate debt market collapse; but when?

The more these type of shenanigans take place, the more volatile the markets become. More and more of all of these practices are being exposed in markets all over the world. The result is increasing uncertainty and risk. It doesn't take much to turn that uncertainty into a default situation like Argentina or even Russia experienced in the 1990s, except the next time it could be on a worldwide basis.

In addition, every time the interest paid on bonds is pushed down further, it requires purchasing more and more of them to achieve the same amount of return. For anyone that counted upon retiring and living off the interest on their savings or bond portfolios, their dreams of a safe (*and fair?*) return have now been crushed. Anyone wishing to safely live off the fruits of their labor is now forced to chase bigger and more risky returns in the private market. Even as the return on government bonds continues to decrease (*to levels not seen, for instance, since records began being kept at the Bank of England in 1696)*, many investors still prefer or are forced into the perceived safety of this *guaranteed* rate of return. Yet for how long?

Inflation, deflation or both?

If you have recently bought groceries, been to a concert, paid a medical bill, or been smart or crazy enough to invest in a stock, you will have probably noticed a price increase. But, if you have recently renegotiated your mortgage, bought a new cell phone, new clothes or gas for your car, you may have enjoyed a drastic price reduction. What gives?

The short version is that with all this excess liquidity (printed and borrowed money) sloshing around the globe, it is causing more booms and busts in different industries at an unprecedented and ever increasing pace. For instance, the junk bond financing of the Bakken shale oil field exploration and development in the U.S.A, while OPEC simultaneously seems to be losing its ability to influence prices, has caused a glut of gas and fuel. The energy shortages and consequential sky-high prices that slammed us less than ten years ago have now been replaced by fuel prices not seen in an even longer while. This has reduced transportation costs on many products, but for how long? The price of oil dropped *again* by fifty percent in less than six months. The cost of producing oil is estimated to be higher than many producers can sell it for. The resulting decrease in drilling activity is causing lay-offs in the oil patch, plus more bankruptcies from companies that borrowed easy money to get in on the game. This erosion of supply will eventually cause a wave of higher prices and the business cycle will start over. Many brush these increasing gyrations off as simply a matter of market timing. How consistently good is your ability to time the markets?

Thus, easy money is metaphorically very much like wetting yourself in a pair of snow pants. At first it is warm and wonderful, but it rapidly becomes wet, cold and uncomfortable. This so-called *financial dislocation* phenomenon is taking place in more markets, as easy money reduces the *borrowing risk* to get into an already crowded game. Trusted names with high legacy costs cannot compete with new, more agile or cheaply funded start-ups. Critical competence and experience is lost with every new bankruptcy. Look no further than home electronics and the cutthroat pricing wars between big box chains and global producers. Even trusted household names such as Sony have been challenged by low cost producers popping up virtually everywhere on the planet. Yes, *borrowing risk* drops (temporarily?), but what about all the other risks?

This entire process causes increased turbulence and creates greater uncertainty when it comes to planning, for example, how much tomorrow's energy costs will be. How can you make long-term forecasts, much less order more raw materials, when you are not sure of how much the product will cost to produce and transport and how much the exchange rate and carrying terms will be? These pricing dangers multiply every time you *look back at your historical records instead of peering forward* towards the financial horizon.

Bigger balloons

As world economy fundamentals continue to deteriorate and our leaders try to prop them up by borrowing and printing more money, it becomes probable that new financial balloons begin inflating and popping all over. This "Whack-A-Mole" trend has become obvious to anyone interested enough to look for bubbles since the so-called 1985 Plaza Accord was instituted to devalue the dollar. The rapid devaluation of the dollar that followed this agreement is now thought to have been the culprit behind the rapidly rising stock prices leading up to the October 1987 crash.

The so-called Black Monday Crash of 1987 forced investors into the perceived safety of Japanese stocks and caused its markets to rise into a second great bubble, which occurred in the Nikkei index in late 1989. When this bubble burst, it was the emerging world market's turn. From the Four Asian tigers to Mexico and Ireland, investment money began to chase yield in these former *third world,* now rebranded *developing,* economies. This was until 1996 when these bubbles too began to pop, causing the agile investors to disregard Fed Chairman, *Sir* Alan Greenspan's warning about *"Irrational Exuberance"* and move quickly to the emerging High Tech market in the U.S.A. Silicon Valley became the place to start your Internet business and young entrepreneurs were financed with billions on the flimsy basis of *clicks per view.* This bubble finally went pop in 2000. With the help of easy money from Sir Alan's now *irrationally exuberant* Federal Reserve, the next bubbles started to quickly inflate in the American Real Estate market, in the raw materials market and in anything Chinese. The so-called Real Estate Bubble burst in 2007 and with crashing house prices, the mortgage market, *which had made those insane housing prices possible* became so bad that the U.S. Government was eventually called to the rescue. The mortgage market collapsed in 2008 bringing world stock markets down with it. This seems to have caused what is now known as *the Great Recession.* The hot money shifted again into raw materials and precious metals until that bubble also popped in 2011.

Since 2009, trillions of freshly printed and digital Dollars, Yuan, Euros, Yen, etc. have been thrown at the problem of reviving the world economy, but views on the resulting successes are at best mixed. The next and possibly final big bubble to fear is in the various bond markets and this alarm may be very under estimated. Since the various debt markets are at much larger than the corresponding stock markets, a loss of confidence or a rapid rise in interest rates could cause another cataclysmic financial *dislocation* that could shut world commerce down on a scale larger than even the Great Depression. With all these bubbles, it is a fair question to ask what the current fair value of your company is? Is it 2-5-10-20-30 times earnings? What will it be tomorrow?

During the big Internet and dotcom extravaganza, many IT/Telecom companies where trading at 100 times earnings and several times revenue. Only recently Pfizer, the Pharmeceutical giant, offered two times *revenue* for AstraZeneca. Sometimes, valuation is a mystery but historically it seems to balance out at around 5-15 times projected earnings. For large corporations, larger multiples must be supported by special underlying reasons. Either they are extremely unique and often only temporary, or they are *fabricated* and subject to collapse, usually when you least expect it.

Often, aggressive growth objectives create their own problems. In Pfizer's case, their enormous size alone, forces them to continue to conduct aggressive Mergers and Acquisitions in order to keep on growing at a pace that continues to excite their shareholders. The excitement can become addictive, mesmerizing and ultimately untenable. Uncertainty increases.

Transactional business versus relational business
Over the past thirty years the focus on the application of technology in business has contributed amazingly towards getting more produced and sold in shorter periods. This process was only made possible with the improved technology available to track and analyze each transaction and do business with a much tighter margin. Great, right?

Absolutely, especially if you happen to be a big box retailer; one who also has access to virtually unlimited credit, at record low rates. You probably also have the shiniest new business system to back it up too. Yet if you are one of those small shop owners on your town's main or high streets, congratulations to you if you are still in business! In fact, how in the world have you managed to survive the increasing level of global competition, drone delivery, and money-back forever guarantees?

If you are still in business, the reason will probably have something to do with the phrase *customer relationship*. That is that wonderful and respectful way of doing business where people will pay you *a little bit more* to feel like they have actually dealt with another human being. It is a form of business that enables you to respectfully see, hear and understand each customer's needs, wants and wishes.

We now have over thirty years of proof that you do not need a human being present to transact business. An entire transaction can now be accomplished by machine and most likely at unbeatable prices. But what happens when something goes wrong or if you wish to change suppliers?

Transactional business only requires *sense* when it comes to measuring stuff. *If you can measure it, you can manage it*, whether it's the amount of money, the color of the item chosen, the delivery dates and/or logistics, to name just a few *measurable parameters*. All of these metrics can be *sensed* using cheaper and cheaper computers or chips.

Sensing, in terms of *feeling* what the customer needs, wants or wishes and how satisfied or dissatisfied they are (before, during and after the transaction), is tragically being forgotten, *because that kind of labor intensive attention costs too much*(?).

As the complexity of the transaction increases, so do the chances of something going wrong during the process. Resolving the situation satisfactorily still ultimately falls back on an *individual in your ever more overworked and frustrated service staff*. Navigating your way through endless telephone trees to find someone who actually cares only increases customer frustration. It also heightens the chance that when you finally do find a sympathetic customer service person, you will be too upset to detect their concern. How agile is this for anyone? More importantly, how important is individual customer satisfaction becoming when it comes to measuring your ability to be agile? How can you ever hope to distinguish your product, service and company from your competition? What if agility now MUST INCLUDE increased soft-skills?

The trend towards transactional business seems to be nearing its peak. The balance between the frustrations of getting what you want, when you want it, and at the cheapest price, is beginning to become noticeable. It is worth noting again the recent figure that 47% of Internet transactions that reach the checkout are never completed. The reason is an unexpected or additional service or handling charge that was added at the last minute. The computer may not feel a thing as it adds this surprise charge, but tracking metrics clearly demonstrate that *your customer certainly does*! Pay Attention! Almost fifty percent of a web shop's business is left in the shopping cart *unsold*, if even only a few pennies are added to the expected selling price! If that sounds high, ask yourself if you would be more or less motivated to buy if an additional and unexpected cost was added to *your purchase*, at the last minute? How easy do you think it will be to regain that lost customer's trust and future business?

Being agile enough to relate to each of your customers, *on their terms*, can be enhanced with the use of technology, but you are fooling yourself *and your future chances of success* if you think technology can replace a personal touch. It is that conscious, human interactive element that will allow you to heighten customer trust and your sales margins.

What if, in our haste for efficiency, we may have thrown the *customer loyalty baby* out with the *relational bath water*, in favor of transaction efficiency and quarterly profit. Short-term, this will goose earnings and possibly even your profit. In the long-term and without constant heavy sales and marketing expenditures, this strategy usually fails, completely. Now it's happening even faster as your typical customer is quickly harnessing the power and reach of social media.

On the other side of this transactional/relational coin, your ability to increase margins in an oversupplied world drastically diminish if all you have to distinguish your offer is a *lower price*. The road to *higher margins is paved with personal and sustainable relationships*. It is further enhanced by an agility to quickly and consciously adapt to volatile market situations and changing customer tastes. These important soft-factors often defy even the best measurement algorithms. This more sensitive behavior demands newer, more agile marketing tools!

The predatory business model
Compounding this problem, more companies and government services are beginning to nickel and dime their customers with small fees on everything. In the beginning it was just another annoyance, now it is morphing into big business. From congestion taxes to drive your car into cities like London and Stockholm to roads that you previously paid to build with your tax money that you now have to *pay a private company to use*. From a charge for every paper invoice you receive, to a hefty sum plus a labyrinth of paperwork to switch telephone carriers. From little or no interest on your money deposited in your bank to a service charge to move it anywhere or take it out of an ATM, these small charges are beginning to add up faster to sums that can cripple a family budget. Each one is an irritation by itself, but together it is becoming a sort of stressful stealth tax where everything is costing more in other ways than just traditional price rises. This practice also insures that any reported inflation statistics will be less reliable.

This practice is now spiraling out of control as more and more companies figure out ingenious and nefarious ways to add charges here and there and those charges are rising at an increasing rate. Look no further than the cost of so called ecological food. It now actually costs a large amount more NOT to have poisonous chemicals sprayed on them! Think of the stress for someone on a fixed income or on a salary that is not keeping pace with these costs, who only wants to do the right thing. The room they have for maneuvering is diminishing almost daily. An increasing number of people are beginning to have to choose between two products that they used to buy without question. If your product happens to be one of them, you may suddenly realize a drastic reduction in sales almost overnight when your customers are forced to drop yours. This situation is not helped should your product or service be the one they resent the most, due to all the small, extra charges they have had to suffer. This is *regardless* of whether or not you were forced to add them just to stay afloat yourself...

Customer capture, the new business model
To add insult to injury and to keep customers locked into current cash cows, a very constraining new form of business has begun to blossom. How many subscriptions do you now have? Have you also noticed an increase in products and services you used to be able to buy one-off to which you must now subscribe?

From cell phone subscriptions to Microsoft Office 365 and others, you are now being forced to pay a monthly or annual fee to maintain access to more services and products. Yes, updates are included, but your ability to switch providers becomes more and more complicated and often you continue to get billed or auto-renewed without your conscious consent. *This information is usually buried on page 37 of the customer agreement you have no doubt read and memorized.*

The result is customer frustration, an increased feeling of helplessness and more time, energy and resources devoted to game changing ways to combat these intrusive and constraining ways of doing business. *This is the textbook opposite of creating and maintaining customer loyalty.*

Explosive growth of mergers and acquisitions expected
Why?

In an era of colossal change and shorter cycles, more companies will try to accelerate the time to market of their products and services through increasingly aggressive M&A and marketing practices. This focus on *marketing synergies*, rather than *operational synergies*, is turning this historically slow process of finding the right operational fit into a frantic search for *the quickest and cheapest way to find, rebrand and distribute a new product or service.* For example, what if Samsung made a deal with Nokia to repackage and sell their products with a Nokia logo? Could a partnership like that have helped one of Telecoms former leaders to at least maintain their now drastically shrinking share of today's telephone market? One they were instrumental in creating?

What this all means is that the M&A process is undergoing its own transformation. Maybe it too should be *rebranded* from finding synergies in R&D and Production to one of finding them in Marketing and Distribution. The crush of *time to market* has now become so unforgiving that to develop a new product often takes more time from its window of opportunity than can be afforded. For instance, if your newest telephone has a sales life of one year, but it takes more than one year to develop and produce it, you have significantly cut your chances of making a decent return on your investment. It will be much more effective and profitable to instead merge, acquire or ally with a company that can develop it faster. Then you can focus precious resources on convincing the market that it looks and feels like your other products.

Therefore, as this trend accelerates, your M&A and Marketing focus will become more important and require more resources, whereas your R&D and Production focus will diminish. Faster time to market dictates the shortening of this make/buy decision. Strategic partnerships, such as the one recently signed between Ericsson and Cisco, will become more commonplace and divestitures will increase when an internal department or unit's usefulness wanes. Yet the tendency will also increase to choose speed over prudence, causing many well-intentioned M&As to crash and burn, due to quick, ignorant or sloppy due-dilligence methods.

Production versus consumption society

Buying stuff has become the new religion. "*He who dies with the most toys wins*" has now been transformed from a cute bumper sticker into a lifestyle. As the Shopping Mall became our new place of worship, our society shifted focus from production to consumption. Indeed, even our ability to produce moved from the West to the East and Asia now produces most of the stuff that we buy. It is estimated by the Federal Reserve Bank, among others, that over 70% of the U.S, economy is currently based upon consumption.

Could it be that in this process we are also *consuming our ability produce?* If this is true, then we are also consuming a large portion of our skills and resources with which we formerly used to produce. The biggest point here is not what has happened to our ability to produce, but *our entire mindset.* It seems we have also *consumed* our understanding of *why losing our ability to produce matters,* especially if, for instance, the U.S.A, the U.K. or even further down the line Germany want to remain global competitors.

Many now look down on those forced to work in factories. Somehow it has even become more glamorous to work in a fast food chain, or some other service job than it is to get your hands dirty on a factory floor. What if we have also consumed our work ethic? Martin Armstrong of Princeton Economics and Bill Bonner of Bonner and Partners have both done very good jobs of explaining that a country's ability to produce what the market wants is what gives it value. According to them, others and a good dose of common sense, 15th century Spain and 1980s Japan exemplify, from opposite directions, the point that the wealth of a nation is not indicated by the amounts of money or gold it holds in reserve, but rather by how much finished product it can produce and sell.

According to Bonner, Spain became extremely rich by relieving the Americas of their gold during the time of the Conquistadors. Unfotrtunately, instead of focusing this newfound wealth on producing things, they spent it buying fineries from all over the globe. After they had spent their gold on a lavish lifestyle and had borrowed even more to finance their continuing wars, the economy collapsed. Other than the current riches enjoyed as a result of Spain's recent travel and condominium boom, the stature it reached as a world economic power, around the time of Cortez, has never been regained.

By contrast, according to Armstrong, Japan has hardly any natural resources of its own. The country began importing raw materials and producing finished goods to sell to the rest of the world, from before the Second World War until after the bubble burst in 1989. Companies like Toyota, Sony and Mitsubishi became household names all over the world. Real Estate prices in Tokyo became some of the highest in the world as well. Even though it has now been mired in a recession for nearly thirty years, Japan is still one of the top three nations when it comes to GDP. This is with a population that is shrinking and aging at an increasing pace. The factor that continues to make them economically viable is their ability to produce things domestically that others, all over the world, wish to buy.

How long will the U.S. and Europe be able to maintain their world dominance while their economies are being *consumed* from within by buying more stuff than they can afford? It has now gotten so strange that since the Great Recession of 2008 Central Banks have gone from lending money at unprecedented low rates of interest to printing it out of thin air to "stimulate" their economies and keep the consumption party going. If there is one thing that historically sabotages a country's ability to remain agile, it is being weighted down with debt that can never be repaid and printing the purchasing power of that nation's money into oblivion.

Buybacks

One of the latest games being played in the boardroom of western companies is taking advantage of these low interest rates to issue debt in order to repurchase their own stock. Since most executives enjoy compensation packages that often include options to buy stock, it is definitely in their interest to inflate the stock price. As they ensure their future security with an increase in the stock price, the temptation to increase that price is too great to be done just through normal increases in sales, research, development and production. Decreasing the amount of shares on the market helps considerably. By also issuing debt to fuel their ability to fund this process and further cutting R&D, they literally *consume* the company's future by jousting for bragging rights to their market's biggest year-end bonus. They get richer by weakening their company's ability to fund new research and development, or to expand, renew and improve the company's production capacity. This short-term strategy of capital consumption invites long-term failure in agility, competitiveness and sustainability.

Simple creative destruction case studies
To really rub this point in, here are just a few examples of trends and game changers that have turned conventional *business as usual* practices into mush. The Internet is shattering one traditional business model after another. If you look at how the path to success in just the following industries has changed over the past few years, you will hopefully sense a trend. That trend is the need to become more focused on what *will happen* rather than what *has happened*.

- **The Recording Industry's** profits have been declining for years, due to both piracy and increased competition from Internet providers. Both now allow you to listen to only the songs you want to hear, *when you want to hear them*. Long gone is the reverse piracy (as well as excessive record company profits) gained by being forced to buy an entire album just because you like one particular tune.
- **The Movie Industry** is suffering from the same online pressure as the recording industry. The distribution of the latest films can no longer be tightly controlled, due to the rise of torrent technology and the ability to stream a film online, *often without paying for it*.
- **The Retail Business** is transitioning from the traditional chain store to Internet sites that are open 24/7. The need for retail space is plummeting. Amazon.com, is just one enormous example. They are opening forty new distribution centers in the U.S.A. alone. "Drone delivery" is being tested. In some parts of the country, entire shopping malls are closing down and turning into forgotten ghost towns, looted for the materials that can easily be pried off the walls and sold.
- **The Banking Industry** has been too profitable for too long not to notice. This is now causing both jealousy and resentment. After the banking crisis of 2008-9, people have slowly begun to wake up to what *Fractional Reserve Banking* really means and its consequences, *on a personal level.* Also, from interest rates to Forex, to commodities, it seems one price fixing scandal is

being revealed after another. Trust in your local bank has drastically eroded to the point that many in the Bank and Finance industry are sarcastically referred to as "*Banksters.*"

With the advent of the Internet and Blockchain technology, more innovative products are being introduced and adopted at a quickening pace. Names such as Pay-Pal, Bitcoin and even Bitgold are offering innovative alternatives to *banking as usual*. Their development is no doubt fueled by almost daily revelations of more shady deals and corruption.

- **The Fast food Industry** According to *Zerohedge.com* there was a recent strike by fast food workers. Their demand was higher pay. In hindsight, the Strikers could not have picked a better time to provide a textbook example how to hasten the demise of their own profession. A San Francisco based start-up called none other than "Momentum Machines[xxiv]" introduced a burger-grilling robot that can produce almost 400 hamburgers per hour (*with no wage complaints*). Possibly sensing the fantastic opportunity that lies before them, yet understanding the dislocation their technology will cause, Momentum issued the following statement:

  "*The issue of machines and job displacement has been around for centuries and economists generally accept that technology like ours actually causes an increase in employment.*"

  "*The three factors that contribute to this are*

    - *The company that makes the robots must hire new employees,*
    - *The restaurant that uses our robots can expand their frontiers of production which requires hiring more people, and*
    - *The general public saves money on the reduced cost of our burgers. This saved money can then be spent on the rest of the economy.*[xxv]"

Whether this is true or just a vain public relations attempt, one thing is for sure. Just as the 18th century "Luddites[8]" found when they destroyed textile machines in the English Midlands (*to retain their jobs?*), progress waits for no one.

---

8   The name of a group of Anti Technology workers named after a Ned Ludd from Sherwood Forest who, between 1811-1816, destroyed textile machines in order to thwart the use of them to replace their own, now outdated labor practices.

Market pricing mechanism destroyed?
The result of all of the above is increasing economic turbulence. This is also the number one reason for increasing your agility. Common sense now hints that the capital markets have been artificially manipulated for so long it has caused the normal market pricing discovery mechanism to be seriously flawed or worse. Simply put, the normal Pricing Mechanism refers to the process whereby two or more parties feel confident that they have enough information to agree upon a fair price. Now large amounts of *hot money* is forced to chase a higher return on investment, regardless of risk or *often common sense*. Investments that can increase production or efficiency (such as rebuilding of infrastructure, modernizing of schools and more alternative energy source development) have often not been undertaken while riskier investments (such as telecom projects, massive building projects, e.g. China's ghost cities and now gambling websites) have had money thrown at them. Thus, with:

- Interest rates at zero or negative numbers
- The money supply increasing due to larger debts and increased printing
- Oversupply in virtually every industry
- A focus on transacting rather than relating

The ability to correctly value and price a product is becoming questionable at best!

This turbulence increases the risk that you will have to change your pricing either up or down overnight to stay competitive going forward. Looking backwards, for more than a moment at a time in this environment, can easily become business suicide.

Finally, the volatility and spread in foreign exchange rates are becoming quicker and larger. Changes in the value of the U.S. Dollar and the Euro, Yen, Yuan and other currencies, which a few years ago would have taken years to play out, are now occurring in months and sometimes weeks. In spring 2015, the value of the Swiss Franc changed drastically overnight when it was announced that it would no longer be pegged to the Euro. As many Eastern Europeans had taken out mortgages in CHF (Symbol for the Swiss Franc) the amount they owed drastically increased, *literally overnight*. Those placing orders in Euros for a product in Swiss Francs or vice versa were forced to radically recalculate if they would be making or losing money after that shift. Even Agile firms like Swatch and Nestle were hit by this quick and radical change in value. This type of arbitrary financial move can quickly and unforgivingly break even a robust balance sheet.

Therefore, the more you can develop tools and tactics both online and within your team, that keep you and your crew *focusing forward* and increasing your flexibility, the more you will be able to handle what tomorrow brings.

Increasing high risk of deep market crisis
The Baltic Dry Index[xxvi] is one of the most followed indicators of world commerce. It measures the cost per day of renting a *cape size* freighter. A *cape size* freighter is a ship so big that it is unable to pass through the Panama or Suez Canals and therefore must sail around the Continental *Capes*. The higher the price, the more robust the need for raw materials and thus, the better the world economy is perceived to be doing. The Index is currently making lows never seen before!

Government activity is increasingly taking a larger and larger slice of the economic pie while business from small and medium enterprise is contracting even further. Also according to the U.S. Federal Reserve's FRED educational website, the current velocity of money[xxvii] (the approximate time it takes one dollar to circulate through the economy) is at one of the lowest frequencies in decades. This is historically interpreted to mean that people are now hoarding their cash in fear, rather than spending it.

Meanwhile, record debt is being recorded in the public and private sector, and why not? Interest rates would suggest that it is safer to borrow money than it has been *since tracking statistics were invented.* Banking and financial institutions are also recording more record profits. What's not to like?

Unemployment looks relatively low, but a peek under the hood at John Williams' site *Shadow Stats*[xxviii] will reveal that official figures are calculated in a much more forgiving way than even a few years ago. A quick look at his figures demonstrates that United States unemployment and inflation numbers are much different, especially if you continue to use the metrics that were originally developed for that purpose. So, how do you make it easy for your team to win? Just keep moving the goalposts to a more favorable position.

These indicators and others portend that while official world trade figures look good on paper, the reality may actually be quite different. Does this contradiction fill you with confidence? How do you plan for the future and *what figures should you use?* Uncertainty seems to be the key word here too. This does not bode well for *business as usual,* but where there is risk there is also reward ... *for the agile businessperson!*

16. GEOPOLITICAL TENSIONS INCREASING

It is becoming clearer to anyone with common sense (and who dares to look behind the headlines) that many of today's geopolitical tensions could be solved if rational dialogue was used instead of saber rattling. It seems that even this kindergarten level solution to an adult disaster will take more time and destruction to resolve. Until we get sick enough of killing each other to understand that *real courage* comes from resolving conflict *without violence,* we need to prepare for more, physically, mentally and financially.

Major geopolitical upheaval
It is no longer a well-kept secret of how to remain the bully on the block. Just make sure your competitors stay mad with each other and you have succeeded in "*destabilizing*" the situation, allowing you to remain in charge. Do it with finesse and you may even look like a savior, even when it was *you who caused the instability in the first place*. Does this sound familiar, especially on a geopolitical level? Study any reliable foreign policy report from the biggest power on the block since at least Roman times and you will probably come across a reference to this type of policy. From Caesar to Napoleon and beyond, all you have to do is successfully *divide and conquer* to remain in power. The key is to get the factions to fight amongst themselves. You get extra points and income by supplying both sides with weapons. Although this type of strategy is getting easier to see, it is still occurring and thus must be reckoned with.

There are also increasing signs that power and wealth are shifting again from the West back to the East. The powers of the Orient are flexing their increased economic might. They are setting up their own investment banks, payment systems and buying anything gold that isn't nailed down. Many of the problems outlined above are exacerbating this shift of power. As China, India and other eastern powers amass great fortunes in production and trade, the powers of the West are going deeper into debt to keep the good times rolling.

Evidence suggest that the age of the Petro Dollar seems to be giving way to a more international payment system. Slowly but surely, countries like Russia, China and even India are looking to pay or buy oil in currencies other than the U.S. Dollar. At the same time China's Yuan has been accepted into the *Special Drawing Rights* or SDRs basket of currencies maintained by the *International Monetary Fund,* IMF. China is also setting up direct payment accounts with most of their trading partners, thus bypassing the need for converting into U.S. Dollars. Along with Russia, they have set up and are now testing an international settlement system to compete with the American SWIFT system. Although this is a relatively recent occurrence, expect its importance to increase over the coming years. What happens when all those Dollars circulating around the world are no longer needed to transact business between two non-American nations?

What was once seen as attractive American humility, up to and including the Second World War, has since morphed into what an increasing number non-Americans are calling arrogance. The rest of the world has now gone from tolerating this, to creating systems to bypass American hegemony. This trend of internationalization looks set to continue; relegating the U.S. to a more appropriate (but diminished) role in a more balanced mix of geopolitics. But, don't think for a minute that this process will go smoothly. Just like a wounded animal feeling threatened, someone used to getting their way often becomes much more aggressive if the position they are used to controlling is challenged or taken away. Since the United States has, by far, the largest military and Military Industrial Complex to support it, they may begin relying on it even more in the future to maintain their so-called *exceptionalism*. Whether the source is American or not, how will you adjust your sails for these kinds of potentially volatile geopolitical winds?

Nationalism again on the rise
Just as in the 1930s, when people feel poorer they look to blame their discomfort on outsiders, long before (or if ever) they look within. Politicians love this as they can create an external bogeyman and focus their voter's frustration on a threat from the outside.

Nationalistic Ultra-Right and Left political movements are gaining ground in most every western country. From Marie Le Pen in France, Jimmy Åkesson in Sweden, Alexis Tsipras in Greece, to war-mongering Demopublicans in the U.S.A, each one still finds it easier to blame national challenges on other parties and cultures, rather than to begin *questioning their own role* and their current way of governing. The biggest problem with this strategy is that if (when?) it is finally exposed, it eventually undermines confidence in the entire system.

Governmental debt equals increased economic tension
If most western governments were to use the same accounting rules *they apply by law* to commerce, most would have had to declare bankruptcy long ago. Since governments increasingly make their own rules, they have *so far* been able to increase their debt loads *way over* what would be acceptable to a responsible company or an individual law abiding citizen. Unfortunately, the gap between governmental fantasy and fiscal reality may be beginning to narrow more quickly. Importantly, more constituents are beginning to notice. Look no further than Trump or Sanders for confirmation.

Although Greece has garnered most of the headlines, when it comes to the effects of austerity and borrowing more to take care of a debt problem, other countries are not far behind. World leaders like France, the U.K, Japan and even the U.S.A. have had their debt downgraded over the past few years. This is due to an increasing level of doubt in their long-term ability to repay it. Even the financial rating agencies that rate creditworthiness have been accused of playing favorites, eroding economic confidence even further.

Many countries have either tried, or been forced into, austerity programs to lower costs. This has resulted in budget cuts on the very social services that *more people have been forced to rely upon*. While health, sanitation and infrastructure costs are postponed or minimized, military budgets are maintained and in some cases increased further, adding more weapons to use during an eventual friction point. For instance, one of the biggest expenses still on the broke nation of Greece's balance sheet is defense.

Fascism gaining

> *"Fascism should more appropriately be called Corporatism because it is a merger of state and corporate power"* — Benito Mussolini

If you care to notice the power and influence that business and banks now exert over our politicians, you will see that Mussolini's definition of Fascism is alive and well. Nowadays, it has more to do with finely tailored suits than with jackboots. Although lobbyists may be making too much money to even think of themselves as the corporate tools of fascism, this may be exactly what they have become. Here are a few examples:

- The government bailout of American banks in the autumn of 2008
- The running of many American jails is now a very profitable private enterprise
- The influence of Big Pharma over health care legislation increases daily
- The increasing amount of money donated by *Political Action Committees* or PACs to U.S. election campaigns
- The selling of public corporations to private (chosen?) ones at very undervalued prices, such as postal and telephone services
- The rise of "natural news" which is another term for news written specifically to promote a product or service (often without the audience knowing it)

These and many other examples should give you a taste that your individual vote may count less and less, when compared to the influence of moneyed business interests. If you are sitting in a good size corporation, this may sound great, especially in the short run. Just remember how Mussolini's life ended. Hanging upside down on a meat hook to be spat upon in a town square. Even if you run a fairly good-sized company, if you are not *in* and playing "*the game*," you are probably *out*. All of these actions further the chances of *business as usual* going forward being more wishful thinking than something to plan on. The need for agility increases.

U.S.A's standing in the world?

Especially with recent events in the mid-east, President Wilson's so-called "*Arsenal of Democracy*" is beginning to be seen by many in the rest of the world as a spoiled, self-absorbed, *exceptional* bully. Foreign policies directed by a motivation to destabilize, and the chaos and death they cause, are slowly being revealed as raw power plays. Which western child, raised during the cold war, could have ever dreamt that Russia would grant amnesty to an *American whistle-blower* whose "*treasonous*" crime was revealing the level of governmental spying taking place *on its own people*?

Rules and regulations regarding international transactions are growing. In their wake, more and more incentives are being created for other nations to work *around* American based systems. An Asian competitor is now challenging the American controlled SWIFT international payment system and even the Washington D.C. based International Monetary Fund or IMF will soon have the Asian Infrastructure Investment Bank or AIIB to contend with. American led international payment restrictions and banking requirements are slowing the velocity of money (the rate of the amount of business being done) considerably, all over the world. These incidents and many others like them coupled with the increasing uncertainty that governmental debt will ever be paid back, is causing a slow but measurable erosion of the image and prestige of the United States and its role on the world stage. Ask any American who has recently tried to open a bank account in another country…

Increased risk of military intervention
As domestic concerns increase, focus upon external military expeditions seem to increase in parallel. Local conflicts are morphing into regional ones and regional ones are attracting larger and larger players. With the United States squaring off against a rejuvenated Russia in both Ukraine and the Middle East, the stakes are increasing as quickly as is the risk of large-scale warfare. Look in any economic history book and it is obvious that the risk of open warfare quickly puts business and society on a defensive footing. This causes already weakening international trade to tighten further. If you happen to be expanding into such an atmosphere, you could quickly find yourself overstretched in a market that no longer exists.

17. Environmental Damage Mounting

People have been preaching to "save the world" since long before the first Earth Day in 1970. Yet only recently have we begun to really observe the impact of those warnings in a way that is finally moving us into action. For instance, we still have unknown quantities of radiation leaking from Fukushima, Japan into the Pacific Ocean *years* after the initial catastrophe. There is also a floating and growing island of plastic waste somewhere in the Pacific Ocean, estimated to be larger than the State of Texas. Entire species are dying off at an increasing rate and Greenpeace now estimates that "*over fifty percent of marine wildlife has disappeared over the past forty years.*" According to statistician Dr. Hans Rosling, our population will continue to increase until the end of our current century. How will these challenges impact our way of doing business?

The Turbulence of the climate change debate

"*There are three types of lies - lies, damned lies and statistics,*" - Mark Twain.

The only thing that has drastically changed in the 100 years since Samuel Clemens wrote this is that there is much more data available from which to create statistics. Now, more than ever, facts and figures can be manipulated back and forth to support, promote or defend *just about anything*.

The debate about whether or not climate change is real is still not over, but most everyone interested in this topic is in agreement that something is happening to our climate and weather patterns. The jury is still out on how our climate is changing. Will it be global warming, cooling or something else? Does it matter?

Many scientists who study climate change agree that human activity is partly responsible for changing the climate. But is this the whole story? Studies on geologic, volcanic, tree and ice samples also point to large and volatile climate waves that span decades, even centuries and date back long before man even existed.

There are many differing opinions but there seem to be two main camps when it comes to climate change:

1. We are the biggest cause
2. Nature is the biggest cause

The discussion always gets interesting when money becomes involved. On both sides of this conflict, a lot of money is being spent to sway public opinion. Once you have the data you want, there are experts who are ready and willing to advocate your point of view, especially if there is some money to be made from doing so. The more money involved, the bigger push you can make. Package your research convincingly and you can create doubt in even the staunchest supporter of a cause. You may even win an Oscar! This debate is bound to cause uncertainty, indecision, gridlock, panic and increased volatility.

One of the biggest actors on the stage on the side of human activity as the cause is the United Nations Intergovernmental Panel on Climate Change (IPCC). According to McKinsey, the IPCC is one of the largest bodies of international scientists ever assembled to study a scientific issue, involving more than 2,500 scientists from more than 130 countries. The IPCC has concluded that most of the warming observed during the past fifty years is attributable to human activities. Its findings have been publicly endorsed by the national academies of science of all G-8 nations, as well as those of China, India and Brazil."

Now, Google the words, "Climate Change Manipulation" and you get 11,300,000 hits and the word "fraud" comes up quite often. For every point brought up by those painting doom and gloom, when it comes to what we humans are doing to the planet, there are valid counter arguments as to why this is not true. The most pervasive of these indicates that some of the biggest names regarding global warming, such as Al Gore who gained lots of attention with his Oscar winning film called "*An Inconvenient Truth,*" still live in homes that consume over ten times the energy of an average size one. Furthermore, instead of cycling or walking to work, they are driven in large limos. If they themselves really practiced what they were preaching, wouldn't it make more sense to lead by example, ride a bike and demonstrate what a small energy footprint looks like? It is also interesting to note that many of the biggest advocates of the carbon credit system have a large financial interest in the market on which they would trade… Isn't that also an "inconvenient truth"?

For instance, an article by Larry Lohmann from Ecotopia reveals the following along with names:

> "*The World Rainforest Movement (WRM) says that many of the authors and editors of the IPCC's "Special Report on Land Use, Land Use Change and Forestry" (LULUCF) - unveiled in June before international climate negotiators - were business people in a position to profit financially from the tree-planting schemes likely to follow in the report's wake.*"

It would seem that here again, certain business people will put personal gain before the interests of society and thereby *further undermine the public's trust in their leadership*. This behavior is guaranteed to feed the growing appetite for uncertainty.

Environmental health
As the world population continues to grow and become more affluent, more strain is being put on the ability of our societies to maintain and increase our standards of living. Issues now being discussed include some of the following:

- Steadily rising crop yields
- Erosion and soil depletion, resulting in less nutritious food
- Big business limiting access to fresh, potable water
- The health benefits and risks of Genetically Modified Foods
- Ecosystems strained to their limits
- Increased risks for big weather

Steadily rising crop yields
With growing urban and suburban sprawl, the amount of arable farmland is continuing to diminish. Therefore, farmers need to continually increase crop yield per acre from the already inflated amounts we currently have. Although yields increased drastically from the 1960s up until recently, the era of sensible "*better living through chemistry,*" seems to be coming to a rapid close as the effects of new solutions become more questionable.

More and more consumers are recognizing that there is a tradeoff between quicker growing crops and the quality and quantity of their nutritional value. For instance, adding nitrogen to farmland provided a drastic increase in the size and speed to crop maturity, but it is also estimated that most oranges and apples produced using nitrogen and other additives have lost fifty percent and more of the nutrients that natural, slower-growing crops contain. So even though there may yet be a further decrease in *time to harvest* and a in *per acre crop yields,* evidence points towards those crops being even blander in taste and weaker in nutrients than current ones. *This does not even include the growing issue of what genetic modification does to a crop and the people eating it.*

Erosion, soil depletion and less potent food
Yearly plowing of the same land makes it easier for rich topsoil to dry up, blow away or get washed downstream during a big rainstorm. The result is less fertile soil remaining to grow crops in and much larger deltas at the eventual mouths of the rivers that flow past these lands.

Take the Amazon, Mississippi and Nile river deltas' rapid growth over the last few decades as just a few giant examples. Not only have they expanded tremendously; they have also created giant dead zones way out into the ocean, gulf and sea into which they connect. These dead zones are caused by heightened algae growth, now traced back in large part to all the fertilizers and chemicals from farmland runoff. It may be worth a moment to ponder the following: if these chemicals are causing so much damage to the water into which they flow, what are they doing to the digestive system and health of each person eating the crops grown with them? Do you know where your food comes from?

Food and water are now big business
The age of the family farm is facing stiff competition from deep pocketed corporate competitors. Corporate farming has become the dominant force in the U.S. and is rapidly spreading across the globe. Stories such as:

- Large tracts of Ukraine's bread basket are being bought up by at least one company in Sweden.
- Thousands of Indian farmers are reportedly committing suicide due to financial stress.
- Lawsuits and harassment by corporate neighbors in the U.S. and Canada on family farmers who are *caught* "using" modified seeds to grow these modified crops on their lands. Although blown there by wind, many farmers, fully committed to planting naturally occurring crops using normal seeds that generate by themselves, are being sued out of business for *stealing* these "patented seeds."
- Big business buying up reservoirs and water rights in regions and municipalities, then leasing or selling that same water back to the community at a

big profit. As usual the poor locals who are affected by this are in no position to complain or resist.

As we continue to use up and pollute our remaining reserves of drinkable water, the shrinking remainder is being bought up and cordoned off by large corporations. They plan to, or are already exploiting this resource by charging those who can least afford it, to regain access to it. Something we took for granted, i.e. access to potable water, is rapidly becoming a commodity to monetize and exploit.

- Whole earth and permaculture farmers who are facing increased scrutiny, harassment, fines and even destruction of their crops and herds by local authorities, due to trumped up "health concerns". SWAT teams have even been called in to harass these normally peaceful farm folk and slaughter their newly legislated "illegal" herds.
- The increased evidence of the poisoning of land, rivers and human consumers due to the constant use of chemical fertilizers and pesticides.
- Many are already talking about water being the next oil. Potable water is being consumed faster than it can be replaced. Aquifers are being drained faster than they can refill. California is currently suffering the longest drought since record-keeping was begun.
- There are also more and more reports that the new oil extraction method known as *fracking* is causing the contamination of underground water tables and there have been many documented cases of fire and water coming out of the kitchen tap!

All of this and more points again towards the increasing trend of *short-term profit triumphing over common sense*. Wiser, more natural and sustainable based farming methods are down, but not out. In one way this era of peak industrial farming is literally sowing its own seeds of eventual destruction by being continually forced to employ harsher and more heavy-handed methods to maintain *business as usual*. For instance, by having more and more legislation enacted with the help of lawmakers who are clearly on the take, the word is slowly but surely spreading to *buy local* and support your local family farmer.

Farmers' markets have been resurrected from the dustbin of history to once again become a local community fixture. Even some local sheriffs are beginning to support neighborhood farmers suffering harassment from unwanted officials. Members of the *Constitutional Sheriffs and Peace Officers Association* have assisted farmers in getting law abiding sustainable farmers out of intrusive government's way. Although these are positive trends, they are still a long way from being the prevalent method of raising crops. As long as consumers still choose price over quality, whole earth farming will have an uphill battle against their larger, cheaper and more "resourceful" corporate counterparts. Staying on top of this important health and environmental issue and it's inevitable shift is important, especially if you want to remain healthy and agile.

The health risks of genetically modified foods
Others more passionate about this subject address this issue in much more detail. The important thing here is that there now seems to be enough evidence to cast serious doubt on the scientific claims that these *manufactured* foods are as safe as their natural counterparts. With larger marketing budgets and more legislators willing to "cooperate", getting an unbiased view of this picture from the Mainstream Media is *challenging*. Luckily, the amount of alternative information sources via the Internet is increasing in both volume and quality. The point to be made here again is that whenever uncertainty enters into the picture, increased vigilance and agility are needed.

Ecosystems strained to their limits
Bee populations are diminishing at a rapid pace in many parts of the world.

Figure 10 Catch of the day, but for how long?

Reasons for this rapid decrease range from the increased microwave activity from cell phone networks to new types of pesticides that were brought to market before they were adequately (or properly) tested. Whatever the cause, bees play an important role in the pollination of the crops we rely on for food. Fewer bees will lead to less pollination, which can result in a drastic reduction in food.

According to Melissa Breyer of the Mother Nature Network[xxix], "*There's a definitive lack of apples, avocados, bok choy, broccoli, broccoli rabe, cantaloupe, carrots, cauliflower, celery, cucumbers, eggplant, green onions, honeydew, kale, leeks, lemons, limes, mangos, mustard greens, onions, summer squash and zucchini — all foods that rely on bees.*"

The same problem is now being documented regarding the rapid decline of marine life that has taken place over the past forty years. The World Wildlife Fund[xxx] recently released a report stating that "*up to fiftypercent of the aquatic life they were tracking has been fished out or disappeared over this time period.*" A certain contributor to this devastation is again the toxic run-off from farmlands. It kills the coral reefs that have been responsible for protecting and nurturing a large portion of the marine life habitat. This trend is still increasing. Many other examples abound, but the evidence that our current way of living is now having serious consequences on our ability to keep living that way is becoming unavoidable.

As consumers wake up to this reality, more and more scrutiny will be placed upon the environmental impact of companies and their products. Getting bad press now spreads instantly and virally over the Internet, *whether or not it is warranted.* Should you, your product or your company get caught in this hysteria, agile actions on your part will be your only hope.

Increased risks for big weather

Typhoons, hurricanes, monsoons, La Niña winds and tornadoes have been increasing in both intensity and frequency during the last few years, causing increased flooding, drought, heat waves and major snowstorms.

Regardless of whether or not this is cyclical or induced by our lifestyle choices, sudden changes in the weather can shut down factories, interrupt transportation and cause general mayhem to all plans to conduct *business as usual.*

Earthquakes and volcanic eruptions have also begun increasing in intensity. An earthquake in the Indian Ocean in 2006 caused a large Tsunami wave that resulted in approximately 250,000 deaths and complete devastation along hundreds of miles of coastline, from Sri Lanka to Indonesia.

Hurricane Katarina pummeled the Gulf Coast region of the United States and practically destroyed the city of New Orleans, Louisiana. Bureaucratic red tape impeded the rescue response time and the FEMA bureaucracy received enormous critique for their slowness to act decisively. For a while the Southern United States looked more like a dithering third world landscape than a robust part of the world's most influential country.

The eruption of the Eyjafjallajökull Volcano disrupted air travel in twenty different countries for a period of six days in April, 2010. This eruption affected over ten million passengers and their travel plans. To even get home during this period required agility.

The Fukushima disaster of 2011 put in serious question the safety and sanity of nuclear powered electricity. More than four years on, we are still not sure of the extent of the damage, further undermining our trust in leadership.

These four "black swan" incidents disrupted lives and businesses on levels rarely seen. These are just four of the most recognized disasters over the past decade. There have been more. The point is that if you look back in time, it is seldom that you find so many powerful natural events occurring in such a short time.

You cannot prepare for everything, but it's increasingly important to be aware of the environment you are sailing into. Right now environmental events are increasing in both intensity and frequency. The better you understand the possible situations you may face and your own capabilities to handle them, the better you will be able to deal with whatever comes.

The Urbanization of society
The migration of people from rural areas to urban ones continues. This trend started long before the industrial period. It really took off once industry began expanding in and around urban areas. Although this phenomenon started in the Western Hemisphere, the eastern one is now breaking all records when it comes to the movement of people towards cities. Estimates of up to 300 million of China's inhabitants shall be moving from the country to the city into the next ten years.

In 1800, just 3% of the world's population lived in cities. By the year 2000, this had increased to 47%. In 1950, there were just eighty three cities with populations over one million. By 2007, the number had risen to over 400. The UN now forecasts today's urban population of three point two billion will rise to nearly five billion by 2030.

In 2000, there were eighteen megacities such as Mexico City, Mumbai, São Paulo and New York City with populations in excess of ten million. Tokyo now has thirty five million making it a so-called Hyper City. By 2025, according to the now defunct Far Eastern Economic Review, Asia will have at least ten hyper-cities, defined as those with more than nineteen million inhabitants. Some Chinese experts now forecast that their cities will contain 800 million of their population within another five years.

Cities are the most inhospitable places to live unless there are effective support systems to keep everyone housed, fed and in good health. As the size and number of cities continue to grow it puts an enormous strain on the infrastructure and resources needed to support them. So far, technology has saved the day when it comes to food, water and energy. Whether or not this will continue is always in doubt. Uncertainty will remain an important factor in the growth of our cities.

Problems that have always accompanied urbanization are still with us and multiply with its growth. Crime, drugs, domestic violence and the spread of disease all continue to increase in direct proportion to the density of population.

On the other hand, with the growth of the Internet and more efficient transportation, selling and delivering products has never been easier. As traditional mass marketing is losing its appeal, micro marketing to larger groups becomes easier as people with the same tastes and interests group together and increasingly share their thoughts online. Although this is an almost embarrassingly simple example of the challenges and opportunities of the urbanization process, it should suffice to underline that doing things as we have always done them is becoming unsustainable. Just the increase in affluence alone has caused the purchase of cars to expand to the point that there is gridlock in most major urban areas on every working day. There are no longer the resources nor the space to add to a developed city's road system without extravagant costs. Even so, more cars are bought each day.

Whether this trend towards larger concentrations of people continues towards infinity or systems start breaking down, human behavior will either continue to adapt or change outright. Looking in your rearview mirror to ascertain when these changes occur will not help you quickly enough to do anything about it. Searching for them on the horizon will be a much more effective way of keeping up, or better yet to stay ahead.

The sixth great extinction

According to several sources such as Stanford University, *The Scientific American* and *National Geographic*, the interpretation of archeological evidence indicates that there have been five great mass extinctions on Planet Earth. According to these sources, we are now in the midst of the sixth. The big difference is that this one, now referred to as the *Holocene Extinction*, has a unique cause - ourselves. This seems to make sense if only from the points above.

Yet according to experts, this newest extinction actually seems to have started approximately 100,000 years ago, just about the same time humans started moving out of what is now Africa. We started by hunting and killing for food to exist. Now we have become so "clever" that we are destroying whole habitats and in the process, our own. This latest extinction seems to be happening quicker than all the others. Estimates by the WWF now put the loss of species currently at about fifty percent[xxxi].

There are the classic cases of the Dodo bird being hunted to death, but now even the bee population is in catastrophic decline. Honey bee Colony Collapse Disorder or CCD is a fancy name for a rapid decline in the bee population. Considering that bees are responsible for pollinating a good many of our commercial crops, this situation could rapidly spin out of control into a food shortage. Agility in this case will include a lot more than just business…

Government to the rescue, again?
With all the hype surrounding our influence on climate change, it is good to keep in mind a quote used again and again by manipulative leaders, "*Don't ever let a good crisis go to waste.*" Interestingly, there is now a major push to *tax* carbon emissions *rather than to eliminate them.* From an economic perspective this makes perfect sense. This will make increased taxation much easier to swallow. A lot of money stands to be made by those people most vocal about the threat of climate on our way of life. Agility is just another tool. It can be used to bring out the most selfless or selfish behavior.

Regardless of the natural versus man-made impact of climate change, the certainty in the equation will be *more new laws*. Well-meant or not, they will be enacted on our "public servants'" schedule, not yours. If you happen to be caught sleeping, you may miss the chance to avoid or profit from the coming changes. Staying on top of your game and aiming your products and energy towards creating a cleaner environment is becoming an unavoidable goal for the businessperson who wants to remain successful.

18. Societal Strains Reaching Their Limits

Many indigenous people express it in different ways, but all point to some sort of mega change for the world and humanity when two things begin to occur with increasing frequency:

1. Natural catastrophes begin increasing in size and frequency.
2. We neglect and ignore our children[xxxii]

Pick up any newspaper or watch any news broadcast and you will certainly see evidence of an increasing trend for both. Natural catastrophes are one thing, but once we take our focus off of our children, and how we guide them into adulthood, we are basically committing societal suicide. From increasing cases of depression and teenage obesity to school shootings, it isn't hard to connect the dots. Clearly, our children are feeling more and more disenfranchised. That is a very wimpy way of saying that they feel alone and unheard. If the message they are being taught and conditioned by is one saying we are too busy to care, what do you think they will teach or not teach their kids?

A reminder of Rome
There is lots of information available comparing the rise and fall of the Roman Empire with our current state of affairs. The major point here is that what started out as an agile step forward in human progress ultimately collapsed and self-destructed into the "dark ages" due to human greed and leader self-absorption. It has been noted that towards the end of the Roman Empire, war, sex,

entertainment and food were the focus of the masses while their society disintegrated. Sound familiar?

The pursuit of personal pleasure in the midst of societal decline became the order of the day. Most people didn't seem to notice when their ability to maintain their lifestyle began to disappear. Most only noticed after the Government had bled Roman Society's money, energy and creativeness dry. At that point, it became easy for the "*Barbarians at the Gates*" to open them and pick over what was left. Any hint of agility seemed to be snuffed out during this end game. Even today, buried Roman treasure is being found that seems to have been deliberately taken out of circulation and hidden. Evidence seems to suggest it was buried by families to hide it from predatory authorities and in the hope of being able to put it to use in building a better future. Unfortunately for them, that future never came.

In short, the great Roman Society failed when an elite few tried to inhibit the creativity, energy and agility of the many. Rome stopped looking ahead and instead focused upon consuming what was already available. "*The older I get, the better I was*" may be a catchy slogan, but it sums up the danger of a person, organization or society that loses that vital sense of focus on the future and their drive to master the ability to remain young and agile.

Integrity or what price vanity?
Current fashion, music and movie trends lay bare the tip of the iceberg when tracking societal values. According to many social researchers, we are living in one of the most narcissistic eras ever. The major focus of many, regardless of age seems to be "look at me." Just as Narcissus spent most of his time staring at his reflection in the mirror, most of us have been conditioned to seek or at least seem to desire recognition from others. The drive to be a *celebrity for the sake of celebrity* is a popular theme regardless of how vain and empty it may be. Want proof? Just watch a so-called "reality show."

It seems that as long as you look good on the outside, it doesn't matter if you are morally and financially bankrupt within. Image is what counts.

This self-absorbing behavior also influences our values and goes a long way to explaining the current epidemic of scandals and corruption that has seeped in to every level of society. The need today for being known for something, *anything* often overtakes common sense.

For those of us interested in running an honest business, this increasingly noisy background makes our quest all the more challenging. As people become more numb to corruption, it becomes harder to maintain a sense of integrity.

Integrity
What is integrity?

Integrity means that everything is integrated and is whole. Just as a balloon demonstrates its integrity when it is fully blown up, a person demonstrates his/her integrity when they stand for, radiate and work from conscious values and principles. Not knowing or selling out what you stand for signals a lack of integrity. You may become rich, but at what price? It is unbelievably hard to *remain agile* or get others to follow when your integrity has a leak.

Integrity also implies a willingness to look deep within, plumb the depths of who you are and consciously choose to improve how you want to be seen and remembered. Those leaders amongst us with integrity and a personal willingness to master life will listen to comments made by others and adjust their behavior according to what they hear. They will consciously do their best to balance this with the principles for which they stand. If their desire is to be more congruent in thought, word and deed then they will be grateful for well meaning feedback. Those lacking integrity will not listen and often sacrifice any remaining integrity by justifying or arguing for why their actions were "necessary." One can wonder how some of them can sleep soundly and there is more and more anecdotal evidence that they do not.

Even casual observations reveal that skinheads, cultists and others with anti-social tendencies are attracted to each other out of a longing for human association. We humans are sociable. We feel better when we have like-minded people around us. Although it may be worthwhile to examine the context sometimes, the principle remains; we feel much better and more valuable when we are in contact with those who hold values and views akin to our own. Some common sense and empathy also helps.

With more and more uncertainty on the horizon, many of us are starting to search for something deeper. The rise in popularity of spiritual retreats and the return of fundamental religious beliefs are both trends that seem to be on the increase. Spirit literally means *everything is connected* and there remains hope that many of us are beginning to realize just how disconnected we have become.

Disconnected from body and planet;
Even in present times, many of our parents or grandparents either grew up on a farm or knew someone close to them who did. Most everyone then knew that food did not originally come from an attractive box or can in the store. Today, many children may have only seen a farm on TV. Even fewer would know how to grow, catch or prepare their own food. The further away our food gets from its source the less nutrition it usually contains. This is due to the processing of it. The shinier and more colorful the package is, the emptier it often is of

nutritional content. Even so, we keep stuffing these manufactured "treats" into our bodies.

Even though we may get an immediate sugar "kick" that makes us feel like Superman, the net result is just like pouring gasoline on a fire. The food often causes more damage than nourishment. Add to this the amount of stress we usually encounter on a daily basis and this pulls us further away from what our ancestors would probably view as a more healthy and natural flow of life.

Not surprisingly, this trend of empty foods dovetails exactly with today's exploding obesity trend. Many of us seem to have disconnected ourselves from our feelings and self-esteem. Many still don't seem to notice or care abut the connection between what we put into our bodies, how we take care of them and how this ultimately makes us feel. Others know and suppress doing anything about it, often out of sheer resignation. Many eat more to deaden the pain and some to create an even bigger "boundary" between themselves and reality. Although some are waking up to this, many are still *asleep at the wheel* of the vehicle representing their own health and well-being. Look around and, if you dare, into your mirror. Notice if "Garbage in-Garbage out" applies.

Working with body language, it becomes painfully obvious, very quickly how little we pay attention to the most important communication tool each of us has, our bodies. For instance, someone near and dear to me works with obese people looking to lose weight, without surgery.

A key element to this life-changing choice is exercise. For many, losing control of their eating habits also means losing control of their bodies' motor function, often with tragic effect. When asked to simply lift up one of their feet, many patients will hear the command, *yet their feet stay put.* The reality of separating their foot from the ground only becomes apparent when the therapist physically bends over and *lifts the patient's foot off the ground!* This has happened too often with too many different individuals to be a coincidence. Could this be shocking evidence that many of us are also "*asleep at the wheel*" when it comes to the reality of converting thoughts into actions? Think of the cause of much of the tragic loss of tourist life in the Tsunami of 2004. How often and in what circumstances do you forget, avoid or neglect to act when action is called for? This disconnection from our ability to act is a giant challenge to everyone on the crusade for more agility.

The term "*guilt money*" is now almost antique, but its consequences will be felt for a long time to come. Parents, even those still living together, who are so busy with everything else, often do not take time to spend with their offspring. Instead, they throw a little money at them to relieve their own guilt and *poof* the problem is solved... or is it? Children are fast learners and most quickly understand this type of behavior. Being kids, they quickly begin exploiting it. What if they begin training their parents and even encouraging them to continue this destructive behavior? What lesson is being taught here, whose behavior is being modified and by whom?

One fourth-grader in my daughter's class discovered that if he threw his cell phone against a wall, went home and told his parents that he dropped it, he would quickly get the latest one. Sure enough, it was true and he *proudly* showed off his brand new phone the very next day!

If these anecdotes are not enough to encourage you to take this social disaster seriously, take a look in any drug store or supermarket at the availability and amount of different types of head, stomach ache remedies and painkillers. The number of people who are taking both prescription and non-prescription drugs are at record levels and it's still increasing. In short, more and more of us are relying upon synthetic remedies and not just to make us feel better. We are increasingly relying on drugs to treat (read deaden) the symptoms. Deadening the symptoms shuts down the search for the underlying causes of your dis-ease and perpetuates the need for continued use (addiction) of those drugs. Not surprisingly, the pharmaceutical companies do not readily demonstrate a problem with supporting and encouraging this type of behavior. Recent resesearch points to that you now have a ten times bigger chance of dying from a misused medication than from a gunshot wound. It seems that quarterly profits have become more important than the Hippocratic Oath[xxxiii] to *"Do no harm"*.

If you have any interest in becoming more agile, yet find yourself resonating with any of the above anecdotes, then it is time to act! *Not doing anything trains you to be less agile just as training to do something makes you more agile.* It always boils down to a choice... To act or not! That choice is yours.

Reflections on human beings/doings, "sheeple" and zombies
When things are going well, you often feel inspired and engaged. When you are enjoying that feeling, you feel connected to what is now often called *the Flow*. When that happens you are usually in, or contributing to, a virtuous circle. In sports, you have entered *"the Zone."* You feel empowered; and with that feeling of empowerment you consciously *become* a bit more *human* even while going about your daily routines.

Unfortunately, we are designed in a way that we can often get so wrapped up in what we are doing that we easily become unconscious to it and start *doing* more without thinking *or feeling* anything regarding the people involved or the consequences. When things spin further out of hand and you become stressed, you tend to *do* more and *feel* less. Your focus turns even more to the task directly in front of you and you become easily distracted from and eventually disinterested in any consequences. You become more willing to intrude into other people's integrity and have less and less concern about preying on others as long as it seems to lighten your own stressful situation. You can more easily throw someone else under the bus, especially if you feel they are of lesser importance than yourself, or if you *are led to believe* this person, group or country may be a threat to you.

Those who understand the psychology involved in this process are also well aware that your willingness and energy to question begins to wane with the more stress you experience. When you become stressed and your feelings start shutting down, you will more easily become resigned to agree and often accept to do more intrusive and predatory tasks. These are often tasks that, under normal circumstances, you would probably have raised an issue with. For many, these types of resolutions usually have an "*If I do this, will you leave me alone?*" factor in them. For others, often burdened with unexplored or suppressed psychological baggage, an opportunity to boss others around seems to fulfill some unfulfilled need or heal some sort of emotional scar. But is it fulfilling, especially if and *when you take the time to reflect over your behavior and its consequences?*

Regardless, the more burdened with *issues* you become, the more distracted you become and easier you are to manipulate. If you also happen to be worried financially, the promise of a steady income will often be enough to get you to go along with all kinds of intrusive, essentially anti-social behavior. This further disconnects you from the flow of good feelings and positive experiences and your stressed anti-social behavior can easily become habit. Since *misery* still seems to *love company*, the more you are surrounded with other human doings and are constantly reminded that this is how things *must be* for society to work, the more this type of intrusive behavior seems to become the societal norm. This type of behavior amplifies resignation. Somewhere deep down, most of us still have some sort of moral compass; yet this process begins to eat away at what is left of that compass, as well as our dignity and our lust for life. Resignation *to do what is ordered* becomes the norm. When the gap between what we are doing and who we remember (and still feel) ourselves to be becomes too great, we often "hit the wall," *burn out* or suffer some sort of nervous breakdown.

Figure 11 Light's on but who is home?

Two terms are now being regularly used to describe this feeling of chronic disconnection and resignation: *Sheeple* and *Zombies*. Just as their names seem to imply, one is more passive and the other more active. The term *Sheeple* seems to refer to those of us who just wish to get on with their lives and off-load responsibility and challenges to their all-too-willing shepherds. It's not that they are against *rocking the boat*, it is more that their stress dampens any thought of doing so. Many of us are so caught up in the details of running their lives that there doesn't appear to be any time left over. If extra time is found, we would much rather use it to collapse or disappear into the excitement of Facebook, Instagram, World of War Craft or one of the many cooking, reality or entertainment programs available on TV. And, as long as you continue to have faith in those in charge of shepherding, it is much easier to *relax* and let them run things.

The problem only arises when those you trust to lead are finally revealed to be more concerned with their own welfare than yours. This is where *Zombies* play a role. Basically they are very much like *Sheeple* with the exception that, just like the mythical and Hollywood character they are named after, they consciously or or not become predators. With all the current questions regarding morals and ethics plus all the high profile corruption cases, this is what now seems to be happening on a regular basis.

We the "Sheeple"

Just like a deer that freezes in your headlights, the more we become dependent on our technology, the more we seem to be losing our ability to be present here and now. The expression, *"The light is on but nobody's home"* comes to mind when you stop and observe how preoccupied many of us seem to be. The term *Sheeple* seems to imply that more and more of us tend to act like sheep and sleepwalk through our day. Just like sheep we often would rather follow the crowd. Take a walk down any crowded street and see how many people you pass who seem present, here and now. Chances are you will notice very few. *If, on the other hand everyone appears to be "present" to you, then you may want to take another look at how present you currently are.*

Take some opportunities to observe the Body Language of people you pass and take notice to how automatic and mechanical much of it seems to appear. Probably the most obvious and frightening piece of evidence to this trend is the following realization. Many you encounter will see you not as a fellow human to acknowledge, but more as an *obstacle to be avoided.* Can you really expect that we are suddenly going to become more agile and pull together in times of great trouble when we currently do all we can to avoid others on the street? This may not be so everywhere, but this tendency does seem to increase in cities and in colder climates.

The more we wrap ourselves up in our little electronic gadgets, permitting people with undeclared motives to dump information directly into our raw senses, the more we succeed in cutting ourselves off from the natural flow of life. Still don't believe this? Take another look around and get a sense of how happy most of your fellow travelers look…

Not very long ago, my daughter's school sent out an alarming notice to all parents. The teachers had observed that the cafeteria had gone silent. The students were still there, sitting in their proper place, but only a few of them were actually talking with each other. Most sat silently, staring vacantly into their smart gadgets. The teachers raised the alarm because these healthy, energetic early teens now sat there like docile sheep totally disconnected from their friends and *life*. What is happening to the agility of youth? Is this the future you wish your children to be raised into?

Many of us who used "*screen time*" as a passive baby sitter in order to handle just one more errand or task in the evening have eventually been *surprised* to discover how hard it is to start a conversation with our now "*screen time conditioned*" children. Once they are trained to seek excitement on line, how can a dull parent compete with the action available just a few clicks away? Quite a few concerned parents eventually seek professional help (often only for their children) when they see how hard it is for them to leave their screen for any reason. Wow!

All of this seems to be contributing towards a society where healthy individuals are being trained to behave more like sheep; hence the term *Sheeple*. The drive to think for yourself and to create something new is being replaced by a fear of not fitting in to the flock. Or there is an overreaction to the other side to begin dressing differently to stand out. Notice the increase in what Psychologists call "Cheap Signaling," meaning piercing, tattoos, non-natural hair colors and "*interesting*" clothes. Now, what if this is the maximum level of protest they can muster or express?

More and more adults and frighteningly many children are now suffering from health problems such as depression. Most of us like to follow the flock and blend in with the majority, but not to the point where we lose our identity. Becoming a Sheeple is a trend that seems to both cause and result in more uncertainty and worry.

Zombies

The increasing number of "Zombified" people among us does not make the plight of the Sheeple easier. These are those human *doings* who have, for whatever reason, decided to take on a task or job that intrudes upon someone else's integrity. For instance, whether or not the threat of increased violence is perceived or real, the increase of those employed in the security and protection sector is currently outpacing the corresponding threat. Taxes and surcharges have also increased to help pay for all this increased protection providing jobs for both

Figure 12 Zombie or tired co-worker?

public and private number crunchers. Big government keeps getting bigger as the encouragement of fear continues to overtake reason, common sense and empathy.

There are unfortunately many amongst us who have no problem with or actually enjoy having the mandate to tell the rest of us what to do. This is the distinguishing behavior factor separating a docile *sheeple* from a predatory *zombie*.

The more we continue to sheepishly react to all the fear around for example, terrorism, the more zombified behavior we are likely to meet *and the less freedom we are likely to enjoy*. As Benjamin Franklin once said, *"The more you are willing to sacrifice your freedom for security the less you will have of either."* If you wish to avoid becoming a Sheeple and the more you understand the challenge your conscience faces when becoming a Zombie, the more you will recognize the value utility in improving your agility.

Some questions to reflect over:

- Have you noticed that an increase in your stress level encourages you to shut out the concerns of those around you?
- Do you *relax* comfortably on a Friday evening or *collapse* into your couch, exhausted after a full weeks work?
- How many choices and tasks can a normal person handle *responsibly* during the day and for how many days running?
- Does your job give you a mandate that requires you to intrude on another's integrity or personal space?
- What if being more agile is also a function of being and feeling more human?

Public servants **or masters**

Let's now limit this broad conversation to just our ability to easily transact business. Do any of the above examples of human behavior make it harder or easier to have a healthy life and run an agile, successful business?

What if, in their interest to preserve their own power, our current batch of leaders are increasingly impeding our ability to conduct business? As the costs, barriers and frustrations of doing business expand, will more or fewer people take the plunge to start a new business? Recently, figures have been revealed that point to a drastic contraction of new business start-ups. Of course, this makes sense. When the economic environment demands a more vigilant and protective behavior, we are wired to respond accordingly.

Since small businesses account for the majority of the GDP of a nation and *its tax base,* does it seem like a wise choice or an effective use of diminishing public resources to try and monitor and control every aspect of a small business? It doesn't take a very high IQ to predict the future consequences of such a poorly thought out plan. Still, most of us have to make a living. In the midst of this drastic increase of red tape, exciting possibilities still exist for agile business leaders who understand and can navigate according to how the future is changing.

This process is sometimes called *Reframing* or creating a paradigm shift. You basically define the tenets that have given rise to a specific industry or profession. Once you have them clearly defined, it is just to challenge a specific one until its weakness is revealed. When this is done, the old, accepted business model will eventually give way and everyone who did not see the change coming will be swept away as the traditional way of conducting business as usual comes crashing down. Once again, look to Uber, Apple's iTunes, Cable TV, Pay-Pal and others for current examples of this process.

This is the same process that ended up fracturing the Catholic Church's grip on Europe when reformers such as Calvin and Luther challenged its dogma and found it wanting. Some unknown genius once stated that, "When you *assume*, you make an *ass* out of *u* and *me*." What are the beliefs of your business model (and indeed your life), which you *assume* cannot be challenged?

There is a saying that seems to be grounded in common sense, which states, "*Pure service is transparent*." What this means is that the more you stand for service, the more you and your ego disappear into the experience you are creating for whom you are serving. Just as an excellent waiter disappears into the background when they are serving you a great meal, so do all other forms of service when performed correctly. In fact, the only time you should even be aware of service is *when it doesn't work*. Only then will the lack of it make it an obvious target. When it's functioning properly, pure service should blend with its surroundings. With this in mind, we again ask why more and more *public servants* now need bulletproof cars and security details, *paid for by your taxes*?

Rethinking societal classes
New challenges call for new ways of thinking about them. The increasing level of uncertainty we are encountering is redefining how we divide up societal classes.

Our culture of entitlement
Entitlement is the belief of an implied right to some sort of benefit. It is basically a form of expected pleasure. Therefore, discontinuing an entitlement can often imply real or imagined pain. Could this be why people are so protective of their entitlements? For instance, all a politician has to do is *hint* they may look at the

growing imbalance between social security underfunding and what you receive in payments. They can then be assured of losing votes at the next election.

How long do you think a system can continue where one civil servant retires and your taxes must then pay for both this new retiree as well as the newly hired replacement? Multiply this by the estimated 10,000 American baby boomers now retiring *per day* and you may sense how the entitlement system called *government pensions* will sooner or later gum up our already overtaxed system, to the point of catastrophic failure. You may even agree that cancelling or decreasing these pension entitlements paid for with your taxes is a very good idea, *as long as your retirement is left alone*!

What if our continuously expanding entitlement society combined with governmental largesse are together destroying the remaining agility in our society?

"The problem with socialism is that sooner or later you run out of other peoples' money"
- Margret Thatcher

Facilitating entitlement through IT
Could this trend, of avoiding pain through increased entitlement, now be supported and encouraged using IT systems? What does putting every aspect of life into a computer matrix or an organizational flowchart do to agility and creativity? What does it do to our ability to remain conscious?

Take Sweden as example. A top Swedish business leader recently expressed his concerns about entitlement by saying publicly that the primary goal of the Swedish workforce has become to create an *"eternal vacation."* After venturing into some Swedish business after spending my whole life abroad, I must sadly concur. Most Swedes now seem to be so indoctrinated and cozy with their "*Nanny State*" of entitlements, that recent polls show that the satisfaction generated from an honest day's work has unfortunately eroded down to a third or fourth place priority. Do you think a Chinese poll would get the same results?

Although it may be noble that family priorities in Sweden still come first in this workaholic era, they are closely followed by travel/exploration, self-development and more "*me time*," These all seem to be much more important than producing a product or service of which you can be proud ... and why not?

First of all, current labor laws in many western countries make it almost impossible to fire someone. Then, even if your company is successful in getting rid of you, the Social Safety Net will probably protect a large portion of your accustomed lifestyle. In short, you will feel little or no pain. In fact, with more and more low paying jobs replacing high paying ones, it actually becomes more economical and wise for a crafty westerner to *look like* they are searching for a job and instead collect unemployment as long as possible.

Socialistic programs have been developed on the premise that we then need a really BIG Mama Government to nanny our every move from the cradle to the grave. What if *"Democracy"* has become *"Autocracy,"* as many vote for those who tell them the best story? What if voting is about whom the voter can expect the best entitlement from for the least amount of personal engagement and strain? How agile is this?

This begs the question as to whether 21st century democracy has finally degraded into mob rule? The most important and enduring aspect of this whole Nanny State structure is the question of who will pay? Paraphrasing economist Murray Rothbard, "*With Government's monopoly on violence, the chances are that when "other people's money" is mentioned it will probably mean yours.*" The trend of increasing social costs and rules for new hires is rapidly increasing. Not surprisingly, the number of low paying jobs with no security or benefits are rapidly increasing while salaried positions with benefits are in decline. This trend ensures that cracks are beginning to be noticeable *and felt* in the ability for leaders to deliver on their promised levels of *public service*.

Look at any of the Socialistic/Communistic failures in modern times, for instance: the USSR, Argentina, the East German "Democratic Republic" and China's transition to Capitalism to name but a few… They all went broke or transitioned into capitalism because the practice of promising everything to everyone eventually was understood to be an unachievable lie. Trust was lost and people bravely looked beyond the rhetoric they had been listening to, sometimes for generations.

Communism and Socialism also have a nasty habit of structuring most entitlement programs on the notion of the "bell-curve." Each program is formed to serve the "average person." Is it any wonder then that mediocrity always seems to take the upper hand? Would the likes of Edison, Tesla, Einstein and others ever have had the chance to contribute their epic inventions should they have been forced to go through any current public school system? In fact, many now argue they would all have been forced to take medication to *tame* their eccentric (or dare we say *agile?*) behavior. Their genius would most likely have been choked off rather than allowed to flourish. This of course, begs the question of, how many gifted, but eccentric geniuses are now having their creativity suppressed with medication or incarceration before it can bloom?

Add to our list of megatrends the one that tries to force the increasingly round peg of a creative individual into the square hole of conformity, although generously *sweetened with entitlement* and you can see why the future is starting to get harder to control. Is the current system the best we can do to promote creativity, resilience and greatness?

After spending my whole life around great people and successful companies, I will also beg to differ. Most people seem to subscribe to the notion of Pareto's *80/20 Principle* where eighty percent of the value of any organization is created and driven by twenty percent of the people. Those twenty percent HATE silly rules and restrictions built for accommodating their "average" co-workers and colleagues.

Now, think about all the rules "good," progressive democratic intentions have created to chasten those who strive for excellence, speed limits, for example. Think now about how rules to increase the entitlement culture have blossomed during this time. What if this whole mediocre process of protecting the sweet spot of the population bell curve destructively undermines the creativity, agility and entrepreneurship needed to remain world-class? Would this also sow the seeds for entrepreneurs to move and find more open cultures and friends, or to create ways to quickly topple this unstable paradigm? Would agile behavior be an advantage? What was it that attracted all the immigrants to the United States between 1850 and 1950? What is still attracting people to Hong Kong today?

Further distinguishing the Proletariat

Over 150 years ago, Karl Marx began exploring what he named the proletariat in terms of the contemporary industrial age filters. They were filters that were just then beginning to take hold. Very simply, he defined the working class as those who created value. He further distinguished workers by also defining the *Bourgeoisie* as the ruling class. Over the next hundred or so years, the working class both expanded and became more entrenched. It began to stratify with ever more "rights and benefits."

According to Professor Guy Standing[9], these included:

- *Health insurance*
- *Unemployment*
- *Minimum wage*
- *Retirement and social security*
- *Job security*
- *The right to organize and unionize*
- *Stock ownership*

---

9 Guy Standing Author of "The Precariat The New Dangerous Class."

Each one of these benefits naturally started out as a good idea, but over time, the "do-gooders" who established these benefits and their followers began to expand these good ideas way past the ability to responsibly fund and support them. This led to an increasing cooperation between aspiring politicians and bankers. Each *well-meaning* program or entitlement gradually became a non-negotiable law. This was not seen as a problem until recently, when employers began to wake up to the increasing costs of it all, *in total.*

These so-called *"social costs"* of employing someone only gradually begin to mount until their growth becomes exponential. The damage to your bottom line begins to reveal itself when you start multiplying them by the increasing number of entitlements, their individual growth and the number of employees you have. The further we get into this cycle of working class entitlement growth, the more each new employment opportunity will cost. To keep in touch with reality, these costs must always be weighed against potential *income and profit that each new employee can generate*. Many employers are now realizing they can no longer justify these new-hire costs and have actively begun seeking alternative ways to get the needed tasks done. The result has been an erosion of secure, high paying jobs. This trend of insecure or *precarious jobs* seems to keep increasing, due to among other things:

- Off-shoring
- Temporary employment
- Contractors and sub-contractors
- Automation

This growing trend has caused an increase in fear and uncertainty for those who still have a traditional and (for the moment) secure type of employment. It also causes growing frustration, anger and resentment in those who don't.

It is now hard to believe that the idea of wage deduction for Income Tax started during World War II. It was sold as a "temporary" solution to financing the war effort. Interestingly, what was *another temporary solution was again never repealed* and quickly became the primary income source for ever-expanding governmental services. Now, even this source no longer covers continuing governmental expansion. Other more creative ways to capture public money were needed and now have been devised. The result is now that the whole "progressive[10]" system is beginning to choke further business expansion. Increasing corporate taxes are now putting more and more tradi-

---

10 According to George Washington University's webpage www.gwu.edu : Progressivism is the term applied to a variety of responses to the economic and social problems rapid industrialization introduced to America. It began as a social movement and grew into a political movement. Theodore Roosevelt was it's first real champion, but Woodrow Wilson would take it to extremes.

tional jobs in jeopardy due to their costs. It has become much more profitable and much less of a liability to have work performed outside of the company, as a business expense, instead of it resulting from an internal, salaried worker's output. This trend will continue.

The strangling of the salariat

Professor Guy Standing's book *The Precariat* is well worth a read as it provides much needed insight into the precarious future of employment. He takes Marx's use of the Roman proletariat and subdivides it further into what he calls the *Salariat* and *Precariat*. The Salariat he defines as those privileged workers who still have a "real" job where there is insurance, job security, sick leave and other benefits. Benefits that most of us *experienced* employees used to take for granted. For the sake of this discussion The Precariat contains pretty much everyone else who now works primarily for money and has little or no inherent security. People in this category can include everyone from migrant workers, cleaning crews, contract workers to certain types of professionals.

As our business environment grows less certain, the Precariat continues to grow in size while the Salariat continues to decrease. As this phenomenon grows it now includes the precarious nature of more and more *company business models*. For instance, in many "developed" countries it is becoming economically suicidal to hire salaried employees to populate a precarious type of business. Sooner or later, the square peg of salaried laws, regulations and taxes will exhaust your round, precarious way of doing business. Needless to say, those still left in salaried positions, unions, and most employees in publically funded (or tax financed) organizations that have relied upon this cozy employer-employee way of working, are not taking this threat to their entitlement-bound lifestyle lightly.

You as captain of an older, salaried crew will inevitably face a situation where everyone around you has been trained and conditioned to feel they are entitled to a certain way of working or a certain outcome, regardless of the current economic weather. One look at the darkening sky and having read *just some of the ideas* suggested in this book, you suggest something else; something more in tune with today's business environment; *something more agile*. How receptive do you think your crew will be? If fact, how can you expect your listeners to even hear your enlightened message, much less decide to adapt to it quickly? Chances are they will probably filter out your message of change; as it is completely alien to what they have been trained and conditioned to do. In other words, the bigger the entitlement legacy, the less listening you can expect, the more resistance you will encounter and the more certain eventual disaster will become. *Think France!*

The growing precariat

All of the above have contributed to a growing sense of disenfranchisement for an increasing part of the global population. Guy Standing has documented in a number of books, the most telling titled, *The Precariat*[xxxiv], a large volume of research and anecdotal evidence to this new and growing segment of the working population. The Precariat refers to all those who could be classified as having a precarious type of employment situation. In other words, their primary source of income is all but secure.

According to him, if there is a positive side to this growing, restless and resentful group of employable people, it is that *so far* their movement has yet to find any type of unified voice. *"Finding one"*, he says, *"is the danger going forward"*. So don't bank on this diffusion to remain! With all the above shifts in both business and society referenced in this book, just about all of them will continue to nurture the growth and promote unification of this group into a powerful, creative force *with less and less to lose.* The Precariat is also overrepresented by *younger people with far less to lose.* We can count on their anger, resentment and (*creativity?*) to continue to grow.

Witness the growing number of young people forced to live with their parents long after they have graduated from school. The price of housing and rents have now increased to way beyond the affordability of most working for an entry-level wage. Worse still, with every table they wait, burger they flip or sale-priced blouse they sell, their skills decrease while their anger grows. This is *not* what they envisioned four years of college would lead to. Now, with *former retirees* competing for those same jobs, automation and the online sales increasing drastically, even these few remaining jobs are now threatened.

McDonald's, Walmart and other low paying companies have to deal with constant increases in the minimum wage laws. Their response is two-fold: reducing the number of employees and automating the increasing number of jobs that can now be automated. The process is often incremental, meaning one small task at a time. As we have discussed earlier, with the rise of technology and globalization, those jobs that can be replaced either by machine or computer/software are growing. This increases pricing (downward wage) pressure on those jobs remaining. Jobs that aren't yet at risk of being automated still risk being exported to lower cost countries, the most blatant examples being China for manufacturing and India for services (Chindia, as this combination is now referred to). Now, how would this *make you feel* if you had just spent four years going into massive debt to get a degree that is less likely to help you land a well paying job?

Some have even gone as far as to suggest that higher education should come with a *money-back guarantee*, should you not get the type of job that you trained for. This may seem a bit outlandish given that a good amount of the work in landing a job has to do with the individual's persistence (not to mention their choice of discipline). Yet the mere fact that it is now on the table *and being discussed* also supports this precarious trend.

Employment dislocation
We are already witnessing a direct consequence of the increase in the precarious nature of working. As more and more private companies reduce staff, the only organizations hiring seem to be governmental. Even with a recent uptick in employment, the number of those who have given up looking for a job stands at all-time highs. This is also notwithstanding the fact that these numbers are not even calculated the same way they used to be. Again, it may be worth visiting www.shadowstats.com to get a feel of how the measuring of economic and employment statistics has become more "*accommodative*" over the years.

Recently, a number of studies from Oxford University[xxxv] and CBRE Genisis[xxxvi] have pointed to the possibility that up to fifty percent of current jobs will disappear over the next five years! The CBRE report further states there will be new job opportunities popping up as they write, "*Organizations with twenty to forty people can be just as impactful as large corporations, and by leveraging technology while being "unhindered by legacy processes and mindsets," they will easily disrupt existing corporate models.*"[xxxvii]

In fact they go on to state the following: "*Corporations will not only need to be lean and agile they must be authentic to attract talent: authentic in their values and in making a real contribution to the social good.*" Are you and your company agile enough to handle this turbulent and increasingly *authentic* employment market as either an employer or employee?

Labor shortage with increasing unemployment
There is another problem that is becoming a ticking time bomb especially in Europe. More and more young people are not even *getting the chance to work*. In Greece and Spain for instance, the number of unemployed people under the age of twenty-five is surpassing fifty percent. The longer these young and energetic people are denied a chance to develop their skills and their self-confidence, the less of a chance and drive they will have to seek employment in the future. As *The*

Trends Journal[xxxviii] forecaster Gerald Celente says, "*People who lose everything and have nothing left to lose, lose it.*" What happens then? This trend of youth unemployment does not look like it will be improving any time soon.

Formal education is no longer the answer.
In the United States it is hard not to notice the increase in elderly workers in both retailing and restaurants. More and more pensioners are being forced back into the work force as saving and investment do not meet retirement expectations. Not only does it tug on your heartstrings to see a sixty or seventy year-old being rushed around by a 25 year-old assistant manager at a Dunkin Donuts, it also means that one more young person who could actually handle this stressful situation has been shut out of that shrinking possibility.

A recent poll showed that over sixty percent of college graduates in the U.S.A. have had to take a job in another area than their chosen field of study. Could they be the lucky ones? There are now also more people, aged up to thirty five years old, still living at home with their parents than ever before. Many of these have student debt and little or no way to pay it back. Yet the number of student loans outstanding continues to break records despite increasing defaults, combined with the diminished possibility of bankrupting their way out of the burden.

Result: The Working Dead
You meet them on the train, when you are going about town, in just about every line or queue you are forced into and often in conversations about politics and money. Their eyes will be either extremely focused to the point that they look hard. It may be the glare of indignation. Or it can be the opposite; a kind of vacant gaze, that gives you a strong feeling of resignation or complete surrender. If any notice of your existence is taken, it is only as an obstacle placed squarely in their way.

Whatever kind of visual contact takes place, it will be distinguished by a gnawing sense that they are not present here and now with you. They are preoccupied with their smart gadgets or a distant thought. They have disappeared unconsciously either into a do-loop of debate, defense or into the resignation of despair. Despite this, they usually keep doing what they are paid to keep doing.

The ultimate result of this detached behavior is the creation of a legion of working dead. The entitlement to a paycheck *as long as you do your job*, combined with a more omnipotent and permeating computer grid that monitors all aspects of life, is creating a sense of "comfortable numbness." This is a state of mind that encourages other people and systems to take care of what to think, for you. As most of us are inherently on the lazy side and like being taken care of, this system has now grown into a comfortable and addictive form of cancer that threatens to kill its societal host and all our individual pleasure and creativity with it.

You may sense this feeling of resignation by noting that:

- Something is not right
- There are too many things to do
- Whatever choice you make, it ultimately won't matter
- You no longer have time to care
- You feel guilty when you are doing nothing
- Someone else should do it
- There must be more to life than inputting more TV and social media
- Acting or speaking up would put you in danger

These and many other thoughts may trigger this sense, but the end result is that it causes you to detach from being fully conscious to what is going on around you. You may see it happening, you may sense that you should do something, but you ultimately remain in a passive, *functional coma*. Look again at those victims who were caught in the Tsunami. Many certainly sensed something was not right, but how many reacted to the threat and ran for the hills in time? Agility? Not!

Now, what makes you different?

Economic deterioration

How can your job possibly be sustainable if it costs your company more to maintain you than the value you contribute? The idea of contributing something measurable to the growth and success of your organization over what you cost has become distorted, but is still mathematically intact. The consuming nature of taking more than you give can work for a while (even generations), but in the long run *it must consume its host*. Look no further than what is left of Detroit, Michigan to see the effects of entrenched labor, unrealistic wages and retirement benefits, in the context of a globally competitive environment. The results can be devastating not just for an industry but also to an entire city! During the 1920s and 1930s, Detroit boasted the highest per capita income in the entire United States. Today they are having trouble funding the maintenance of the city's water system.

Is collective bargaining an anachronism?

One of the most powerful forces in labor for over one hundred years has been the power of collective bargaining. Trade unions existed to force management to reassess the relationship between them and their workers. Great headway was made to improve the worker's situation and environment during this time. Like almost every other cycle we have talked about in this book, the reliance on the collective bargaining cycle may now actually be hastening its own demise. In many countries, the power of the unions has decreased precariously over the past generation. The U.S.A. is a prime example of where unions had once been powerful enough to force companies to accept unsustainable wages. Whole industries that were influenced by collective bargaining have now moved to areas with cheaper production costs and where unions are either weak or non-existent. Two prime examples of this are Detroit with regard to automobiles and New York City with shipping.

Right up until the 1960s, New York Harbor bustled with shipping and docks bristled with active cranes. This was both in Brooklyn and the entire west side of Manhattan Island. Yet a very disruptive technology made its presence known on the docks in the late 1960s and early 70s in the form of the Shipping Container.

Up until this time, each ship had to be loaded and unloaded piece by piece. The only people who could eventually do this backbreaking work in the Metropolitan area were card-carrying members of the Longshoremen Unions. With a lock on dockyard labor, they charged a price way over what the market would soon reveal was actually competitive. When containers began appearing more frequently, the unions went on strike and for a while maintained their grasp on the shipping business in NYC. Ridiculously, they forced shipping companies to unload the containers on the boat, carry the contents off the boat and then repack the container on shore. The reverse was necessary for filling up outward-bound ships. What would you have done if you were a cargo ship owner?

It didn't take too long for shippers to reroute their cargo to other ports where containers could be used as they were designed. Now, fifty years later, there is hardly any trace left of this once robust industry in The Big Apple.

Collective bargaining can temporarily give its union members a false sense of security. Evidence in N.Y.C. and Detroit would also suggest so. It may even last a few decades; but change will eventually prevail. Skim through David Halberstam's 1986 book *The Reckoning* and observe the difference between how Ford Motor Company and Nissan chose to handle the emergence of a worldwide car industry. In retrospect it is obvious what the outcome had to be, but it is still amazing to read about the devastating effect that insulated arrogance had, leading to the slow erosion of an entire industrial Mecca. The difference between adapting to change and the old adage of, "*Give him enough rope and he'll hang himself,*" come to mind.

Entrenchment from the top down.
Inhibiting change not only happens from the factory floor up, it is just as devastating from the ivory towers of management downward. H. Ross Perot, former presidential candidate and founder of Electronic Data Systems, was given a seat on the board of General Motors when GM purchased his company, EDS.

A few years later he doubled his money when he was "politely" asked to leave the board and was forced to sell his shares back to GM. His agile style and his harsh Texas honesty clearly did not fit in with the "traditional" way of doing things at GM. In order to silence his criticism and attempts at reform, could he have been offered a large enough bribe just to walk away? Whether the following anecdote is true or just an urban myth, the following story is offered. The drop for this decision reportedly came when he addressed GM's board with something that had *more than a hint* of stinging Texas sarcasm. Mr. Perot was supposed to have said, "*I cannot understand why it takes six years, from concept to showroom, to build one of our cars and it only took four years to win World War II!*"

Did he possibly have a point? Automotive history seems to support him. There was a time when it was said that, "*When General Motors sneezes, the U.S. Economy catches a cold.*" Increasing international competition has now eroded that time and the destructive arrogance that accompanied it. It may be worth a moment of reflection on what could have happened if GM's board had opened up and listened to Perot's comments and chosen agility ...

Government agility?
Perot's focus was always said to be on the customer and this focus kept him, those who worked with him and his business endeavors agile for the times. It is interesting to note that a strong reason why many believe that he was not taken as a serious candidate for President in 1996 was that his agile style of leadership would have upset the way *politics as usual* was conducted. This was deemed to be too uncomfortable for those who ran the show. Has this trend towards comfortable entitlement changed?

Now, a generation later we have more outsiders contending. It will be interesting to follow Donald Trump's and Bernie Sanders' progress in listening to and also responding to the American Market of eligible and now even more disenchanted voters. Why?

Continue reading...

Get agile or change the law?
With the rise of the Lobbying Industry an alternative to training to be agile has become to stack the legislative deck in your favor. According to Lobbyist.info,[xxxix] there are now 37,000 lobbyists populating 4,600 firms in the Washington D.C.

area. On the other side of the Atlantic, the British Newspaper *The Guardian* estimates that there are over 30,000 lobbyists now working the corridors of the EU in Brussels.

Paying former lawmakers lots of money to talk their friends, who are still in the Legislative Branch, to write a law in favor of you and your product or industry is now considered sound business practice. These laws usually exclude others from entering your market. This comfortable strategy has worked brilliantly for the past generation or so. Among other things that have been enacted into law are:

- Legal stipulation regarding the size and curvature for European bananas. This law strangles African and Asian competition by championing the interests of a few well-known Multi-Nationals with expert lobbying skills.
- The use of Genetically Modified Foods in the United States and the increasing use of patents on certain types of food and grain.
- Energy saving light bulbs to replace incandescent light bulbs. Both in the EU and in the U.S.A, the traditional and cheaper alternative to light up your room was outlawed for the more expensive energy saving ones. Yes, they do save energy in the long run, but now you have no choice, *especially if you are on a limited budget*. If you look at the profits General Electric and Philips have generated by this legislation, it might be worth pondering how much of it was generated from a few advantageous changes in the law.

The only problem is that, as this way of doing business has expanded and the laws become progressively more outrageous, the legislature further loses touch with the realities experienced by customers/voters. Morals, environmental concerns, fair trade policies and ultimately profits all suffer. More and more people are beginning to wake up to the fact that they have become victims of a system that is becoming harder and harder to enter or keep up with. There is a growing feeling of alienation and it is beginning to dishearten and anger these voters and consumers greatly.
You can't fool all the people all of the time. With increasing awareness of the option for us to vote with our wallets, entire companies are rising to success and falling back to failure at a frantic pace, due to public perception. This is without discussing the impact of those High Frequency Traders, which author Michael Lewis refers to as the "Flash Boys (Lewis)" who can now make and break companies and their stock price in nanoseconds. Whether this practice is illegal or controversial, it can still rain havoc on the capitalization of your business in the blink of an eye.

MASTERING AGILITY

The increasingly precarious nature of the organization
The precarious nature of employment is not happening in a vacuum. The turbulence brought about by globalization, and the competition it causes, has put enormous stress on business margins all over the world. A certain rebalancing between the high wages and benefits of the West and the low ones in the east is causing massive dislocation of work from one end of the globe to the other. In order to survive and thrive, companies have been forced to seek out the most efficient places in the world to get what they need done. The destination keeps changing. This of course, adds to the instability of employment and quality ultimately suffers. For those of you old enough to have purchased a "standard pair" of blue jeans forty years ago and compare them to the quality to a standard pair today will notice a distinct difference between price and quality.

How can you be expected to concentrate on doing a good job when you are preoccupied, worried about what you will be doing when this latest temp-job is over? Just as importantly, how can you as a business leader concentrate on delivering a quality product when you are focused on saving costs and moving locations all the time?

The death of socialism?
A controversial but thought provoking issue to consider is the question of which socio-political domino will be the next to fall? What if this friendlier cousin of communism may be the next political ideology to be found wanting?

Consider the amount of debt that has been issued since the Progressive Movement started in the end of the 19th century. Recently debt has begun multiplying exponentially as the financial shockwaves from the 2007-9 Great Recession continue to reverberate through the global economy. Without going into the detail that can easily be found by Googling the phrase "World debt," one question stands out: "How will governments (*meaning you, dear taxpayer*) ever repay all the debt that is now outstanding?"

Getting votes by promising more than you have resources to pay for has become a way of life for our *career* politicians. The only way this system has been held together so long is by the use or implied use of force. To paraphrase economist Murray Rothbard again, what if "*The power of the State resides in its monopoly of violence*"? What if the cornerstone of socialism is the government's legal ability to take from you the money you have earned and then distribute it to others? How is this accomplished? It is done through the implied threat of violence (a police officer's gun), the threat of incarceration (prison) or both. The more voters a savvy politician can turn into beneficiaries of *other people's money*, the better their chances for re-election. The tighter the grip on power, the more promises need to be made. What if this works until such a time when the amount promised can no longer be taxed, borrowed or printed? Increasing evidence suggest that this is the reality we are now finally waking up to.

Just like the erosion of quality in blue jeans over the past forty years, no matter where you live in western society you are probably beginning to notice deterioration in the quality of public services offered. You don't have to believe anything above. You are still offered an invitation to observe the increase in crises occurring and the corresponding increase in laws and regulations sold to you as, "*For your own good.*" This situation may still suggest that becoming more agile is a prudent choice.

Volatility, confidence and trust
More and more evidence is now being revealed that points to the theory that economic booms and busts are not financial in origin, but rather a phenomenon based upon levels of trust and confidence. When people are confident in their futures, then they are more willing to spend and thus the economy grows. As Armstrong Economics points out, "*We are more willing to take a loan out, regardless of the interest charged, if we know with confidence that we can make money on it.*" On the other hand, when confidence in the future begins to wane, the economy begins to contract. People begin saving and hoarding.

Confidence. A cellular phenomenon?
Research in the growing field of epigenetics (the study of genes and their surroundings) by Dr. Bruce Lipton[xl] and others points to each cell in our bodies having two basic operating states: growth or protection.

- When a cell perceives its environment as safe, it naturally opens up its cell walls to confidently take advantage of the positive surroundings, to attract and receive information, nutrition and energy, moving towards this positive environment and to grow.
- When a cell perceives a hostile environment, it does the opposite. The cell shuts down and protects itself by cutting off all contact with the surrounding environment including food and moves away from the perceived threat.

What if this basic biological principle is also the basis of our behavior? What if we are always either open, trusting and willing to grow, closed, protective and ready to defend, or somewhere in between? Consider that even this basic process also occurs in waves. As a society, we have now been in a positive, open and growth oriented state for the last thirty plus years. What do you think can we statistically expect going forward? It is also worth taking into account that up until the present one, these longer cycles usually lasted approximately one generation, averaging about seventeen years from bottom to top. The current growth cycle is now over thirty years in duration and, as we have seen, is becoming increasingly shaky and uncertain…

A coming collapse in confidence?
Although many have written both positively and negatively about finance as the ultimate confidence game, research by Martin Armstrong of Princeton Economics has tracked the collapse of societies going back further than the fall of Rome. His well-documented conclusion is that what ultimately causes a country's or region's economy and then its society to collapse is a loss of public confidence in the contemporary system and the ability of its leaders to lead.

Take a closer look at what is happening in Europe, particularly to Greece, Italy, and Spain. Look at Japan and what is now being referred to as *Abenomics* and see if you can make common, logical or business sense of it. Look at how much money is owed by each citizen in the U.S.A, especially if you include what is both *"on budget"* and *"off budget."* Estimates range from the official seventeen trillion dollars to over 200 trillion dollars if all future governmental commitments to pay are included. Divide that number by the 309 million citizens, or better yet by the estimated 150 million who actually pay taxes and you may begin to get a sense of why anxiety and distrust continues to build.

Our current global economic situation is deteriorating, while we simultaneously wake up to newer and stronger laws regarding taxes and money flow. More and more, it seems just a question of time before we *are forced to* collectively look for more agile, *outside the box* solutions, which may increasingly *not have the blessing of our current batch of rulers.*

> You need look no further than the turmoil against *politics as usual* to see that the public seems to be losing faith in their ruling elite and their *"market tested"* message. From Brexit to the US Presidential elections voters are starting to turn their backs on the candidates and advice served up to them

via traditional Main Stream Media channels. What is even more shocking is that the more these "correct" options are pushed into our faces the more enticing the likes of Nigel Farage and UKIP are in the UK and Trump and Sanders are in the United States. This wholesale rejection of politics as usual is spreading all over the globe cultivating increasing uncertainty for the future. Could another term for this rising interest in *outside the box politics* be *agility*?

Crash and burn is an option

"Everybody has a plan until they get hit in the face." - Mike Tyson

With human nature being what it is and with human history documenting our nature again and again, it should be of no surprise that current behavior often becomes habitual, until some great crisis or catastrophe forces us to change. It is Dr. Lipton's *growth* or *protection* again. This is the nature of both cycle theory as well as our tendency to seek pleasure and avoid pain. In other words, we are programmed to try to avoid pain and just get on with our lives until the pain becomes (often ridiculously, sometimes tragically) unavoidable. Could this be the situation we are again beginning to face?

This behavior also gives us a physiological explanation as to why agile growth, *from a cellular level upward*, predictably morphs into a protective type of *business as usual*. Therefore, considering the incredibly good run we have had for the past thirty plus years and unless human nature has fundamentally changed, we can expect another cycle of crash and burn to appear on the not too distant horizon. Keep in mind that down waves usually happen quicker and with more force than the upward ones. With the Laws of Physics being also what they are, the longer you postpone a given outcome the larger and more powerful the consequences usually become.

Yet even during the height of the Great Depression, fortunes were made for those who chose to look forward and gingerly responded to the prevailing market conditions. For instance, Charles Ives, a famous composer of that period, made a fortune up to and during the depression by running his own insurance company. In 1930, he retired from business and eventually won a Pulitzer Prize in music. Another story was that of Irving Weiss, a young investor who sold all his stocks before the depression and borrowed money from his mother at the market low in 1932 and began buying trusted names, *at bargain basement prices!*

The dangers of *business as usual*: the Titanic revisited

Figure 13 The Titanic on that fateful night

We cannot start a serious discussion about being agile and using sailing the ocean as a metaphor without one last, reflective look at a saga-like catastrophe, known to the world as the *Titanic* disaster of April, 1912. Imagine being on the maiden voyage of a ship reckoned to be so safe that the management only installed half the lifeboats needed, ostensibly to make more room to walk on deck! The ship was commanded by a certain Captain E. J. Smith, who was on his final cruise and had been taught to speed up when entering an iceberg field to *get through it faster*. You were to be saved by a crew that had little or no emergency training. A ship that was so big and had such a small rudder that turning quick enough to avoid icebergs turned out to be impossible. Safety was compromised again and again in favor of headlines and firsts. These mistakes and hubris cost two thirds of the people on board their lives. Although the term wasn't invented until much later, the *Titanic* and her crew had all the characteristics of being "*Too Big To Fail*"; yet it failed miserably. It might be more food for thought that this catastrophe occurred in the middle of a crystal clear night on a mirror-like sea.

This is before we even consider that there may have been manipulation in the background. For instance, why did most of the firemen, those who shoveled the coal, decide to quit and leave the ship when they reached the first port of Southampton? Why did J.P. Morgan, a major owner of the White Star Line and never one to shun free publicity, decide to cancel his ticket, at the last minute, on the maiden voyage of the biggest, most prestigious ship, which he owned?

Today's challenges, some of which are mentioned above, are dangerous all by themselves. Yet they can exponentially increase in danger due to their increasing interconnectedness. This fateful *comedy of errors* phenomenon was much in evidence with the loss of *Titanic*. Moving away from our nautical metaphor and back to our own era, all of these forces are increasingly becoming interconnected and are building in intensity at a growing rate. Being able to meet them will require an extra strong dose of agility coupled with a much faster and more decisive response time.

19. Does the Future always go to Agile Entrepreneurs?

Entrepreneurship is often mistaken for the ability to be agile. The fact is that many entrepreneurs can be extremely hardheaded and stubborn and *not agile or flexible at all.* They just happen to be in an environment without inhibiting legacies or just in the right place at the right time, happily riding a new wave or new business that is independent of the current established way of working. Anecdotes abound about Apple's Steve Jobs stubborn hardheadedness and his genius. Many new and successful companies also have or are creating legacies, but most of them won't show up until things get tough.

"Luck is opportunity meeting preparedness," - Deepak Chopra

Preparedness is great, but what if you can further increase your chances of success by listening closely to what your market is saying and then being agile *and* entrepreneurial enough to act upon what you see developing?

No guts, no glory! To be successful you need to act; and acting requires good information, agility and a resolve to trust yourself. Is there any better way to sum up the successful traits of an agile entrepreneur? The level of your success will probably hinge upon these traits along with the quality of information you have to work with. Basing an overwhelming portion of your focus on scanning the horizon will also make you more successful than by just showcasing your past performance.

SECTION THREE

Get Agile NOW!

Get Agile NOW!

Congratulations! You have now successfully navigated through some exciting megatrends that we see are now influencing us. You have also been introduced to our collection of favorite major storm warnings now appearing on our horizon. Making it to this point in the book you can now justifiably take a breather and ask yourself the best business or life question there is:

"So what?"

Our answer to this important question *and our heartfelt invitation to you is*:

Get Agile and Do It Quickly!
If you already understand and agree with us why agility will be the deciding success factor going forward and now wish to get some practical management tools and advice on how to use them, please feel free to skip directly to section four.

Regardless of whether you continue on a rosy megatrend path to growth and success, or "crash and burn" as forces of a perfect storm overwhelm you (or experience a powerful combination of both), one thing seems unavoidable; *the rate of change looks likely to increase with every breath you take.* Success can, of course, crush you as easily as failure. The most sensible and effective path is the one leading to surviving and thriving in this uncertain world. *The name of this path is Agility.*

Returning to our nautical analogy, success in sailing a large boat depends upon seizing the moment, acting wisely, forcefully and nimbly. The tactician must see and understand how market and environmental shifts can affect stated objectives, then quickly determine and implement alternative actions. With this information your navigator plots the optimal heading to reach the objective and your skipper is there to coordinate all actions and, when necessary, override ineffective decisions. We see this same proven combination in the business team of CEO/COO, CFO (Chief Financial Officer), CMO (Chief Marketing Officer) and CHRO (Chief Human Resource Officer). Each of these officers must contribute as a key player in the integration and building of an effective sailing team. Please read on to discover what their toolboxes will need to contain going forward. Learn the steps of how they can listen, collaborate and better work together towards success.

Our book describes how any corporate ship, even those with thousands of logged miles at sea under their keels, can practice and master becoming more agile. The following deck plan gives you an idea of our suggested cabin configuration. You will notice that the front of the boat consists of those cabins or departments that are *and should* remain focused upon the horizon. In the middle of any boat and placed somewhere above the middle of Marketing, R&D between Manufacturing and Operations is the bridge. In the back, focused on creating and maintaining a powerful and true wake, is your powerplant and all your ship's supporting systems. These consist of Finance, Legal and all Administrative functions. We suggest your corporate ship be set up in the same way. This will offer you maximum agility. The key here is to keep your corporate yacht on an even keel even when the weather turns against you. Often it is too easy to run towards the back of the boat and to check and recheck your power plant and gauges instead of focusing upon the horizon and the storms and rocks dead ahead. Just by staying in the more stable and comfortable part of the back of the boat will in NO WAY calm the seas that you will shortly be sailing into. Vigilance and a clear view will be necessary to maintain agility.

Figure 14 The deckplan of your corporate ship.

Very often, established companies such as those that have been honing their business models for the longest time, can have much better staying power and resilience than many entrepreneurial start-ups. Their biggest challenge remains to get their systems, organization, culture and processes in more agile shape and then refocus forward towards the horizon. To encourage this process, the above deck plan may be worth framing an putting up on a prominent wall in your corporate bridge.

The final and crucial ingredient is the ability to overcome the most common inhibitors to this process and take conscious and decisive action. The first batch of our powerful tools to help you will be discussed in the fourth section.

The prior two sections, *Megatrends* and *The Perfect Storm*, strive to convincingly describe how increasingly volatile our world is becoming. They also indicate that globalization, information and new technologies will create exponential growth and encourage radically new ways of doing things. This massive wave of innovation and disruption will continue to *dramatically shorten all product, service and business cycles!*

This fact will naturally create new challenges for the leaders of both corporations and institutions. As some of the more potent new technologies, such as Big Data Analytics evolve, targeting, speed and accuracy of decision-making will improve further, *leaving **execution** of those more accurate decisions as the greatest leadership challenge.* Here, many leaders will be found to be weak, irresolute and lacking integrity. They will be discovered to have no clear muscle when it comes to achieving short or long-term aims under increased pressure. Many leaders who have consistently received high scores in their rhetorical prowess will find themselves cornered by serious circumstances and will receive zero scores in measurable action. *These windbags will be looking for new jobs.* The consequence of shorter product/service cycles will force the governance of corporations and institutions alike to get serious about practicing:

- **Exceptional navigational ability** and the need to stringently focus forward towards the horizon instead of the wake.
- **Dramatic improvements in both strategic and operational agility,** to better anticipate and execute the next move. They must be nimble enough to act quickly and decisively *through the company's entire business process* to continually improve their competitiveness
- **Building a selective, quick and effective cost/value culture,** *where people know what a leak or threat and/or an extra value opportunity looks like, as well as what to do.* They must practically respond to stop more leakage by selectively adjusting the value, price or cost on popular products and features.

Smooth sailing AND batten down the hatches

There are many ways to describe the roots of human behavior. Since this book has a nautical theme, let's stick to it. When sailing, you either have favorable weather conditions or not. The more favorable these are, the more sails you can set and the faster and truer your course will be. In stormy weather, crew behavior can quickly deteriorate into an *"every man for himself,"* survival level. Then the outcome ends up depending upon how watertight your boat really is and how well you have trained your crew. This can be metaphorically compared again to Dr. Lipton's *growth* or *protection* states inherent in each one of our individual cells.

Practicing to both grow and protect, then training your agility to change quickly from one to the other, will help you better adjust to uncertain business seas and weather. This will also lessen the risk of missing a big change in the weather. For instance, when things are going well, how often do you feel like changing your course or your behavior? Then, when you have been hunkered down in protection mode and the wind starts to lessen, how long before you dare trust your sense that the weather may actually be improving?

Ironically, when you have the hatches battened down and are struggling to survive, that is often when you are forced to learn and grow more. Yet how agile do you feel at that particular moment? On the other hand, when things are sailing along smoothly, do you also go out of your way to inhibit change? Think about it. You are up on deck with a nice drink in your hand, the sun is shining and you feel a warm breeze at your back. How much energy *and what level of danger* will it take to motivate you to get up and change course; even if you start seeing clouds way out on the horizon?

It is usually more fun to remain in entertainment mode, save work and learning for later. We have already seen that we seek ways to prolong the fun and actually impede change. The process of enjoyment actually *encourages* you to be a bit resistant and helps to hinder any interruption of enjoyment. Now given that we are all wired more or less the same, *do you really think any of your colleagues, customers, partners or suppliers will behave any differently?* How can they if they are hard-wired into the same genetic growth and protection system as you? This is the origin of our human habit of inhibiting change. Although we might start out being wired the same way, *the perception of our circumstances* or surroundings may become totally different just around the next island, *causing major differences in behavior.* Trying to maintain or increase your and your crew's agility, when you are all relaxing and enjoying yourselves, is about as effective as pouring molasses all over your crew while ordering them to pick up the pace.

MASTERING AGILITY

Factors that make the molasses of inhibition thicker:
Below is a partial and random list of just some of the factors and situations that can inhibit your crew's agility.

- **Rules, systems, processes and regulations**, written and unwritten
- **Culture and hierarchy**, organizational, societal and individual
- **Politics** within your group, your company and even in your society
- **Moods and behaviors** of the people involved. Simply having a good or bad day can influence how you interact, decide and act
- **Experiences,** history and your interpretation of it. We use experiential filters every time we are reminded of *that* good or bad situation/decision.
- **Points of view**, opinions, combative attitudes and assumptions. Everyone has these, yet are they relevant right here and now? Are the most important opinions being expressed in a way that can be heard, understood and acted upon? And...
- **Listening:** How many people you meet are actually interested in you and listen to your message, compared to those who are just waiting to speak? What about you?

This is not nearly an exhaustive list and it can constantly change. However, it should contain enough examples to make our point that agility gets more challenging to maintain or enhance as time passes and these and other behaviors become institutionalized. This molasses effect *naturally* slows down the whole *decision to action process* until after a while, a less encumbered, more agile person, organization or society enters the picture; then runs circles around you. Whether they arrive with a game-changing technology, business model or new way of thinking, the result is usually another round of creative destruction where only the agile survive and only *the most agile of them thrive.*

I had the opportunity to work for Digital Equipment Corporation in its final days. Even though DEC had been one of the most agile and successful competitors in the mini-computer marketplace, that market died a quick and almost unnoticeable death. The PC quickly took its now extinct *mini-computer* market share and DEC lost its *raison d'etre.* Suddenly, there was no need for minis any longer. This great company with about 120,000 competent, well-meaning and dedicated employees, could not change the course of their proud ship quickly enough to save the company *or their jobs.* Even though bold, then increasingly desperate decisions were made, those tasked with changing company behavior would not or could not do it. Add to this that most employees had made careers out of DEC's own brand of *business as usual*. How open do you think they were for someone preaching that their way of life was now doomed and radical change was needed; FAST?

DEC is not alone. The molasses of their culture, internal systems and the *DEC way* of doing business inhibited their ability to change to such a degree that it destroyed the company. Just like a major storm, the market is unforgiving. It just is. The question you and your crew will continue to face is what can *and will* be done when faced with a rapid, unforgiving and market-changing shift in your *business as usual?* These changes are coming faster and more furiously with each passing day.

20. GET AGILE OR DIE?

Want to know what happens if you choose not to personally get agile? Take a bus, train or look into most cars on the way into any major city during rush hour and notice the quality of life around you. Are you inspired by what you see? Chances are that you will witness the "Working Dead" we have already mentioned.

More often than not, you will probably be surrounded by those who are still lucky enough to have jobs, sitting there in some level of resignation. Look closely at their level of enthusiasm and:

- The way they shuffle and drag their feet
- How *little and seldom* they breathe
- How they stare through the windshield and tightly grip their steering wheel
- Notice the preoccupied, *lights on, but nobody's home* look in their eyes
- How they treat you as an obstacle in their path

The older they look, the more resigned they often appear. On the way to work, most are trying to distract themselves with their smart gadget, book or music from all the stuff they will soon face when they get to work. On the way home many will have their eyes shut or their headphones in to block out as much stimulus as possible, while they seem to collapse into their seats. Granted, there are those bubbly, intrepid people that you meet that seem to thrive on adversity and always land on their feet. But look around, most of your fellow travelers will probably look just a bit more subdued. Is it any wonder why watching Zombie movies has recently become so popular?

It is now pretty much accepted that most people still working are responsible for the tasks of what two to four people used to do, only a generation ago. Not only this, but when you subtract inflation, current average wages have now shrunk back to levels not seen since the 1970s. Does this inspire you? Prices have risen drastically since then and most of us need to work much harder and much longer to make ends meet. The prognosis looks to be more of the same or even worse. How are you, as a leader, going to get your increasingly urgent message of *yet more change* to move these resigned, system-oriented, *business as usual people* into decisive often radical action?

As computers and robotics continue to improve in performance and dexterity, many jobs and even careers that were safe a few years ago, are now in jeopardy of becoming extinct. We mentioned that McDonald's is responding to employee demands of 15.00 US Dollars. per hour wages, **not** by caving into these demands, but rather by installing new self-service ordering and grilling machines. There are now capable robots that can take orders and payment; others fry hamburgers perfectly, without the need for coffee breaks, and have no wage complaints. Can you guess what this means to an unskilled, non-agile service worker? For the rest of those workers in retail, the thought of self-service machines combined with drastically increasing competition from the Internet spells a perfect storm in the traditional brick and mortar retail model. Even Walmart's continued success *and bottom line* are now being questioned. Is it any wonder with paychecks shrinking and the threat of unemployment rising that the amount of inspired looking commuters is reaching all-time lows? And this increasingly precarious situation is occurring without even being called an *official Recession*!

Make no mistake. This same phenomenon described by Joseph Schumpeter as *Creative Destruction* works on both a personal and company level. The bigger the company or ego, the more it takes to retain or enhance your agility.

Regardless of whether you are unemployed and capable, unskilled and working, middle class and worried, a successful entrepreneur or a rich and fully invested corporate titan, the quicker you become more consciously agile, the more you will be able to remain being *The Captain of your ship*.

What if it really has become, "Get agile or die"?

Is becoming agile any longer even a choice?

Too Big To Fail vs. Agility

One of the biggest impediments to change, as well as the ultimate reason that we will be hard pressed to avoid the inevitable perfect storm, is the advent of *Too Big To Fail*. It seems to have started in the banking business, but has quickly spread; and how could we forget about TBTF government. In each of these cases, companies and governing bodies have merged and grown into global behemoths. If we believe their well-paid-for hype, they are now so big that it would create tragic consequences for society, should they be allowed to fail. Even a rudimentary understanding of history or a memory of that childhood saying, "*The bigger they are, the harder they fall,*" will remind you that this will not end well. Now ask yourself if this behavior makes any business sense at all?

Who besides the benefactors will benefit from something that, by all rational measures of business performance, should have failed, but is forcibly kept alive (often with your money)? Just in the context of this book, if something is destined to fail, *propping it up further, to continue to do business as usual is about as far from agile as you can get!* Add to this that these organizations are so politically connected that they routinely lobby for laws to further protect their existence and thwart younger, more agile competition. If this isn't enough, in the last crisis, public companies were bailed out *with your tax money* to keep them afloat. If we pay attention to history, all these Band-Aids will work only until they don't. If you are not agile enough to respond when this house of TBTF cards finally collapses, good luck.

This adds yet another dimension to the words *business agility*. What business agility really means is that you not only have to be agile enough to handle the megatrends and the perfect storm brewing on the horizon, you also have to be agile enough to handle all the laws being enacted to protect a privileged, connected and moneyed few. This is probably the toughest challenge, as they can and usually have, changed the playing field over a night or weekend to better suit their needs. This trend of TBTF combined with Crony Capitalism is no longer even hidden in the shadows. For instance, the recent Trans Atlantic and Pacific Partnerships are laws made by your elected officials, *which are so secret* that their contents will not be revealed to the voters by their "*public servants*" for another five years! *This stunning, extremely anti-democratic fact is public knowledge for anyone interested in knowing!*

Don't forget that when the famous 2010 Obamacare Health bill was up for a vote, Nancy Pelosi, an elected representative ostensibly for the people of the State of California and Minority Speaker of the U.S. House of Representatives, was quoted as saying, "*We have to pass the bill so that you can find out what is in it, away from the fog of the controversy*"[xli]. Do you sense a disconnect in the "*Representative Democratic Process*"? Who now represents whom? This method of doing business depends directly upon who is in power at that moment, their personal agenda and often to whom they owe a favor. This is a public confirmation of, "*It's not what you know, but who you know.*" Avoiding being agile enough to sense who knows who, leaves you one new piece of legislation away from business catastrophe.

For the honest and agile businessperson, this creates an extra dimension of stress, as whom, being of sound mind would dare take a promise at face value any longer? To even act *at all* may turn out to be the wrong decision. Yet not acting may also be equally as destructive. How will you know when the situation can change and then change again overnight? We humans are designed to change behavior to accommodate new situations, but if we do not understand the situation or are blindsided by some totally unexpected occurrence, we will probably end up acting irrationally, further helping to cause the market to "dislocate." As economist John Maynard Keynes once wrote, *"The market can remain irrational longer than you can stay solvent."* Yet, the longer these imbalances persist, the smaller the catalyst needs to be to create havoc. Think of that one extra snowflake that lands on an imbalanced ledge of snow, high up on the mountain, causing a catastrophic avalanche into the valley below... Agility is nothing without timing.

This uncertain environment supports and indeed adds fuel to the precariousness of both the market and your employment situation. It absolutely confounds the ability of even wise and experienced corporate leaders to plan for the future. For now, there doesn't seem to be any complete solution for the precarious nature of today's market and the moneyed players; *yet becoming more agile will certainly help.*

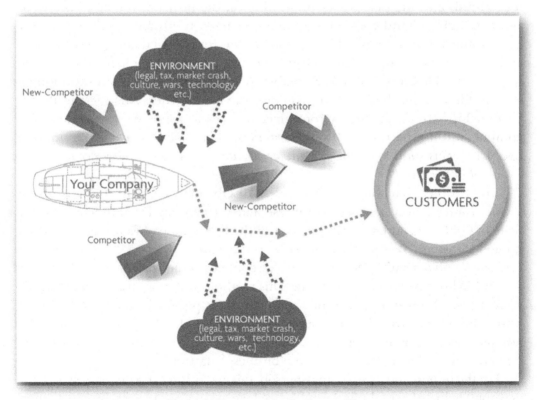

Figure 14 Your need for business agility

Becoming more agile to avoid customer capture

As we have mentioned, an interesting side effect is increasingly noticeable in especially larger TBTF companies it is something known as customer capture. This is a subscription-based model where you are forced into a monthly payment for your phone, banking services, magazines, make-up, tampons or whatever. Have you noticed that it becoming more and more challenging to cancel or change that subscription? Could this be by design? The idea gets even more complicated as it seems to be that if the rules are hard to understand and the service is irritatingly slow, you will then resign yourself to stay put. That may be true for a while, but what happens as frustration builds?

Although the following observations may not be in the *stated* plan, it is interesting to notice a molasses-like effect when faced with some of the following small but accumulative irritations:

- Paying extra for paper invoices
- Not being able to easily find how to cancel them
- Having to hunt for a telephone number to call.
- Being forced into a telephone tree only to end up being referred to a chat line or email when you only wish to ask a simple question
- Getting late fees on your late fees
- Not finding your simple question answered in their FAQ (Frequently Asked Questions).
- Not knowing what your problem is called or how to express it so you can even begin to seek help.
- Getting even more paper invoices after you have spoken with a representative who promised you there would be no more; again.
- Standing in a long line to "automatically check-in," getting sent to another line with an equally long wait to finally be sent to a third, attendant-based line, because it is discovered that you have some "priority level" you were not aware of.
- Then finding our you have been paying a premium for this extra level of service for years.

In days gone by, you would have had the time to deal with these small irritations quickly, but now when you multiply them by a factor of twenty or thirty similar business models, and they keep recurring, it slows you down. These irritations drain your energy to the point that you (and millions like you) resign yourselves to the reality that it is easier to continue paying these few extra bucks than have to hassle with fixing it, again. Automation makes the process of nickel and diming us out of money here and there even easier, as a computer does not have a conscience. The irritation still registers and festers.

Interestingly, if you look behind the scenes with these highly automated companies, they often have the highest employee burnout and turnover rates. In some telecom companies, up to eighty percent of some sales staffs can now turn over in a single year! With the quickening spread of information via the Internet, even a big company's reputation can now be quickly ruined by too many complaints posted in rapid succession. For the moment at least, TBTF companies can still use their money and muscle to prevent genuine competition and dissent, but is that a trend that can hold?

New business models encourage new behavior and luckily *this is where the agile businessperson can now succeed!* What if, just by treating each customer as a *valued and respected individual,* helping them to extract themselves from the prison of your competitors *Customer Management System,* you could become an overnight success?

21. Defining and Distinguishing Agility

The word agility comes from the Latin *agilis*[11] and simply means *quick movement*. Although this doesn't look so sexy at first glance, if you begin to see how inaction, resignation and indifference are slowing our society down, agility becomes something not to be caught without. Granted, not everyone is slow and in fact, those who act usually make out better than those who don't. Action now increasingly represents a threat to those who, consciously or not, would rather remain docile. Being agile can actually cause debate, hostility and sometimes even sabotage from those who would rather just be left alone.

Definition
Donald Sull from McKinsey defines agility as: "*The capacity to identify and capture opportunities more quickly than rivals do.*" But what if this definition is *too* limiting?

Wikipedia says: "*Agility is the ability to be quick and graceful on the basketball court or in the courtroom. The noun agility can be used for both physical and mental skills in speed and grace. Your mental agility might allow you to follow two conversations at once. We define it as the power of moving quickly and easily. Nimbleness in response, time is the key.*"

Think of the metaphor where you are the skipper and see a boat coming directly at you. Even with a successful career of avoiding boats and icebergs to look back upon, Captain Smith, of the *Titanic* missed just one, on the final voyage of his career and the result became the icon of maritime disasters.

---

11 The Free Dictionary By Farlex

Does it rhyme with stability?

According to the absolute latest from Wouter Aghina, Aaron De Smet, and Kirsten Weerda of McKinsey, you still can have your cake and eat it too. In their article *Agility: It rhymes with Stability*, they point out that, "*Companies can become more agile by designing their organizations both to drive speed and create stability*[xlii]," they make the case that even big organizations can extract themselves from inhibiting traps, act entrepreneurial, be more agile while retaining chunks of their bureaucracy. Is this possible or just wishful thinking?

If we understand it correctly, their point is that their *preliminary findings* point towards that you can take all the "good" from a start up mindset and become more agile as long as you have a solid core or "*backbone of stable elements.*" Well, maybe… Yet ask any back surgery patient if they feel better and have more agility after they have fused a few vertebrae together and you usually get a resounding "NO." Yes, the pain may subside, but that fused core makes being flexible much tougher to achieve. Our version of agility is to make the whole package flexible and to continuously figure out new ways to transform inhibiting traps and inflexible bureaucracy into a more agile way of doing business. "*A flexible organization around a stable but flexible core*" is absolutely a step in the right direction, but with the pace of change increasing, your whole organizational structure needs increased capacity to flexibly respond or eventually risk breaking completely.

The tools below will help you identify where major inhibiting factors and overwhelming bureaucracy is draining life and agility out of your organization. Then you can take suggested, proven steps to loosen up the knot and add more flexibility to it. Tools such as Rolling Budget, Forward Decision Drivers and *Carve-Outsourcing* can provide a strong, supple and responsive backbone to your organization, plus keep you vigilant for changes happening in front of you on your economic horizon.

The properties and qualities of conscious agility

If we really want to become more agile in our lives and our businesses it is important to get a better grasp of exactly what we mean. Being agile is a good start, but right off the bat, wouldn't being *consciously agile* give you a sharper edge? What other words would help us get a better understanding of a bigger possibility for agility?

Here are some suggestions:

Flexible
To move, you definitely have to be flexible. Unfortunately, this word may not go far enough to describe what we are looking for. A piece of hose is flexible, but does it consciously know what to do with its flexibility?

Lithe or supple
This takes flexibility to another level. Sense if you can the soft fluid-like presence in these words. Maintaining a supple or lithe corpotate or human body takes work, as does remaining agile, but the payoff is usually less stress and more measurable result.

Soft and receptive
Soft may not mean just "silky" soft. It may mean the *spongy like* ability to receive, absorb and respond to information at a quicker rate. Ask yourself, "Do I like to listen for understanding, or do I just wait for the opportunity to talk"?

Vigilant
Keeping watch for storm clouds is more informative than reading a book about weather. The more you tune into sensing what is happening around you, the more you may just make it to a safe hill before the next tsunami, be it financial, environmental or otherwise.

Quick and decisive
Hesitating can sometimes mean the difference between life and death or riches and poverty. For instance, the more you can decisively *kill the alternative* to act or not, the quicker you can later adjust or relax to newer changes.

Wise
"We are creating a generation of intelligent idiots." - Unknown

There is a difference between being intelligent and being wise. This difference usually shows up in stressful situations. Your ability to think things through under pressure may take more time than a snap decision, but if that decision is taken too quickly it may do tragic damage. Never forget, sometimes it is even wiser to do nothing at all.

Vulnerable
This word has little to do with being weak and everything to do with being prepared, present, relaxed, vigilant and ready for anything. For any serious practitioner of Martial Arts, being vulnerable means having all your physical, mental and even spiritual resources at the ready, to immediately meet your next threat or opportunity with full energy, resources and enthusiasm.

Responsive
Responding means possessing the wherewithal to go past an automatic, programmed reaction, reflect upon the situation together with your options and only then, *answer back* to stimulus. Responding moves beyond those sticky behavioral patterns and those pesky emotional triggers. Agility allows you to use your wisdom, blended with quickness and respond accordingly.

Respectful
Treating everyone with a sense of curiosity and wonder will energize you and them both to do what needs to be done *together*, even in times of stress.

Compassionate
Dealing with others with passion will make you a more attractive leader to follow. Empathy and compassion will also distinguish you as a leader of people from most other management types who have checked their emotions and feelings in the closet, in order to be more effective. What if a good dose of compassion will help you to sense what is going on much more effectively than just reading tables and charts?

Present
Dealing with the here and now *directly* is much more effective than dealing with your idea of it. This may sound obvious, but until you can separate what *you think*

you see, hear and experience from what is actually happening *in real time,* your ability for agility will remain a dangerous and filtered shadow of its true potential.

Courageous
To act or express from your heart is the origin of this Latin based word. This is where intelligence gives way to heartfelt and active passion. The better you can express your thoughts with heartfelt conviction, the more followers you will inspire into action.

Compression versus expansion, regarding agility
Agility has to do with expanding a possibility into a measurable action. Business as usual is about status quo and limiting or inhibiting new possibilities. When we talk of incorporating agility into an organization it may be wise to compare your corporate body to your own. Compressed tissue stops the natural flow of blood, causing tension and pain. It uses more energy and results in increasing stiffness, pain and entropy. Relaxed tissue is expansive and blood flows through it much more efficiently. It feels good and increases your agility and resilience.

What does your ability to sense compression and expansion have to do with communication, relationships and business?

This question may be better framed as what sensing compression or expansion *does not* have to do with communication, relationships and business?

I recently witnessed an interaction between a board member and his accountant over an important accounting question. The answer to this question would basically mean a difference between the company breaking even or being stuck with a large debt on the books. The board member was used to and very good at driving his point home with a series of well-structured arguments and justifications. The accountant was used to bullet proof accounting practices that would stand the most determined tax office scrutiny. The challenge was that the board member needed the accountant's support to implement his well thought out solution. Although legal and viable, his solution landed a bit outside the comfort zone of his accountant's standards and his meticulous accounting practices.

What made this interaction so interesting was that the more the Board Member brilliantly argued for his case, the more he compressed the accountant's willingness to help and drove him deeper into his defensive shell. Both people wanted to solve the situation, but their well-used communication tools and accompanying behaviors were now working against them. The board member was now caught in the common trap of using his favorite tools, the ones that had brought him so much success, in a situation where their use was making matters worse. The accountant (used to employing standard "business as usual" solutions that he knew would make it past the tax authorities) began to look increasingly uncomfortable and tense.

Agility on a personal level means exercising your senses more and training to notice how you are, in this case, pushing your accountant further away from your goal with each extra word you say. What if instead you tried a few curious and inviting questions, then sought some expert advice from your accountant?

In fact, this ended up happening. At a critical moment in their discussion, the frustrated board member asked the accountant to please give him some feedback on what he saw for possibilities. With this little, delicate bit of coaxing, the accountant thought for a moment, then picked up his phone and called his tax expert to explain the situation. The tax expert responded by going methodically through a SWOT analysis before agreeing to look into how the proposed solution could be implemented. A bitter argument that had been festering for months was moved measurably forward; just by employing a curious question, presented as open invitation to dance.

Now, think how often this same compression phenomenon happens in conversations and relationships in your organization, on a daily basis. Just think of how many times your company's relationships and business flow are measurably inhibited by such compressions as:

- A Salesperson who oversells someone. In the process he gets politely thrown out, or the customer sheepishly buys what is being offered, only to embarrassingly return it the next day and never be seenor heard of again.
- A Manager who commands his staff to spend their increasingly precious time filling in useless reports for Headquarters, without explaining the reason.
- Rumors start circulating about reorganization, yet management refuses to confirm or deny them. This causes everyone to begin spending more time and energy on protecting their livelihoods and looking for new jobs instead of performing their mission-critical functions.
- A customer service agent, who is so eager to demonstrate his expertise and efficiency, that his *well-intended and correct* attempts to solve a complaint are interpreted as downright rude. The customer, who feels neither heard nor understood, keeps getting interrupted before she can finish expressing her thought and leaves the call totally frustrated, never again to return.

In each one of these all-too-common situations the conversations become *compressed, as do* the relationships and everyone's resulting ability to do business. The listeners go from *growth* into *protection* mode, batten down their hatches and thus impede their ability to hear other possibilities. Where is the agility or service in the speaker's presentation or behavior? Keep in mind that in each situation described here and in many others, *everyone had good intentions,* but did it matter?

Becoming agile means practicing *to sense* when a conversation or relationship begins compressing and using the correct conversational tools to halt this process. This is usually as simple as asking a thoughtful and inviting question. Then you can invite your listener to brainstorm other possibilities by using tools that expand the conversation.

This is leadership! It is the kind of give and take increasingly necessary to get anything done with co-workers in today's stressed environment. The simplest and most agile conversational tools for this process are curiosity, questions and invitations, followed by a good dose of listening, understanding and action.

Creating Agile Awareness

Agility becomes more powerful, the more you become aware of what it means. As we are creatures of habit, we usually do what we have always done until we get hit over the head with the realization that it no longer works. With all the stuff you have to do during the day, how often do you go out of your way to find new alternatives when older, trusted methods or behaviors already exist?

Keep this in mind when you are communicating to customers and colleagues alike. Unless you can clearly demonstrate that you have a better, more agile suggestion that can produce measurable results, your listener may politely listen, but chances are they will continue to do what they are comfortable with anyway. We get bombarded with more and more information every day. This makes it even more important that what you say is not only technically correct, the message also has to emotionally "*move*" your listener into action as well. The more agile your ability to communicate becomes, the more chances you will have to accomplish this.

Practically, this means that you need to inspire and engage your listeners with both facts and feeling. It is no longer enough to leave your listeners with more bullet-proof logic; you have to generate *actionable understanding* of what you want them to buy or do. Remember, "*Knowledge leads to debate, understanding leads to action*" and measurable action is what gets things moving.

Think of the metaphor of something you *know* sitting in a box on some high, but inaccessible *ledge*. Then think of that same bit of information that is anchored from *underneath*, *standing* tall and attractive for all to see and connect with. How often do you leave your listeners with more *knowledge* instead of taking them to the active level of *understanding?* This is more often than not a question of simplifying (instead of complicating) your message. Simplification is much easier and quicker to action upon than unnecessarily complicating it with more alternatives and bigger words.

> "*The Mind cannot argue with simplicity*," - Patrick Collard

To move into action, the left and right hemispheres of the brain need to synchronize on the thought. The right hemisphere is more concerned with aesthetics, form and feeling, whereas the left hemisphere is more concerned with results that can be measured. Synchronizing and harmonizing these two hemispheres is no easy task. Often, if you break your message down to the least common denominator and add your heartfelt passion to its essence, this potent blend will definitely help. Break complicated topics down into bite size chunks and add a bit of emotion and you will begin to *feel the agility* this practice brings to your brand of leadership. You will be appreciated and followed as a leader who can explain things. This is the door leading to mastery.

Peril and agility
Navigating in the Swedish archipelago during a storm is a bigger challenge than a similar storm on the high seas. The reason? Rocks! There is literally a mountain range directly under the surface. Disregarding this extra, unseen level of challenge puts you, your boat and your crew directly in harm's way. You need to monitor your depth gauges even closer as well as develop an intuitive sense of what lies underneath the water's surface.

The Swedish language has a word for this, "Lyhördhet." It means to *listen with all your senses*. From a practical sense, how can you expect to increase your physical agility without simultaneously increasing your ability to *listen with all your senses?* To do this requires you, as a leader, to go against current corporate convention. Increasing your ability to listen with all your senses means practicing to conscientiously *feel* and intuit what is going on around you. Behaving like this in the current international corporate atmosphere can still get colleagues talking behind your back or get you thrown out of the macho, good ol' boy network. In fact, the biggest critique of this book is this chapter and it's focus on "warm and fuzzy" soft-skills. What do manners have to do with running a large and prestigious company? What if the times as well as customer and employee expectations are changing fast?

This *head-in-the-sand* type of behavior of not listening with all your senses can quickly become a liability to those who consciously or not believe in *business as usual*. We have now *raised* one, possibly two generations *who have no allegiance or respect for their elders*. They are now beginning to flex their business acumen and muscle. They also are expressing their growing distrust and often disdain for habits used by those currently in charge. Therefore, should you need to, you can justify practicing this non-conventional, *soft behavior* and compare it to the soft, agile behavior of a samurai or native american warrior. Both were taught to develop and sharpen a keen and intuitive sense for what was happening *within themselves as well as all around them*, in real time. Compare that type of behavior to the poet Tennyson's soldiers[12] who were taught, "*Theirs not to reason why, theirs is but to do and die.*" Then ask yourself if you would rather be an agile warrior with your senses highly tuned for any and all input, or a dutiful soldier blindly following orders. Who do you think risks the biggest chance of becoming the business equivalent of cannon fodder?

Ask most soldiers who have survived battle to describe the rigors of combat and they will usually say that it was those most perilous moments, within an inch of death, when they **felt** *most alive*. In fact, from soldiering to sailing, to leading others, the closer you come to personal peril, (real or perceived) the more heightened your senses become. Now what if this ability to heighten your senses can be practiced and *mastered?* How much better would you then become when also armed with the best tools and equipment that current technology and experience have to offer? Would this give you an edge?

Not just agile decisions, agile executions

This book is about being agile enough to execute important decisions effectively and appropriately in real time. Therefore, this book is NOT written just to show how to make more agile *decisions*. **It is written to help you to master** *executing those* **decisions** with increased agility.

If we are successful with this book, then you will have better tools in your toolbox and more effective equipment on your corporate yacht with which to act upon important decisions swiftly, *even when they are unpopular. Political Correctness* is not agility. In times of uncertainty, count on someone's feelings getting hurt. Acting decisively and engagingly is an unavoidable part of being, "*lonely at the top.*" Decisive action is demanded to become a respected leader who is worth following. If a child is playing

---

12 From Alfred, Lord Tennyson's famous poem *"The Charge of the Light Brigade"*

in the street in front of an oncoming bus, the situation requires *action first, then explanation* - when safely on the sidewalk.

The art and practice of decision-making has been in focus for many years and there is more than enough good literature available on how to best decide. In fact with improved artificial intelligence applications, your computer can handle most decision-making processes much more effectively and objectively than you. What is still sorely lacking are simple, understandable and powerful tools to implement these decisions, plus an effective way to measure and fine-tune the effectiveness of each.

The tools you will soon read about in section four will help execute and implement critical changes quickly and are the major part of what makes this book unique. In the final part of our book, you will be introduced to these tools. You will also be instructed as to the fundamental steps to use them. You will learn to change course quickly and to implement procedures and systems that can prevent you from falling back into *business as usual*. Practicing to do this by motivating your listeners, rather than dictating to them will further insure success.

Therefore, the purpose of this book is to demonstrate beyond a doubt for you, dear reader, that to go forward, it is to not just to *get agile or die*, but *to get agile and thrive!* Doing or living *business as usual* is no longer enough to ensure your company's or your family's survival, much less your success. Training to be and act consciously agile, as we suggest, takes an enormous amount of commitment and energy for even the most healthy and smartest amongst us. Many of the tools go stridently against convention. But what is the alternative?

As the pace of change quickens and both the opportunities and storm clouds increase in frequency and size, you will need to develop your ability to *sense* what is happening and *sense* it in many dimensions. Then you must quickly act, and do it decisively; to motivate your crew for them in turn, to execute their duties with power and grace. Missing a key bit of information or misreading an emotional turning point could result in financial and/or personal disaster.

This time is different...
The greatest challenge is that when things have been so good for so long, human nature signals us to let our guard down. We then justify this and convince ourselves that life will always be as good as it is currently. Intuitively, you probably understand that life just doesn't work that way. Yet we are wired so good times encourage us to think that this time *is really different*. Regardless, this comfort zone *of pollyanna thinking* is most likely the biggest risk you will ever face. It represents being lured into an unfounded, false sense of security. Just think about the fate of

many honest, law abiding German Jews living there during the 1930s. Many had even fought on the frontline during World War One. Some surely boarded their last train still thinking that this couldn't possibly happen in the country of their birth... Wouldn't you?

Now the good news is that regardless of whether the future is dark or bright, can you see any downside with training to be more consciously agile? If nothing else, there is the possibility that you may develop further, learn something new and be even more successful than you have already become. Agility is your razor sharp edge! So regardless of your darkest fears and even if you are looking forward with hope towards a promising future, get ready for some tips to help you to better survive and thrive.

Much more nimble in steering our ship
Becoming more nimble is a function of being able to be present to, and gracefully handle, what is going on right here and now. Being burdened by thinking too much or having to remember the policy on your corporate rulebook's page 132 will inhibit your capacity to be agile. You will be constantly filtering what is happening through all the preconditioning you have ever received. The more you commit to developing systems to handle your *stuff*, the more you will increase your capacity for curiosity and creativeness. These are critical factors that need to be developed to stay agile.

22. The Age of Agility is here!

"Lead, follow, or get out of the way" (Found on CNN's founder, Ted Turner's desk)

What do all these opportunities and challenges point to? They demand an increase in agility in order to lead, follow or get out of the way. If you want to remain in a profitable and sustainable business, the demands to do so keep rising. There is no sympathy for those who miss even one important market signal. Make one bad decision or miss one important new rule or piece of legislation and you may be out for good! And this pace of change is accelerating!

Viral agility
Agility needs to become a lifestyle; one that is taken on at all levels within an organization and by each individual. At this point you may agree that the decision to get agile is a no-brainer, but what if that makes it akin to implementing a budget cut?

Everyone is for saving money! *As long as the cuts occur in someone else's department…*

The process of becoming agile is bound to reveal traditions, behaviors and systems that are not only ineffective, but also well entrenched and desirable to some, EVEN YOU. Resistance to changes in these *"legacy"* issues are bound to cause irritation and confrontation, but to *really* become agile they *must be addressed*. In terms now used on the Internet, *agility needs to go viral*. It needs to seep into every nook and cranny throughout your organization and into each individual team member's cells in it in order for it to really make a measurable and sustainable difference.

With agility, both privilege and risk increase for those in responsible positions. Getting everyone on board and empowering the whole team, even in the face of understanding all the Megatrends and The Perfect Storm clouds, will be challenging! A new level of agile collaboration and connection will be needed that stretches from your shareholders to your boardroom, throughout your organization and ultimately extending out to *each individual customer.* Heartfelt cooperation between workers and management, focused upon customer needs, wants and wishes demands to be constantly strengthened and cultivated.

Every process needs to be looked at and increasingly revisited, throughout your entire organization. This means for instance, even looking at traditional HR and the antagonizing role of unions. To be effective going forward also means eliminating the fear of internal competition and the destructive behavior it encourages. Finally, it is critical to begin appreciating and cultivating a culture of empowerment. What if *knowledge* is power, but *understanding* is empowerment?!

Good parents usually feel they have accomplished the task of correctly raising their offspring when their children enjoy better life, filled with more opportunity than they did. This mindset needs to become the norm for business leaders too. Management needs to tackle their role and transform themselves into worthy leaders, capable of *mastering their role* of cultivating people to become better than they are.

For instance, what about basing leadership promotions and raises partly upon the *number of employees or contractors who surpass you* in the organizational structure? Why should your ability to cultivate your colleagues' skills, to the point that they are better than yours, be seen as a personal threat or failure? Instead you and your ability to *master* teaching others to practice the skills needed to make your organization more agile and successful should be acknowledged, celebrated. Your skills to bring out your colleagues best, should be trumpeted as part of your success!

What's better, to manage or to lead an agile group?
To become agile, fundamental traits and roles will have to be re-examined. Tools, methods and work roles developed for the industrial age no longer provide the same level of impact. They are increasingly becoming a heavy drag on development. For instance, what if something as accepted as the conventional manager role is also a stubborn holdover from the industrial age? What if traditional role of Manager has now become an anachronism?

Think about it. The role of Management was developed during a time of scarcity; scarcity of resources, time and capital. Resources in those days included bricks, wood, nails and water. Resources also included an extra pair of hands and a stronger back. As we have discussed, we now live in an era of abundance. Resources are cheaper and more accessible than at any other time in human history. Unfortunately, this designation often still includes "human resources."

Most Millennials have never known want and are irritatingly used to having their way. They are also the most educated generation ever and *although they often don't act like it,* they are very responsible and capable. Most of all, they will accept being inspired to do something, but they absolutely do *not* like and usually resist being told what to do.

Now, what is a manager's traditional role?

Their job is to apply scarce resources in the most effective way to produce or accomplish a result. This involves taking decisions, directing resources (both human and not) appropriately and monitoring the results. After all, *"you have to break a few eggs to make an omlette."*

Right here and now we have:

- Decision-making software that can take more objective and more effective decisions much faster than any human.
- RFID chips and ID cards that automatically monitor where people are and give a very good picture of what they are doing.
- Cameras and surveillance that are well above and beyond what is necessary to ensure someone is working effectively.
- An educated workforce that can be given a goal and then encouraged to figure out the best way to achieve it.

What is the point of someone still lodged in an administrative role, commanding others while being paid more than their colleagues, when those doing the work are actually charged and responsible to produce the result? This type of *management role* is beginning to be revealed as the predatory (and costly) role that it has become.

These are all reasons why *managing* people rather than *leading* them is rapidly becoming antique. Sophisticated software programs can now allocate resources and streamline processes very well, thereby freeing up managers to begin focusing on leading and encouraging their people rather than just managing them.

Rear Admiral Grace Hopper once eloquently observed that, *"You manage things and you lead people."* The more you make people feel like things, the more they will either resent it or *resign themselves to it.* Regardless, their dignity as human beings will suffer and their energy will dissipate. The ultimate result will be that their quality, creativity and efficiency will suffer. How does this affect your bottom line?

As we have noted already, a large part of being agile has to do with being open, receptive and compassionate, to name a few qualities. Interestingly, a leader who easily attracts followers demonstrates those exact same qualities. So, if you want to become more agile, learn to lead. If you want to lead better, become more agile.

23. Incorporating Agility

Incorporate is such a versatile word when it comes to agility. It conveys the importance of integrating agility into not only your business structure, but also into the minds and bodies of each individual in your organization. Incorporate literally means to *put into a body* and that includes in every type and definition of what a body is, from yours to the incorporated body in which you work or which you run.

Therefore, to really incorporate agility will require you to:

- Question everything
- Listen with all your senses
- Increase personal and business capabilities
- Lead rather than manage
- Make better use of soft-skills
- Practice looking forward instead of behind
- Employ new and effective business tools

Question everything!
With everything changing at an ever increasing pace, holding onto outdated information, beliefs and dogma becomes a tangible risk. Gone are the days when you could run the same process for decades and enjoy the same result. To be agile requires you to be open, curious and question everything from new ideas to behavioral patterns; some of which are so ingrained that they have become invisible.

Agility demands a new level of discovery and wonder. The more you can view yourself and your organization from your customers', suppliers', and employees' perspective, the better access you will have to invisible behavioral patterns that used to take you farther from your goal of loyal customers and increased business. The more you question, listen and observe what is happening, the more you will be able to see the positive and negative ripples that certain behaviors cause. Increasingly, you must accept *and celebrate* that your customer comes first, last and always. In the end, it is each individual customer who pays your bills.

Increase personal and business capabilities
Increased customer sophistication and the extra demands this causes screams for a constant review and increase of personal and business capabilities. To do this and remain competitive will invite a new and innovative look at on the job training. This demand for state of the art knowledge is already encouraging all kinds of new applications of *online and blended learning*. Preparing now for a time when learning and working become so intermeshed that you will not know where one ends and the other starts.

Lead rather than manage here, now!
As we have already mentioned, your ability to attract willing and engaged followers will be critical in your bid to become agile. Distinguishing management from leadership will be a critical capability for successful organizations and key people from here on. The simple explanation is that coercion and force are becoming less motivating factors. Metaphorically speaking, the stick is losing its effectiveness and the carrot is becoming more essential.

Young and capable people do not fear losing their jobs like previous generations did. Even though the traditional job market is shrinking, new, more precarious and exciting ways of earning a living are on the increase while more and more people are testing the waters of becoming self-employed. Many are doing this *along side of working full time*, with the specific goal of being able to support themselves, regardless of the job market. They somehow have realized already that the luxury of relying on only one income stream is no longer prudent. This is agility and this is the type of person you *must attract*, retain and learn to lead, going forward. In fact, as colleague and leadership coach Jörgen Khilström says, "*Our parent's generation could reasonably expect to stay at the same organization for their entire career. Our generation has probably had, on average, six employers. The next generation is beginning to understand that it will need to have multiple income streams to insure a steady lifestyle*". Do you really think they will take kindly to being managed?

Make better use of soft-skills

This topic will be the subject of another book as its ramifications are now just being noticed. As our world of transactional business gets more structured; as we get more involved with our electronic toys and gadgets; as we become more and more stressed with the increased amount of work and chores that need to be handled, your ability to communicate in a way that gets things done will become more dependent upon your ability to use soft-skills. Why?

As we sink deeper and deeper into the complex world of technology, we become burdened with more stuff to do. People who listen, respect and understand us will become more important as we will be more desperately searching for someone we can trust. Right now, many of us seem to be further alienating ourselves from one another, suspicious of anyone who seems to want gain your confidence. What if anyone training to *authentically* buck this trend will begin to stand out more and become more attractive? In the rapidly unfolding future, knowing how to communicate your sincerity in a way that makes your listener feel seen and heard, plus using your body language to help get your message across in a way that *moves your listeners to action*, will help to distinguish you as someone to know and do business with. For instance, did you know that by just introducing yourself and saying your name to someone whom may want to cause you harm, you will decrease the risk of being attacked by fifty percent? Studies show that it is much easier to rob a "*mark*", someone you don't perceive to know. It seems there is now science to back up that fact that we become just a bit more *human* when we strive to connect and get to know each other better.

People need people. People go out of their way and will pay more to be treated with respect. Don't you?

Practice your soft-skills and see if you not only notice more people being attracted to you, but also notice whether you begin to earn more money too…

Some important *Soft Buying Factors* that can help you win the race are:

- Listening in a way that makes the person speaking feel specially chosen
- Contagious trust, that ripples out of your people and company
- Personal service, that secure feeling demonstrating that you and your team will run *that extra mile.*
- Leading edge design and front-running perception of suppliers
- Better perceived quality, of your supplier's products and services
- Attractive status and prestige of being a buyer who buys from you
- Feeling loyal enough to warmly and spontaneously recommend a person, a product and a company

Practice looking forward instead of behind

"*The older I get, the better I was*" (Spotted on an "Old Guys Rule" T-Shirt)

Spending your time looking at past performance indicators will keep you focused upon the past and prevent you from seeing the sunshine or icebergs directly in front of you. This is the quality of being vigilant. Lose your vigilance and your risk of being surprised, by something you should have seen coming, increases drastically.

We are trained to and feel comfortable with looking back at what has already happened. This can and often does block or filter our perception of the future tremendously. Make no mistake; being vigilant is not the same as being naive. Vigilant comes from Latin and means watchful. It refers to you staying awake and aware of your surroundings and being prepared to act. With all the distractions of twenty first century life, you no longer have to be physically asleep to lose your watchfulness. Learn to constantly "*check your six*"[13].

Add to this our cult of measuring the past. Most measurements that are applied to our success are based on past, short-term, performance, e.g. quarterly and yearly results. The greatest challenger to your bid for agility undoubtedly is your budgeting process. This process can and often is used as defense for decisions that might or might not have been taken. Budgeting has resulted in truly catastrophic long-term results even if well-meaning management really *did not see* the "iceberg" coming until after the budget was done. We will deal with this issue more in the next section.

Employ new and effective business tools

Some of our favorites will be the focus of the final section of this book. We have developed and worked with a number of tools that now have proven track records of drastically increasing an organization's agility and success. They cover sales, marketing, HR, R&D and management, to name a few. These are areas of vital importance, when it comes to creating a brighter future, *regardless of the weather*. The following portfolio of tools is still growing. Even today though, you can create an absolute advantage for yourself and your crew by employing them to *get agile now*.

While you cannot immediately change large trends, such as the tax code, the legal system, wars or your own competitive environment, you can improve your ability to navigate these challenges and even have more fun and make more money. That is what agility and these agile tools can mean to you and your organization.

---

13 Checking your six is an espionage term referring to checking all four directions around you, plus above and below you for threats and opportunities.

SECTION FOUR

Incorporating Agility

Incorporating Agility

Not only are your customers getting more sophisticated by the day, so are you. So when you read about the following tools, *you are invited and encouraged to be skeptical*. From our experience, they have proven to contribute measurably and dramatically to those companies that commit to them. Your commitment to them will be up to you. We therefore encourage you to test them as well as others. As long as they measurably contribute to a more agile stance for you and your crew, they are worth pursuing. As we have written, *agility is a lifestyle* and will develop over time, just as each of these tools will. We also encourage you to join us on the path of *mastering agility*. We look forward to your reflections and contributions to this important conversation. Our blog, www.masteringagilityblog.com should be up by the time you read this and you are welcomed and encouraged to read and contribute to it. The more we share ideas about the best way to master and incorporate agility into each other and our organizations, the healthier, richer and more agile we will all collectively become!

We again choose to use the word *incorporate* here consciously. What if just implementing something is no longer enough? Implementing can still leave room for miscommunication through intellectually based misunderstandings, abstractions and interpretations. These mistakes may be in direct conflict with what you actually wish to accomplish. *Incorporating* goes a step further. By focusing on the practical implications of executing and managing what you want to do and then *blending this with the spirit or feeling* of accomplishing your goal, you add another dimension to the individuals and organizations involved. Just as there is a tangible difference between the letter and spirit of the law, there is also a difference between the *intellectual* and an *incorporated* application of agility.

The word incorporate not only refers to building a corporation, it means to personally embody something. The more you personally incorporate something, the more it's absorbed into your system right down to your cells. The more this process is taken on consciously, by each person involved, the more effective, profitable and *sustainable* your results will be. It manifests, resonates and becomes part of you. This is the level of the commitment we see needed to successfully implement these tools in a way that can cause permanent change in your individual and organizational behavior.

24. Some tips when incorporating agility into your organization

Build your vessel (organization) to last. Make it sustainable. That means starting by plugging the leaks. You cannot realistically think about winning a race or sailing smoothly into the sunset if you are taking on water. Therefore, focus on first things first. If your company is losing money, the first step is damage control. Focus on finding each financial leak and plug them all.

"When the tide goes out you will see who is wearing their swimsuit."
- Warren Buffet

Remember, a rising tide lifts all boats. Don't confuse intelligence or business savvy with being lucky enough to be enjoying the right trend at the right time. Strive to consciously figure out *the Mechanics* of how and why you are winning. A gift is a gift and is dangerous to confuse with a tool. When you figure out how and why your gift works and where it is most effective, only then will it become your tool.

One of the most obvious examples of this is conscious use of body language in selling and leadership. Ask most successful salespeople or leaders, *"What is it in your body language that makes your message attractive and engaging?"*, they will often have trouble even understanding your question. It is only after cracking the code that they are able to begin consciously using it effectively. Until then it is a gift, pure luck.

Always strive to improve your position. This sage advice for driving is also applicable for sailing, business and living. Continued success requires constant vigilance and a will for sustainable improvement. Remember, what may have worked before may not be the best choice going forward.

25. OVERCOMING THE BIG INHIBITORS OF CHANGE:

It is easy to talk about incorporating an agile business model that goes viral and saturates your organization. Still, count on the change necessary to accomplish this being met with resistance. Why?

Because as you grow you will inevitably run up against one or more of the following biggest inhibitors of change:

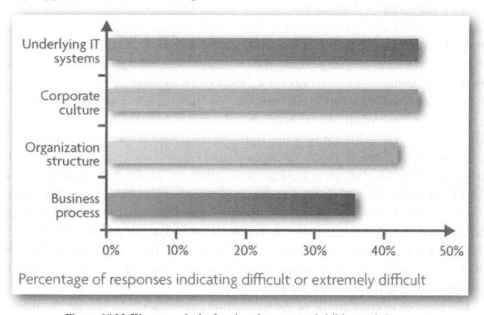

Figure 15 McKinsey analysis showing the greatest inhibitors of change

Systems are (surprise) inherently systematic; otherwise they become art. Processes are designed to follow a specific and measurable course to a predetermined result. Deviate from a system or a process and their integrity and effectiveness rapidly diminishes. Organization and structure bring in the human elements, but only slightly. An organizational structure is created so that everyone knows their role and how to systematically *react.* Corporate and personal culture is probably the toughest nut to crack as it varies in accordance with those involved, their feelings, behavior and everything else. These factors also change over time. Finally, culture contains many unwritten rules that you must "*sense*" and practice *even if there are no clear signs to guide you.* Discovering these requires curiosity, listening and presence to everyone around you.

Each one of these inhibitors should be constantly reviewed and improved, especially as the pace of change accelerates. The more you monitor how efficient your people are at adapting themselves to changing markets and internal conditions, the more flexible and resilient your organization becomes. The more resilient you become, the more you can handle future developments and ensure a sustainable level of success. Below we will take a closer look at each of these inhibitors to get a better understanding of how they work and how to handle them. Handling them will require another book.

When IT rules rather than serves

It always starts as machine code. At its roots, Information Technology is made up of either Ones or Zeros. Each *One* represents an *on circuit* and each *Zero* represents an *off circuit.* In many ways, it is very much like Dr. Lipton's cellular *growth* (open) or *protection* (closed) behavior model, only on a digital or binary level.

In our cells a One would represent an "*on*" or *growth* circuit and a Zero would be an "*off*" or *protected* circuit. This limits behavior to being a derivative or shade of either "*on*" or "*off.*" This sources the rigid rules and processes necessary in the IT paradigm. For instance, if your company runs on an Oracle or SAP system, their performance is based upon adhering to the strict *one or zero* rules of that system in order to produce the anticipated output and reports. This rigidity is often the root cause for a lot of the debilitating reaction times and the frustration of figuring out what particular input is causing the malfunction in the output. Moreover, by the time management input reaches the factory floor and all the field offices, the ripple effect of a misunderstanding or misinterpretation, especially in a larger organization, can multiply many times over.

The most obvious example of the frustration surrounding IT is security. Although a good case can be made for its need, think about how much time is spent (often wasted) logging in and out, recreating your password if it is forgotten and fixing a security issue if it's compromised. If you forget your ID card you most likely need to return home to collect it, otherwise you will be locked out of your office, functions and reason for existence. You often cease to exist without it. With the increase in business done on the net and all the temptations it causes, the level and frequency of this annoyance are also increasing.

Teleconferencing is also wonderful, when it works; but when your system doesn't function, it can still cause more communication problems and frustration than it solves. With the explosion of different communication channels, the challenge of choosing the most effective one is also becoming critical. As one colleague observed, "*It seems the more ways we have to reach people, the harder it is to get in touch with them.*"

Culprit of IT inhibition, the Data

If you are in a decision-making position, you are certainly familiar with the infamous *Budget Crunch* that takes place at end of the year. *Crunch time* becomes an extraordinary inhibitor of change for a number of reasons:

- Being administrative, the process chews up valuable sales and service time.
- It inevitably creates friction between internal groups who already have, and those who want more money.
- As your company grows, it usually becomes more complicated, political and time consuming.
- It is often tough or impossible to adjust something that needs to be changed until the next crunch, even if it is detected *less than one month into the new budget.*

Why do we even use a yearly budget? This yearly process is a legacy left over from the agricultural age. Agriculture is of course, a cyclical growing pattern based upon the four seasons of the year. In order to maximize your harvest, you had to make sure you budgeted your time and resources appropriately for the season. With the exception of the few farmers who may be reading this book, how many of you have a business or product that is still critically affected by the four agricultural seasons?

For the most part, our way of living and doing business has moved on. Yes, taxes need to be reconciled every year, but even they can be adjusted to your fiscal year and divided up during the year to cushion the shock. What if there is a more agile way of mitigating the *budget crunch*?

The Budget Process is also a fine example of what is known as, "*Garbage In, Garbage Out*" or GIGO. The output of your budget process is totally dependent upon the quality of the input. Every number entered hooks into so many other functions and assumptions. If what you input is only based upon your best "*guesstimate,*" then what can you expect to come out on the other side?

A budget is no more than a very sophisticated spreadsheet, which in turn is a fancy relational database. Put something in and out comes the result based upon all the functions to which it is connected. This information then spreads through the whole organization and sometimes beyond, often instantaneously. We will look at the budget process more closely very shortly, but here we want to plant two questions worth contemplating:

- How the quality and reliability of your input directly influences your output?
- How rigid and relevant the yearly timeframe of your standard budget is, really?

In other words, if your guesstimates are too optimistic, pessimistic or just plain wrong, it may take another year before you can change any of the input or the assumptions you base them upon.

Add to this the swamp of over fifty different communication platforms, portals, different or new standards, non-compatible protocols and your whole IT situation can quickly become a pit of quicksand.

For instance, at one point the Swedish telecoms company Telia had three different accounting/billing systems in use in different parts of the company *at the same time.* This caused massive incompatibility issues, wasted lots of time, due to having to re-input figures multiple times. This situation caused extreme frustration for among others, the sales and billing teams. Then there was the internal battle over which system should prevail... The merger of these systems took a longer ramp up time than expected. Then the additional time required for training and the need to adjust the system during implementation was enormous. The whole process was a huge source of frustration for employees, suppliers and customers.

A further example is the Swedish seed company, Nelson Brothers, which nearly went bankrupt upgrading their IT/Business system. What was promised did not function and by the time it was fixed, it had taken a few different companies, installing a few different systems to create a fully functioning solution. This process exhausted most of their cash reserves, money that had been saved up over generations.

Another poignant example was Y2K. This was the situation at the turn of the last century where billions of dollars and untold hours of manpower were invested because of the need for one extra zero. Great fear was generated out of the worry that all computer driven systems would come to a halt at Midnight on New Years day 2000. After lots of worry and a lot of reprogramming, hardly anything occurred at the appointed hour, even to those who chose (correctly) to do nothing.

You can absolutely count on your computers delivering accurate information. Keep in mind though that its accuracy is directly related to the quality of your input. If the input is wrong, a guess, or is out of date, it will iterate further and further from reality. Systems are based upon models, not reality. How closely can a model mirror real life and its challenges? Budgets will always be based upon models, but those models can be a lot more flexible if they are based upon today's reality instead of yesterday's planting cycle.

Finally, how often do you question a prepared report?

Most people we have surveyed, *including many decision makers,* don't usually question a report. Whether it is due to time constraints, comfort or plain laziness, most of us take a printed report as the truth, regardless of its flaws. Agile systems demand constant vigilance, more accurate input and healthy questions.

In short, changing input in just one place in your system can create an enormous leveraging effect upon the rest of your organization, often without realizing it. Even when an accounting system is integrated correctly, it still takes a long time to close the books and get accurate information. The agile Skipper needs that information immediately. Why can't you close the books every day with just revenue and cost? Because even today, most systems won't allow it!

Life in a spreadsheet

A little over a generation ago workers were still in charge of their jobs and lives. Computers worked alongside them as a support or aid function. Fast-forward thirty years from the invention of Lotus 1-2-3 and the cataclysmic shift it provided to modeling, calculating and predicting results. The power and presence of Information Technology is now ubiquitous. It is now impossible to remain competitive, let alone agile in today's business environment without IT support.

While this has boosted productivity throughout the organization, it has also handcuffed workers to the rules, regulations, constant monitoring and evaluation of their performance. All of this comes with being relentlessly under the digital microscope that has now become IT. This intrusive monitoring and measuring now causes an enormous amount of strain and frustration in the organization and within the individual *humans* who comprise it. In the beginning there was much "fat" to be trimmed by *reengineering* organizations. Profits soared by decreasing unnecessary costs. As systems became more sophisticated and individual performance was monitored more and more closely, this boon to profitability morphed into a threat for those who could not keep up. Now monitoring and measuring performance has become so sophisticated that it is impossible *not* to feel you are being watched. This causes frustration, stress and can contribute to burnout or worse, lying.

Data stress

"There are two types of computers, the ones that have already crashed and the ones that will" - Computer proverb

Think about all the extra steps your day consists of just to be able to use your IT system. Are you:

- Constantly logging in or reactivating a lost or forgotten login code?
- Often having to upgrade software and apps?
- Wondering whether to call for software or hardware support?
- Defining which hw/sw supplier is actually responsible for the glitch?
- Going crazy trying to figure out what the name is for the problem you are having?
- Often rebooting your system when something loads up incorrectly?
- Required to be constantly vigilant for viruses, bugs, phishing and other threats?
- Explaining your obvious problem to your clueless techie repairperson.

No matter how agile you pride yourself on being, working with IT takes time and puts an enormous technical and emotional strain on you and everyone you interact with. Even so, it is necessary since the alternative is shutting down the system and choking off the information and financial flow to your company. Yet is there a better way?

Reliance on processes
It was too late to change the direction of the *Titanic* once the iceberg was spotted, when put in motion most processes can only result in the planned result. That planned result is most likely based upon historical data rather than real time or future predictions. Could the solution be, rather than focusing on *Garbage In, Garbage Out or GIGO*, to look forward, measure and appreciate the present, then season this information with a little historical perspective? Getting this recipe right can drastically increase your ability to anticipate future conditions.

Varied research has shown that corporations are usually looking in the wrong places for information on which to base forward looking decisions. This is especially true when it comes to risk assessment. According to research, "*the biggest risk factor is strategic at 86% followed by a distant 9% of operating risk*". Our experience confirms this data presented by the Harvard Business Review, July-August 2015[xliii]. This further argues that the greatest amount of time spent by auditors is *"reviewing operating risks (42%) followed by strategic risks at 13%."* How can you steer your ship correctly into the future, when these actual figures represent looking in the opposite direction of where your focus should be? This fact is further multiplied by both your banker, who finances investments using the exact same, *completely misdirected* and often backward looking filters as most auditors. This will affect your board's decisions and the subsequent marching orders handed down by management, often sending teams off in the wrong direction. This often causes focus on trivial and unnecessary operating issues, while concentration is lost on the more important strategic ones. *This is a very serious flaw in our current management behavior and its response to risk!*

This sort of makes logical sense since all popular *Key Performance Indicator* or KPI systems are based squarely upon historical data and its analysis Thus by nature, all KPI and quality processes become constraining. For the reasons mentioned above, even well-meant, KPIs, as well as all the processes built upon them, inhibit agility because the KPI process corrals and eventually kills off individual and organizational creativity.

Deliberately bad data doesn't help

For many insecure or lazy managers, accurate data represents a clear and present danger to their careers. The more accurate the data is, the more the information can be used to objectively judge their performance. Especially in a large organization, middle management has traditionally had ample time and opportunity to neglect, postpone and fabricate performance numbers in order to look better. In accounting circles this used to be refered to this as the *"Fudge Factor."* In the selling profession this process is sometimes known as *"sandbagging"* and is practiced to skew sales figures by *more experienced* sales people. They simply take their last few sales of the month and delay inputting them until the beginning of the following one. This makes the current month look decent and provides a great start for the next one. This process increases greatly, skewing the numbers even further, when there is a sales competition the following month. It can even be compounded if the sales manger encourages it *department wide,* to garner a better monthly or *quarterly bonus*! How accurate will ordering and billing be with this going on?

Context is key

Therefore, an agile captain needs to always place accurate data in its appropriate context. A simple story that ascribes the dangers of becoming obsessed with the process of measuring everything without understanding the correct context is the tale of the Two Archers.

Two archers compete by shooting three arrows apiece. The first archer, William Tell, shoots one light grey arrow into the outer border zone of the target. His other two arrows miss the target, but land very closely to his first arrow. Even though all three of his light grey arrows land very close to each other, he only earns ten points. Not only that, he only actually hits the target once. The next archer, Robin Hood, lands one dark grey arrow in the bullseye, and the other two miss the target by a wide margin. Yet his shooting earns him 100 points. The Judges that day are either statisticians or technicians and are focused entirely on the rules. They correctly declare Robin Hood the winner. What could be wrong with that?

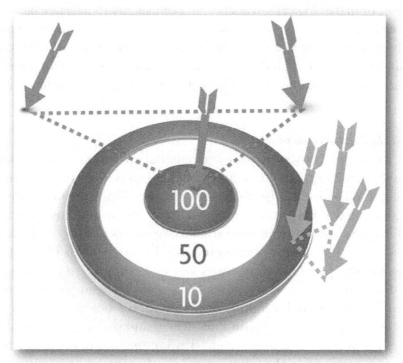

Figure 16 Robin Hood's Arrows are dark grey, William Tell's are light grey

Taking a closer look at how the two archers landed their arrows reveals that although Robin Hood received more points and won, his arrows were spread out over a much wider area. In a broader context his marksmanship can be seen as less reliable. In terms of quality control, his accuracy was lower than that of William Tell, who landed all three arrows in a much smaller, tighter area.

All William has to do now is to shift his aim in closer towards the bullseye and the quality of his shots and the points received will increase *dramatically*. Yet, this important quality issue is not picked up when dogmatically analyzing the now historical statistics. *Without taking notice of the broader context, the difference in quality between the two archer's marksmanship is not fully appreciated.* If the context is broadened at the event, in real time *with an eye on the future, a different result and winner could be anticipated.* Statistics do have a place, but sometimes they (forgive me) *miss their mark* when improperly analyzed, or placed in an improper context.

In this example, just counting the number of points misses the point! This is analogous to today's current dilemma of relying on analysis without honoring its context. All comprehensive measurement practices or systems that just measure hard numbers can easily miss the *big picture*. This can lead to very damaging assumptions and conclusions. For instance, in the case above Robin Hood's score would most likely make him the best candidate for a promotion. William Tell could easily be chosen to go in the next layoff. Accurately capturing and analyzing the *soft factors* and the context involved in any decision such as buying, selling, restructuring, etc. is important, if you want to get a real understanding of the whole situation. Don't get caught trying to *analyze* with *anal-eyes*. Train to sense the difference.

If you can measure it, you can manage it
… but at what cost?

This is the challenge with any process driven data system such as Six Sigma, Lean or a comprehensive reporting system such as SAP. They are all designed to take the art of measuring, the use of historical data and stringent procedure to even stricter and more extreme levels. *Policy eventually replaces life* and people, *especially creative ones*, get stymied by strict routines, like flies in a spider's sticky web. They will suffer by being bound to these often-arbitrary constraints.

For example, creativity is a *soft-skill* and is therefore hard to measure. Bright ideas, more often than not, explode onto the scene in bolts of creativity, just as a lightning bolt strikes. Put a creative person into a protected or controlled process and count on their creativeness to eventually wither and die. In the meantime, they will probably focus all their remaining creativity and energy on executing an escape from your process *and organization.* This is *regardless of how effective and well meaning your system is meant to be.*

Every investment disclaimer's fine print somehow reminds you that, *"Past performance is no indication of future returns."* This warning should also be put on most KPIs. They are almost always focused upon measuring processes *after they are already complete.* At best they take a snapshot of the present, which starts aging as soon as it's taken. This is instead of using indicators to better help you anticipate and prepare for the future.

Mediocrity rules

Any process driven company *has to* become mediocre sooner or later. That inevitable outcome is due to its focus on implementing the most general rules and metrics available. This is done *intentionally* to make it easier for more members of your staff to follow them easily. A successful process is intentionally designed to harness the biggest statistical slice directly in the "sweet spot" of the bell curve of *normal distribution*. Just as in the Goldilocks fable, the process then becomes "*not too much, not too little, but just right.*"

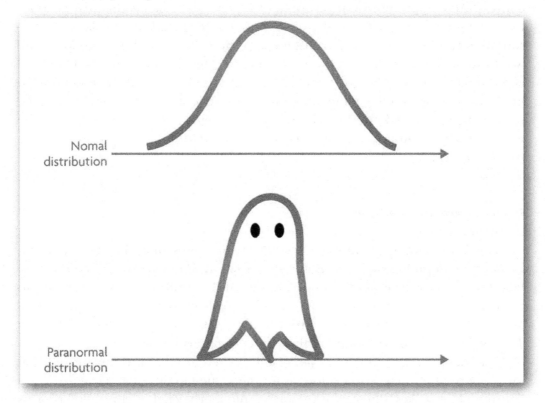

Figure 17 Normal distribution curve and... (Originally from the National Association of Psychologists)

This seems contrary to how life actually works. Excitement and creativity do not happen in the middle. They happen on the edges! Think about the middle versus the edges of forests, oceans and *of course, human interaction. Creativity and inspiration exist on the edges of the bell curve,* not in the middle. Just as every rule is made to be broken, it is only by breaking rules that we get to see what is on the other side. Therefore, by focusing on a process to exploit the *sweet spot* in the comfortable middle part of your business curve you will only encourage those bureaucratic individuals who are most comfortable with the status quo. This is while you limit and ostracise the bolder few, who thrive on its creative edges.

Look no further than the once great company Motorola. This is the company that invented *Total Quality Management*. What remained of this once innovative giant has now been totally broken up and sold off. All the creative genius slowly drained out of it to greener, more creative pastures. What happened? Their exodus was due to the fierce commitment of management to religiously heed to the suffocating constraints of TQM. This very well-thought-out process becomes the *Achilles Heel* of the very creative spirit of the company. Instead of creating and nurturing an environment of freedom and support, management created a prison from which its creative inmates only wanted escape. Compare this telecommunications disaster to Google.

At the same time Google has grown into a behemoth, it has somehow managed to both maintain a sense of *on-the-edge* entrepreneurship, while creating just enough processes to ensure that it presents one face to the market. This is a very tough balancing act, especially as a company continues to grow rapidly while the business environment gets more uncertain. To maintain this balance, *it pays to stay agile.*

Ironically, Google bought up parts of Motorola's telecommunications business. It will be interesting to see if and how they can revitalize that strict culture, which seemed to have doomed Motorola. With any luck, there are still some agile thinking, former Motorola employees left. Those who can appreciate and promote, *to other less agile colleagues*, the opportunity that Google's open and agile atmosphere presents.

Agility is about steering your organization *forward*. This doesn't make history irrelevant, but emphasizes that input from what is ahead as *more relevant*. Working from history makes you more reactive and less proactive. Forward risks are much more important than historical ones and the awareness of this fact must be raised. Maybe it's just human nature that makes us focus upon history instead of anticipating the future. Yet history is already finished. It is now historical fact and thus it is much easier and safer to measure and analyze. The risk is lower and should you care to spend precious time and resources to *anal-eyes* it you absolutely lower your risk to be proven wrong. This may make it seem safer career move, but (especially in the long term) is it really?

Organizational structure

"*There are no rules! We're trying to accomplish something!*" - Thomas Edison

Business leaders who ran most corporations after World War II often created structures based upon their own personal experience of the C3 military model of Command, Control and Communication. Leaders being groomed today often have little or no relation to this rigid structure other than it being the *traditional* and the textbook way to run things. The good news is that *tradition* is being increasingly questioned and challenged. What is the reason for this?

With shorter cycles everywhere, companies must become increasingly flexible and agile. You must anticipate future requirements while avoiding treating individual humans as a flock of sheep that require rules and babysitters. Many companies are still falling into the Industrial Age Management Trap of telling employees exactly what to do and how to do it. Do you get inspired when dealing with a resigned robot who is so worried about his/her *program generated performance indicators* that he/she tells you exactly what to do and when? Feeling helpless in a system crushes both responsibility and creativity while it rapidly breeds mediocraty.

Increased competition makes it harder for customers to distinguish between your competitors and you. You can have the technical and organizational stuff down pat, but most other serious competitors now have that too. *Soft-skills* are rapidly on their way to becoming *the distinguishing factor of choice*, yet by their nature they are harder to measure and assess. Soft-skills are not easily captured in market research instruments or total quality assessments and that irritating fact limits your company's ability to be agile. As the precariousness of both the company and the worker increases, *the HR person will need to become their champion.* HR now needs to actively voice employee concerns forcefully, in order to create more stability and encourage creativity. This shift in roles will lessen worry, resentment and resignation in a time when each individual employee is counted upon to continually do more with less. This shift will also go a long way to healing the artificial rift between unions and management. In our increasingly competitive and unstable business environment, *everyone needs to know their roles in the same metaphoric boat,* or one unexpected wave could easily capsize it and drown everyone on board, *regardless of rank or affiliation.*

The *Human Resource Dilemma*
Do you like being told what to do? Productive and creative people usually don't, especially from people with no practical experience and who are also removed from your organization's core business flow. This is the tenuous and sometimes treacherous position in which your HR people now find themselves, without wishing it. They are usually stuck in a corporate backwater, with little or no practical experience from your company's field operations, They are usually seen as an unwelcome and extra cost.

This is the dilemma facing most of today's Human Resources Departments. HR's role has evolved into more of an administrative and un-respected function compared to the "Hot Shots" in Finance, Sales, Marketing, R&D and Production. Agile leaders are finally recognizing the obvious; that companies do not do business with companies, *people do business with people.* Therefore, relationships play *the critical role* both internally and externally. Put a capable, happy person in an efficient environment and things just function better.

The popularity of the HR Department can be tracked in direct relation to the health of the economy. When the economy is slowing and the labor market is slack, HR becomes a nuisance. Why? The most vocal critics of HR claim that its focus is too much upon administration and that (often correctly) HR people tend to lack both experience from the line as well as critical strategic insight. Therefore, HR has often been seen as a hindrance to business development rather than a positive facilitating force. Whether HR is the chicken or the egg in this situation, which came first matters less than how HR will be valued and used in the future.

Interestingly, Human Resource Management is not handled the same way in all countries. For instance, in Japan HR is often represented in the C Suite. In India it is an integral part of management. In Europe the HR department seems to be growing in importance. Evidence would suggest that HR becomes more vital in countries and cultures where the people that deal with the biggest societal issues get the most power. For example, environments where work related legislation is a big deal, such as Sweden, HR is naturally stronger and more influential. In the U.S.A. it's marketing and sales. Even so most of the comments on HR below are focused on the U.S.A. market, but you are encouraged to compare and contrast those comments with your experiences in your own location and situation

Just the continued use of the term *Human Resources* should give cause for worry. How does it feel to be a resource? Resources, like iron ore, lumber *and livestock* are usually managed, exploited and ultimately depleted. Many current managers throughout today's organizations still look at new hires as just that - Human Resources - or sheep to be farmed. How does it feel to be a resource, *livestock?*

This *management* type of behavior, often unconsciously, creates big issues of resentment and resignation within a company. Think of all the paperwork or screen time you waste filling in reviews, questionnaires and evaluations many of which you never hear about again. In a large telecoms company, one department of highly talented and well-paid engineers dutifully filled out yearly evaluation forms that asked for their suggestions for improvement. After *seven years* and seven evaluations, *without any feedback or acknowledgement of their suggestions,* they were extremely frustrated when the eighth year's evaluation arrived. An enormous amount of time and energy was wasted discussing the pros and cons of filling it out again. They felt, and rightly so, that they were not being seen, heard or cared about. Their performance and morale suffered accordingly, *as did their output.*

This lack of love for HR also stretches up into executive offices too. HR is often excluded on long-term strategy issues. It is very seldom that is HR is allowed to take a leadership position. They are often not invited to be members of the C Suite for two reasons:

- First, with so much time being spent on brushfire management today, there are often *few to zero* long-term strategic discussions to discuss.
- Second, HR is often consciously excluded. This way, management can react faster. They can decide quicker without having to suffer through hearing about employee concerns and issues. This creates the effect of making the situation of each employee even more precarious and unstable.

HR's role to assist, advise and support leaders in workforce planning has been undervalued at best. It is seldom that you see an HR person transferred to a line position. Most HR people come fresh out of school, trained more in administration than in handling individuals and their problems. Unfortunately, HR has also been considered a backwater that is far off the path to the executive suite. Therefore, sharper and more decisive personalities are seldom attracted to this particular career choice. This also creates a stigma where HR becomes a hindrance to career development *within the organization it is trying to develop.*

This ultimately causes further alienation, resentment and resignation. HR often gets the blame from above and below. In fact, we have experienced that only about one third of the HR departments surveyed were consulted on who should be dismissed during the Great Recession of 2008. Imagine the potential talent that was lost as well as the *extra stress* and resentment this precarious decision placed upon those *lucky enough* to remain.

On the other hand, very few outside of the HR department understand how important a structured, well-executed interview process is, in new hire selections. Many people with little or no interview training are too often put in charge of this important hiring function. This short sighted approach often results in labor disputes, increases the costs of litigation and drains precious time, energy and resources for cleaning up the mess caused by poor hires. Adding insult to injury, people in line-management positions often prefer to use external search companies than their own internal HR department for advice on new candidates. After all, HR in their eyes, is just a group of administrative inhibitors of change. How much extra does this cost?

Especially with younger workers, arrangements such as working from home are often still resisted by line-managers, even though this solution may actually be the most efficient and most motivational one. The HR people are often some of the only ones who recognize the growing importance and value of working from home.

When it comes to HR management, most of the appraisal systems out there are questionable at best and often are resented in their fabricated design and objectivity. Because of this situation, the best consultant firms such as PWC have abandoned standard performance appraisals. Instead they are now moving towards a continuous discussion and thus taking this process even further away from the traditional HR power structure. Still at this writing, most firms remain stuck in the *Business as Usual* morass of traditional appraisals.

The problem then becomes that *HR is seen as more of a long-term play, while your business cycles constantly shorten.* This paradox creates a damaging mixed message, which is that although people are acknowledged as the most important asset in your company, *they are still treated as resources, things.* Now more than ever, personnel issues must be seriously addressed, *even before strategy,* and on as human and personal a level as possible. If you have the right people in place and they are happy, then company strategy and tactics usually take care of themselves.

Rethinking human resources

Therefore, this is an agile time for HR to take the same leap as Finance has already done and become a bona fide member of the management team. Just as the CFO and CMO the *Chief Human Resources Officer* or *CHRO* should become a valued and trusted partner of the CEO. Expanding your management team to include a CHRO is the best way to link company financial performance factors to your individual team members and their *growing personal concerns*. The transition to this new and improved HR department will go a long way towards refocusing on your company's most important resource and it will send a positive and rejuvenating signal to your marketplace.

This will correctly elevate the important task of marrying motivated people blessed or trained with the appropriate skills and the optimal position or task. Each person's profile should generate a balance between IQ and EQ to get each job done with optimal efficiency. For instance:

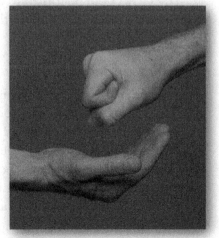

Figure 18 HR hard (administrative) skills versus soft (personal) skills

- How are you going to reach your results if you have a brilliant technician, who insists upon solving everything himself, yet is in charge of a group of and inhibiting creative but frustrated troubleshooters who are itching to apply their talents?
- How will you get your sales people to sell more effectively when your sales manager is more interested in going on sales calls himself, usually just to show-off rather than teach his/her sales skills?

The result of both of these cases of insecure leadership is usually the creation of a huge sandbox of upset egos instead of a homogenized and focused group of professional team players who enjoy supporting and helping each other.

Ask yourself how can your HR leader become a true strategic partner when she/he is still seen *and treated* as a bureaucratic administrator? To accomplish this transition, their knowledge of organizational functions and lines will need to be greatly improved. This transition of getting your HR people accepted on the same level as the management team will take time. What if time is running out?

Your new HR leader still needs to be able to talk about human capital in business terms, but with a heartfelt respect for each individual in question. They need to be adept at analysis to make workforce decisions, yet they must be able to make measurable predictions about the types of skills needed going forward. They also have to retain a good sense and appreciation of the soft-skills each employee brings to the table. That information is not necessarily available to the HR people at all times, nor is it well understood. For the agile company it is imperative to improve the access to and appreciation of this important information of its value and its application.

The CHRO will be forced to take on a more strategic function in the organization due to a number of factors that include the importance of:

- Having the right people, with the right skills, in the right positions and *with the right workload*
- Understanding the leveraging effect in appreciating what makes each worker happier and more productive, especially in our current environment of decreasing resources and increasing time constraints.
- Being able to increase the creativity and efficiency of each employee by understanding what makes each individual "*tick*" and providing the right type of environment and training to make it happen.
- Understanding what is happening within the company regarding relationships and morale and then *translating and conveying this important information into business and analytical terms* for the C-Suite's understanding.

- Making each individual worker feel more welcome and secure. This will happen naturally when HR is placed in a decisive and more appreciated organizational position and given the mandate to speak with authority. This shift will help minimize employee concern about their employment security.
- Training and encouraging each worker to be more self-confident, self-sufficient and self-motivating for three reasons:
  - They can do their job better and earn the firm ant themselves more money
  - This will naturally encourage workers to *choose to stay* because they are motivated and enjoy the feeling of team-spirit in this type of atmosphere.Should they be let go, they will know exactly what to do and how to quickly handle finding income somewhere else.
- Ensuring that when people are forced to leave, they do so as amicably as possible and insuring that the door will be open should other opportunities arise.
- When all the above occurs, would you feel the need or want to look for another job?

Another idea is to rewrite the CEO, CFO, CMO and CHRO roles to cover the essential pieces of company strategy. Your HR officer should absolutely be someone who has come from a line function and knows what it is like in the "trenches." The more they understand the situation from practical experience rather than abstract hearsay, the more confident they will be to execute their role. HR now needs to be considered part of the management troika. The time has come!

It will also be a plus if HR gets rid of both routine administration functions and training. Admin functions such as attendance and compensation can and should be done on a much lower level and increasingly by a well-designed app. *Training should be more closely tied with the eyes and ears of your organization,* Marketing. In fact, we believe that your internal and external communication departments should quickly evolve to become the new natural home for all of your training groups. There, your training staff will experience greater kinship and more appreciation for all their skills and technology. There will also be more appreciation of the valuable information training routinely gathers and interprets. Combining training with communication will be a considerably more synergistic and relevant placement than the current, typical configuration that places it in a forgotten closet in the HR department.

Training's new role

The important role of training is often defaulted or dumped into the HR department. Yet take a step back and think about this. Aren't skills training such as sales, marketing, IT, media and advertising more naturally aligned with internal/external communication? A free flow of communication, from each customer to the boardroom, is critical to maintain and improve, *if your company is serious about remaining competitive.* Budget concerns often take first priority and training is usually the first thing to be cancelled when times get challenging. This borders on crazy and correcting these priorities will become a critical survival factor going forward! As your market shrinks, people are going to pick and choose what they buy and from whom they buy it much more closely. If your company's people are not the most updated, effective and service minded in your market, *prepare to lose market share.* How can you maintain and improve your level of service without the constant, relevant and timely improvements interactive training can provide?

Customer, sales and service training decisions should be held at a divisional level. It is important to remember the value of being able to spread critical knowledge throughout the organization as efficiently as possible. To survive and thrive, training must now be considered as a corporate appendage rather than an irritating corporate expense. Therefore, training departments need to be strategically managed from the Corporate Level. Strategic yet sensitive programs, based upon efficient learning management systems need to be implemented. Operational training, such as distribution and product training should be executed by the respective product or market segments and/or regional organizations, especially in large corporations. In the end, a decision must be taken in the main office about the role of the corporate parent regarding HQ involvement. Are they running the company in a *"hands-on"* fashion from the parent or taking a laissez-faire *"hands-off"* approach? The responsibility of the parent compared to the subsidiaries must be defined! That is another issue we will address in our next book.

Training must also become more of a two-way street. Effective trainers constantly have their ears to the ground, looking for changes in the market and shifting trends, both internally and externally, from all of their customers. Trainers must stay constantly vigilant for new and better ways of doing what your company does best. Tips for this come not only from listening more closely to course participants, but also from the competition and from the **Forward Decision Drivers** we will discuss later.

Professional training departments increasingly need to employ the very latest techniques and tools as well as the most effective pedagogical platforms and vehicles available. This allows them to change participant behavior even quicker. Therefore, small and medium sized corporate training departments can, and increasingly should be, subject to takeovers by more specialized, "Pure-Play" outsourcing companies. These pedigreed training organizations can then offer their acquired employees greater experiences and more challenging careers. Becoming a pure-play training company, they can now serve several companies with their skills and experience instead of only one. Their skills will be sharpened further by having to answer to many different clients and situations. This will increase their understanding of their profession and add a new level of responsibility and finesse to their job. They will now be responsible to create customer loyalty (and more business) by listening more closely and being agile enough in their response to satisfy all their clients' various needs, wants and wishes.

Thus, this new "Pure-Play" model will be a real win-win-win for the company agreeing to an outsourcing of their training department, for their former training department employees, as well as their new outsourcing employer. The result, increased customer loyalty and:

1. The Company gets an upgraded training resource that is now an empowered open market competitor.
2. The company gets increased market intelligence and information flow from those most qualified to listen.
3. The former company employee now gets a more important and expanded role by having to serve more than one client. This can also lead to more advancement possibilities or deeper specializations within their chosen field.
4. Each former company employee suddenly gets the chance to be rocketed into the center of the action within his former company as the hired specialist and *soon to be hero*. This is instead of trudging along as some nameless "grunt" buried in the bowels of a hierarchy, which has little or nothing to do with his/her chosen craft.
5. The Outsourcer gets to expand while enjoying economies of scale by being able to make more efficient use of specialists and sophisticated (therefore, more expensive) technology and programming. Their reputation and success should also benefit as word spreads of their "*pure-play*" offering.

Corporate culture and tradition
Within the greatest inhibitors of change "Culture" sticks out as the most potent. It can easily become culture for employees to use the other major inhibitors (IT, Structure and Processes) as an excuse for poor execution or total avoidance of change.

In fact, one of our primary inhibitors of change is the inevitable institutionalization of a thought or an idea. As Deepak Chopra has said about the institution of religion, "*Before Christianity there was Jesus, Before Islam there was Mohammed and before Buddhism there was Buddha.*" What he seems to mean is several world religions, that followers have defended to their deaths, were originally based upon the personal beliefs of three single individuals. Evidence would suggest that these beliefs and hundreds of years of interpretation, development and stratification by committees, whose members increasingly have a more comfortable lifestyle to defend, have twisted and manipulated these personal beliefs into dogma, *way beyond their original intention.*

A good little story highlighting this point of missing the forest for the trees, from a slightly naughty, religious perspective is:

A very curious monk working on updating old scripture brazenly asked his master, "how do we know these new translations have anything to do with the original texts?" His master and colleagues were horrified at the newcomer's insolence. They became very defensive, to the point of being angry and screamed in unison, "The texts could NEVER have been misinterpreted! Now, to get back to work." The next day, after a frustrating night's sleep and deep contemplation, his master returned. With a judgmental look, he said to the monk, "OK! I will go and check." The master disappeared into the depths of the monastery and went missing for three full days. At the end of the third day, the new monk's worried colleagues forced him to go look for their master. The monk finally found him in the deepest, darkest and oldest part of the monastery archives, relentlessly banging his bloody head against a stone pillar. When asked why, his master responded,

"You were right my son; we should have been more careful to accurately check the original texts. I have now looked at one particular passage which states, "*The men of our calling are to serve, support and safeguard their flock to the best of their ability. Then, on every Sunday forevermore, once the service is complete, they should go celebrate.*"

But the next translation was mistakenly updated to read, "*The men of our cloth are to serve, support and safeguard their flock to the best of their ability. Then on every Sunday forevermore, once the service is complete, they should **go celibate**.*"

What a difference even a simple spelling error can make, when the context is forgotten, overlooked or not challenged or questioned...

Now take the idea of Political Correctness and intolerant belief, what do you think Jesus would say about people being burned at the stake because they disagreed with the Church, founded in his name, on whether the earth was the center of our solar system? What do you think Mohammed's comments would be about killing innocents, in order to die a martyr and spend the afterlife with 74 virgins?

Rather than listen to reason and create a flowing dialogue, people have historically defended their points of view and shut out all opposing ones, even to the point of killing others to silence them. Add a bit of money to the mix and watch the intolerance of others' views and rules to support *business as usual* increase further and faster. How agile is this?

What if the same exact process occurs when a corporate culture takes root? Unwritten rules can often carry more weight than the written ones, causing previously efficient processes to bog down in conscious and unconscious committee wrangling and miscommunication. Unwritten legacy issues often accompany documented legacy costs such as retirement. These weigh down established organizations with outlays that other, younger competitors laugh about, all the way to the bank. Below are some of the biggest.

Policy versus empathy
There is a ferryboat in the city of Stockholm that takes passengers for a beautiful fifteen-minute boat ride from the City's Amusement Park on the East side of town to the South side. Recently, one of your authors noticed an elderly Norwegian couple trying, in vain, to buy a ticket with their bankcard, but the machine was broken. Although they had Norwegian cash, the ticket taker would not accept it. They finally left the boat totally frustrated as the ticket taker was heard to shout, "What if I accept everybody who cannot pay...?" To add insult to injury, the attendant also refused to allow me to pay for their tickets since they had just abandoned their place in line. At that point, I also left. Not content with this, the attendant concluded by screaming; "We have rules, you know."

"*Policy replaces life*" - Patrick Collard

Out skiing one time I ended up in the local village hospital with a friend who had fallen down hard. In line in front of us was an unlucky skier who had obviously broken his right thumb as it was now bent straight up in the air, far from where it should naturally be. He was in pain! Even so, before the physician would even look at his thumb, he was forced to sign a whole stack of legal and admission papers. The pain was clearly increasing with every signature, even though he wisely chose to sign with an X using his other hand. This is a rather tame example of when the rules and policies we set up take over our capacity to be human. An extreme version is a famous quote from the Vietnam War "*To save the village we had to destroy it.*"

Going forward we need to be more agile *and forgiving*. Just as Captain Barbosa famously said in the movie *Pirates of the Caribbean*, "*They're not so much rules… they're more like (long smiling pause) guidelines.*" As greater portions of our lives come under the rule of technocrats, bureaucrats, bankers, accountants and their computer algorithms, we may also be facing peak compliance too. All too often these technicians put their measurements and rules in front of the overall picture. This seems to be the source of the current rise of third party politics opposed to our old batch of career politicians. After all who likes to be told what to do when the big picture is either unknown, ignored or *intentionally hidden*; or when:

- You never personally agreed to the rule or program to which you are now forced to submit.
- Both your common sense and integrity tells you to do something different.
- It either feels disempowering or just wrong.
- There are other people, rules and programs that tell you what to do, many of which, *upon simple reflection*, are in conflict with each other.

Saying *No* or even, "*let's stop and think about this*," may not require as much agility as it does plain old common sense *and guts*. Importantly, it requires the curiosity and *backbone* to question the appropriate authority *for the common good*. Yet how willing are you or anyone else to challenge an authority figure who may hold the keys to your next promotion, your continued employment, or *whether your next stop today is home or jail?* To make matters worse, for the first time in a number of generations, a rise in intolerance has even been rising in our younger generation, especially on college campuses!

Recent polls show that a growing number of students would rather limit the subjects and speakers they wish to hear than be open to other than alternative opinions. This is a worrying trend, since college used to be the most open and receptive time in a person's life. It was originally designed to challenge and test what was accepted as knowledge. To paraphrase a speech Ralph Nader gave at my college long ago:

"*You students are now at the ideological pinnacle of your lives. You enjoy a cozy, pre-work-life reality and have the luxury of access to all types of information and opinions from all different sources. Don't let this moment of openness and learning go to waste!*"

Consciously or not the opportunity to entertain different points of view, *possibly the basis of what makes the pursuit of higher learning so valuable*, is now being shut down. More and more pampered students would rather muzzle dissenting opinions than have to listen to and engage a conflicting point of view. Comedians such as Chris Rock and Jerry Seinfeld have recently declared they will no longer perform on College Campuses, ostensibly because of the dissent and heckling they now receive from the audience. Does this sound like the breeding ground for open, agile leaders to you?

More and more of us are being forced to either confront situations that are either completely outside of our integrity or to kowtow to that authority figure, only to have to *wrestle with our conscience in private.* Maybe this explains why, for example, there are now more Viet Nam veterans who have died of suicide than were killed on the battlefield.

PC no longer means personal computer
One of the biggest inhibitors going forward, with regards to open and free flowing communication, is being *Politically Correct.* Knowing what to say and carefully choosing how to say it so as not to offend someone or some group, is reaching plague levels. Your authors absolutely support non-intrusive behavior, but *that has nothing to do with full self-expression.* How agile is it to have to respond quickly, yet have an extra barrier of figuring out how *not to offend* various listeners' capricious and constantly changing tastes and beliefs. How can, for instance, your HR department do its job if just bringing up the topic of Sexual Harassment causes offense to certain employees? Agility means toleration and the ability to hear conflicting points of view in order to make better-informed decisions. Judging from Donald Trump's progress in the current U.S. Presidential election, this trend of Political Correctness may finally be waning, yet…

As Sun Tzu once famously said, "Choose your battles," as some are worth fighting and others are not. Could a bit of increased tolerance *and empathy to sense the difference* be where increased agility can play an important role? Could your ability to listen, understand and empathize with your customer or colleague now need to be expanded and practiced religiously? This process is often more about unlearning than learning more…

Sticky thinking
Have you also noticed that the older you get, the more you have to think about and the more you have to do? What if not only we ourselves work like this, but companies, governments and societies also? Things pile up and with experience, there is naturally more information to draw upon. This causes more opinions, debate and doubt; ultimately leading to increased indecision.

Needless to say, the more you have to think about, the slower and more cautions you become when taking decisions. This is part of our human nature. The more experiences you have to share *and the better you get at articulating them,* the more you want your point heard. This takes time. We call this *The Molasses Effect,* as the deeper into a discussion you get and the more opinions need to be expressed, the more the conversation takes on a texture resembling swimming through thick and gooey molasses. Discussion easily degrades to a debate and often to an argument. This is the extreme opposite of agility and makes it harder to do what needs to be done to reach your goal in the time allotted to do it. How can you streamline conversations and transform debates and heated discussions into dialogues? How about asking more questions?

The disease of inaction
Inaction can take the many different forms such as:

- Not doing anything
- Watching too much TV
- Too much curiosity to the point of indecision
- Eating too much
- Being worried or scared to act
- Force of habit
- Debating to win rather than compromising and moving forward
- Babbling *around a point* instead of communicating towards it
- Being preoccupied with a smart gadget
- Physical or mental challenges that confuse or amplify the situation such as ADD, ADHD or Asperger's syndrome.

Inaction can range from annoying to dangerous, as many unfortunate victims of the 2004 Tsunami found out. Reference again the many stories about animals running for safety while people stayed put or even went closer to the water to get a better look at the receding surf.

Look in every public place these days, from restaurants to buses and trains and you will see the same thing. Most faces staring into a little smart screen of some sort. Everyone is so caught up in their little gadget that many prefer the company of their electronic entertainment than warm and active conversation with a fellow human being. Anecdotal research seems to be confirming that the underlying motivation to turn off the world and bury yourself in your electronic gadget is an increasing level of stress. The need for some time offline, alone is on the rise. Many are learning that just looking like you are pre-occupied with your gadget often blocks others from approaching you.

There are other social media phenomena that are not simply explained by stress and are increasingly inhibiting commerce. For instance, it has reached the point that restaurant owners, confused about packed evenings with fewer profits, discovered their financial squeeze was *due to smart phones.* They discovered that their waiter or waitress now needed to come back to each table more often and over a longer period. First, their dining guests now had to "check in" on Facebook, take pictures for their Instagram posts and finish texting their friends before they could finally settle down to order. In short, tables that used to be occupied by a group for ninety minutes now consumed up to fifty percent more time. Slower turnover and fewer guests per evening mean fewer meals served and less profit, even on packed evenings. This trend of lots of people and lower profits is also increasing.

The amount and quality of information needing to be processed is slowing down the whole communication, decision and action process. Just think of how many hours you burn weekly just by taking care of the following issues:

- Bank, investment and retirement accounts
- Telephone bills
- Switching TV channels
- Social media choices and comments
- What to eat this evening and how to prepare it

This short list is offered just to get you thinking seriously about how many distractions there now are that cause you to lose sight of your purpose. Just look in your store next time you wish to buy a box of cereal, or a bottle of shampoo. You will be faced with a whole wall of alternatives. How often do you have or take the time to study the labels of all 200 plus bottles of shampoo or fifty boxes of cereal to choose the best choice for you?

Is it any wonder we may be losing the battle of staying conscious long enough to choose?

Entitlements that inhibit
According to an aging article by Bill O'Reilly[14]

"During the last two years, '09 and '10, the feds have spent more than a trillion Dollars on programs to help poor Americans.

- *Most of that money goes to what is called "means-tested entitlements." That's direct assistance, Medicaid, food stamps, childcare and nutrition, etc.*
- *Since 1970, means-tested entitlements in America have increased… ready… an unbelievable 5,500 percent.*

---

14 Bill O'Reilly's talking points about, "Is the entitlement society strangling the U.S.A. economy

- *Now an astounding 150 million Americans live in households that receive some kind of government assistance; almost half the population.*
- *Since President Obama has been in office, federal welfare spending is up about 41 percent. Food stamps are up about 135 percent since 2007, from thirty billion to 72 billion a year; disability payments… up 116 percent from a decade ago."*

Getting something for absolutely nothing creates behavioral trends. Once you get used to something for free, why would you ever again want to exert yourself to work for it? Agility demands energetic engagement and a heightened ability to think for yourself. Unfortunately, when you are conditioned to rely upon entitlements and other people's opinions, it seems to become human nature to begin expecting freebies as some sort of right. Take them away and you risk social unrest. Evidence would suggest that we are reaching Margaret Thatcher's economic inflection point where we are *"running out of other people's money."* What happens next? What happens to people who have mastered the art of receiving entitlements as a right instead of training to be agile?

Reputation
None of us want to look bad. Therefore, those people who quickly and humbly admit to their own mistakes (and learn from them) are few and far between. This becomes especially true when there are prestigious business or governmental decisions on the line. Many a company has gone belly up due to someone concealing what later turns out to be a bad decision or investment. A number of investment houses have been crippled by so called *rogue traders* that hid massive losses and even "doubled down" on them rather than revealing their mistakes and seeking help. Interestingly, the sums involved with Barings and JP Morgan's famous *Whale* make their management's "surprise" both a little hard to swallow and hard evidence of a *critical need for more agility*. How much more face do you save and how much more agile do you look by *not being aware* when you are in charge, compared to knowing and being wrong? TBTF anyone?

HPPO (Highest Paid Person's Opinion)
Another form of inhibition is being forced to "politely" concede to the *Highest Paid Person's Opinion*. The further we go into the twenty first century, the clearer it becomes that the relationship between the highest paid person's opinion and the most appropriate or effective one is not always one-to-one. Money still talks, and

all too often the highest paid person also has the seniority. This assumption is often based upon past glories rather than a reflection of the current situation. What if it really is easier to bite back verbally challenging someone and, as a good friend Patrick Collard once quipped, *become polite?* He used to say that, "*Polite also means Pissed Off Lightly!*"

Confidence

If you are sending people off to a course to improve their skills, it is important to do this with a clear motive. It is not necessary to attend every training course your staff attends, especially when it has to do with *their specializations,* i.e. a technical or tactical part of their jobs. Yet it is important to make a conscious and confident showing or even attend the training or event that has to do with team building or some sort of kick-off event. Being *too busy to attend* can be dangerous. Who, nowadays isn't too busy? Behave in this way and your status as a leader could become tarnished quickly.

Dumping versus delegating

Overworked managers often have too much to do and take opportunities to offload uncomfortable tasks on those who cannot say no easily. The resentment of not being allowed to participate in such a choice can build quickly. It's all about confidence and providing inspiration rather than ordering others to act. Asking the opinion of those affected will go a long way towards gaining their heartfelt co-operation and producing positive, measurable results.

Good and bad habits.

We venture to say that most of the processes, cultures, organizations and systems in a corporation are currently designed with the intention to *make it easier for employees and staff to act without thinking!* An expression often heard in the corporate corridors is, "*we have to dumb it down so that people know what to do.*" This is an extremely condescending, disempowering and increasingly dangerous attitude, especially when creative, entrepreneurial behaviors are involved. In the end, most managers just want their crew to act like "mini-me"s on their demand.

This is very hard when ingrained "habits" are involved. "*This is how we have always done this,*" is a common expression by those who will potentially be affected and are fearful of or just habitually opposed to change.

The consequence? It is an immediate delay of action and one point for the opposition. It also increases the risk that the danger will increase. We can also make the argument that this hypothesis is a major culprit in stimulating exploration. Tests have been made that show neurons in the part of our brain called the Striatum are much more activated during exploration than after a habit has become imprinted. By then, we act without thinking; why? *Because it worked before*. In too many teams and typical grouping of individuals from corporations to the military, such traits are encouraged and promoted.

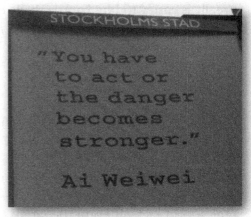

Figure 19 Ai Weiwei, Chinese artist & activist

"*Do not think, just do as I say,*" needs to be use sparingly, if at all and in the correct context, or the consequences can be anything from discontent to mutiny.

This might be OK if El Capitan is ultimately proven correct but what if the decision is wrong? Regardless, can we at least agree that it is true that we still are mostly creatures of habit? If so, then change and transformation will naturally be hindered by unconscious behavior and habits that are further enforced by those systems, culture, organization and processes designed to make work easier and thought-free. This is a problem that will need more attention going forward in our new brave world of constant change. Do not despair yet, some practical things can be done to enhance business agility and we are getting to that rapidly.

Inhibitors and Zombification

All of the above cultural and systematic inhibitors DRASTICALLY contribute to turning good hearted, well meaning and ambitious people, like yourself, into sheeple and zombies. All of these human and system based friction points wear you down and drain precious energy. Slowly but surely, your integrity can begin to erode as maintaining your stand in front of continuous peer pressure and multiple complex systems, nibbling away at you, begins to take its toll. After a while it becomes easier just to agree and just resign yourself to shuffling along with the flock. Can you say Baa? Should you find yourself one day being promoted and in charge of enforcing rules and regs that would have made you cringe in the past, consider yourself *zombified*. By then, any thoughts of agility will have disappeared, probably never to return.

The Consciousness of agile collaboration

An interesting discussion between we two authors occurred while writing this book. Hans, comes from the Corporate Transformation, Structural, Strategic, Marketing and Tactical side of the agility question. He has trained in and made a good living using tools to help companies become more agile. He wanted to focus upon the tools and leave the issue of consciousness as a footnote to the process. Kurt's contribution came from a more "artistic" background in sales, *sensational soft-skills* training, teamwork and body language. He also happened to end up writing a good deal of the verbiage based upon Hans' structure and ideas. The results became this unique and powerful blend of hard and soft-skills, which now seems a perfect and agile match for these exciting, dangerous and increasingly emotional times.

One of the main points of this book is that technology and systems are beginning to take over our way of living. The more we become subjected to policies and regulation, the more people begin to become frustrated and act *anomie* (according to Emilie Durkheim this means a feeling of passivity born of despair)[15]. In other words we are losing our individuality, creativity and drive as we become more a *part of an uncaring system* or we "lose it" and begin flailing at it out of our desperation. Either way, our *reactions* to these stimuli cause us to become *human doings* even more quickly, further suppressing our feelings and abilities rather than reaching our full creative and cooperative potential, together.

The reason?

Consciousness.

We humans are creatures of habit. This reliance upon unconscious behavior patterns is now coming back to haunt us. For some reason we feel more comfortable doing again what we have already done, even when it is no longer useful or efficient. It's is the evolutionary equivalent of still using Microsoft's Word 1.0 when the latest version will save you time and accomplish exponentially more.

Conscious action

There is nothing new in saying that understanding customer tastes and marketing conditions are the new holy grail of business success. This has been the secret for a long time. The difference is now that with increasing competition and customer sophistication your ability to create and maintain relationships really begins.

---

15 Guy Standing, The Precariat,

Look no further than your own process of selecting someone to do business with. How have your selection criteria changed over the last few years? Not long ago your selection of possible suppliers was more limited and in many cases the quality of both the product and the post-sale service were much broader. With each passing year and with the increasing intensity of the hunt for efficiency and lower margins, businesses were forced to cut more and more corners in order to survive. The fat was trimmed long ago and now most surviving businesses are cutting into their corporate bones to remain competitive. As more and more people are applying for the same positions, even the cost *and quality* of employees is eroding. Those employees who still have some sort of work ethic left are being forced to work longer and harder for less pay, increasing stress and the inevitability of making a mistake. With this and the help of more regulation, competing products and services can easily homogenize into a grey, profitable center. Just look at how much alike different car manufacturers have now made each class of cars.

Creating a more agile organization that customers can distinguish from the rest demands more automation as well as an increased sensitivity to customer needs, wants and wishes.

Some conscious soft-skills
Here we include a number of ideas, issues and examples that can help you *consciously* enhance your agility into a new dimension of *sensational* performance. Breaking out of the mechanical and automatic is more important than ever, if you still want to think for yourself, become successful by attracting and retaining more loyal customers. Still, when you are being bombarded with increasing amounts of information and are kept off balance by decisions you are forced to make (on someone else's schedule), the challenge to remain conscious increases drastically.

To effectively use the skills presented in this book it will help enormously to practice being here now and bringing a conscious touch to whatever you do.

Here are some simple tools to help you in this pursuit.

Is the Fax on?
Before the age of broadband, when telephone cables were the primary way to transfer voice and data to someone else, we relied upon tele-modems and telefaxes. What these communication tools essentially did was to translate your message into a package

of electrons that could be transmitted over the wires and then retranslated back before entering the receiving machine. To accomplish this these two dumb machines needed to *shake hands* first, in order to agree upon how the data would be translated back and forth. This process could be interpreted to sound something like this:

Machine one	Machine two
Hello	What?
Hello	What language?
Hello	Oh, English!
Hello	Hello!
Hello	How can I help
I have a message	I'm now ready to receive it.

At this point these two dumb machines had established the so-called "handshake protocol" and now could begin communicating.

Your question is, how often do you send your message before making sure your listener's fax is on and ready to receive?

Even though these two dumb machines are smart enough to connect to each other and make sure they understand the same language, how often do we begin talking before we even look to see if anyone is ready willing or able to receive our message? Have you ever thrown a ball to someone who wasn't looking at you?

Collaborative Urgency
If you feel pressed for time and that you have to make up your mind on someone else's time-line, then chances are you are being sold. After all, if an expert convinces you that time is being wasted, it must be the truth right? Have you possibly begun to notice that the more someone is telling you that you *must act* within a certain time period, the more it will probably be wise *not to?*

The Collaborator will also bring up deadlines, but the difference will be that they serve everyone and strive to be mutually beneficial. You may still sign and commit before the end of the month, but you are more apt to be aware that your collaborator will now get to go on that bonus cruise. This makes him/her even more inspired to agree to help you with something special upon returning. Win/Win! An authentic collaboration will be transparent in nature. You should be invited to discover all the profit and consequences of acting together within the timeframe, but the *choice will still remain yours to make.*

Relate and Challenge

In every era there is a prevailing formula for success. In our post-industrial information age, transactional business was the way to go, as it allowed organizations to expand quickly, *emotions be damned*. Now, as we approach important limits in virtually every business dimension, the importance of creating loyal relationships is becoming a critical factor in customer retention. The price for finding brand-new customers continues to increase and each customer is becoming more sophisticated. In fact, it is not unusual now to see someone talking with a salesperson at a store while simultaneously Googleing the competition. This forces the salesperson to use a broader set of sales "arguments" which has to include soft-skills that focus on a better service experience. *What if the only real value left to add is increasingly personal?* Making each customer feel special and even integrating them and *their competencies* into *your sale* will create the basis for a sustainable, collaborative and profitable relationship.

Yet there is one even more important skill that is worth taking with from the golden age of transacting. That is to relate to your customer while challenging to do even better.

Research undertaken during the Great Recession of 2009-2011 showed that when times got rough, two types of sales behavior maintained or increased their sales numbers. These two types of personalities were: those that were pros at creating and maintaining relationships and those who challenged their customers to be even better. Not surprisingly the ones who created and maintained relationships *maintained* their numbers whereas, those who challenged their customers, from a solid relationship *increased their sales figures*.

Developing Trust

In both winning sales models *trust is key*, yet here too there might be an important distinction.

- In the transactional model *trust is focused on the tools, methods and systems.*
- In the collaborative *trust is focused upon the people involved*. Part of that trust depends, of course, on their ability to effectively use those tools, methods and systems prescribed, but trust becomes a powerful leverage point when people and emotions are welcomed and encouraged.

Figure 20 Do you want to live life fully or just transact it? Is working equal to living?

Consciously including the human factor in collaboration is metaphorically a bit like transforming a two dimensional black and white picture into a three-D color one. But don't stop there, what if feelings and your ability to sense and express emotion is what makes you human? Do you want to live a life of quality or just exsist and transact?

Leveraging agility via confident leadership

The need to get agile is grounded in the emerging crisis of confidence. You can have the best change management and business tools available from the most well known business consultants in the world. Yet if you as the leader do not feel and radiate confidence, you and your crew will still founder in the growing seas of uncertainty. It is also human nature that during times of greater volatility and uncertainty your average crew member will instinctively look to you, for positive signals and reassurance from his/her confident leader. You need to be confident and ready!

The causes of uncertainty

IBM and other IT companies have sold billions of dollars of hardware and software by playing upon management uncertainty. By heightening feelings of fear, doubt and guilt they understand that management will shell out large sums in order to lower risk and feel safer. If their sales people fail to demonstrate authentic confidence in their story, the chances of selling themselves and their products rapidly diminish. Fearing the unknown causes uncertainty. The more you feel you can predict what will happen, the more confidence you will project to handle it. One of the keys to increasing confidence is your ability to break large unknowns down into smaller manageable components. This allows you to put a measurable handle on your uncertainty. Looking forward instead of behind will also help.

The physiological mechanics of confidence

There is one more area needing to be addressed and that is the area of conscious leadership projection. It is important to sense its effect on your level of confidence, your ability to decide and to effectively lead others. What if simply by adjusting your posture and breathing more you can leverage your ability to decisively inspire and engage others? What if *increasing your confidence is a function of the congruency you create between your thoughts, words and deeds?*

Thoughts

It is now almost universally accepted that what you think, influences what you experience and express. Thinking positive is a good start; but combining this with *feeling* positive will drastically boost your confidence. A simple way to increase your chances of feeling positive is to smile. Did you know that regardless of whether you adjust a few muscles on your face or the source is a warm and fuzzy feeling from deep within your heart, smiling will release endorphins into your bloodstream that promote well-being and healing? Take a moment and smile and see if you do not start feeling better. When you feel better you also project that out to those listening. You become a more attractive leader and project more confidence during the process.

Words

Words and conversations can be either compressive or expansive. The words you choose to think and express influence your cells to either focus upon growth or protection. Positive conversations cause your cells, and consequently you, to open up, expand and actively participate in more of what is happening around you. Negative conversations will encourage your individual cells to close down and compress for increased protection. You become stiff, silent and can look like someone to avoid. That defensive message is then broadcast out to your surroundings either vocally, as in angry remarks, or as stone cold silence. That old childhood rhyme of, "*sticks and stones will break my bones but names will never hurt me,*" may not be as true or comforting as we were led to believe. Start noticing when your words and conversation are expanding the listening of those around you or compressing and shutting it down. If so, change course!

Deeds:

Want to inspire those you are talking with? Let's start with where the word *inspire* comes from. It is Latin in origin and literally means to "*breathe in spirit.*" Take a long, deep and inspiring breath. How does that affect the way you are feeling? Chances are no matter how good you felt before, you are now feeling just a bit better.

Also, as we are essentially wind instruments, the more air we allow to pass through our lungs and larynx, the more of our cells will resonate with the words we speak. *Increased resonance invites increased trust.* Why do you think most successful radio and TV announcers have a deep, dark, rich voice? Because it inspires us to trust them more and to buy whatever it is they are selling. Their voices are simply more attractive.

These are just a few of hundreds of tips to consciously increase the impact of your projection to overcome fear, doubt and a lack of confidence. The more you can align your thoughts, your words and actions into one congruent package, the easier and more effective you will be in delivering it and the more your listeners will be *moved* into action.

In our current world of uncertainty there is a distinct lack of confident leaders. Distinguishing them from those confidence artists and sociopaths who have learned to use their body language to deceive us is an important bonus of becoming more conscious of your own body and its language. If you really want to lead others into a brighter future, get more agile. Get more conscious of the message you are receiving as well as the one you are projecting with your entire self. Make it authentic! Make it something that excites, inspires and engages everyone!

Getting past behavior
The more understanding you create, the more agile you will become. Those of us who have a few years under our belts come from a past where there was more time to reflect before acting. Now, shorter cycles and increased volatility are forcing leaders to do away with that attitude. Their crews must learn to adjust their course much quicker than in the past. This implies being agile enough to run the gauntlet of your listener's behavioral triggers. These include all those psychological buttons that you can easily push, sending them into a familiar "do-loop" that shuts down their listening and sets them onto automatic pilot.

This can take the form of:

- Causing a debate
- Taking offense
- Anger
- Checking out and day dreaming
- Nodding approval with a blank stare
- Confusion
- Checking their phone
- Polite but clearly detached listening

These are some of any number of other pre-recorded, unconscious inhibiting behaviors.

Collaboration, we're all connected
Each system is intrinsically connected to many others. For example, next time you board an airplane take a moment to reflect on how many people and systems are involved in getting you safely from one place to another. Think about all the:

- Travel agents and their booking systems
- Programmers that developed the code and the factories that built all the computers and networking systems.
- Miners that dug up and processed all the raw materials and resources that were used to build everything.
- Architects, engineers and construction workers who built the airports, roads and rail systems that got you there.
- People and processes that built your airplane.
- Airport staff and the crew of your airliner and all the people and systems that support and train them.

This by no means is a complete list. In fact, this list could include just about everyone on the planet, depending upon how broadly we define connection. The point is that we are all connected and the sooner and more inclusively we recognize this, the sooner we can start appreciating and using this tremendous leverage to our collective advantage. Then we will be able to accomplish more, together.

Successful vibes
In the movie, *The Secret Behind The Secret,* Jerry Hicks explains how he found and examined the original draft of Napoleon Hill's *Think and grow rich.* Somewhere, he had heard that essential information was edited out of the first edition. What he found was that every reference of the word *vibration* was removed. It must have given the publisher some *bad vibes…*

It would be an interesting discussion of whether this omission of the word vibration was a disservice to the millions of readers who have read this amazing book or if the book would have ever been published had Mr. Hill insisted on keeping this controversial concept in the book. Regardless, this discovery adds more power to this powerful concept of attraction. There really are good vibes that you can create and send out to attract even better vibrations back. Even more than a century ago, the likes of Carnegie and Morgan were talking openly about soft-skills. *Don't believe us?* It may be worth considering that Napoleon Hill's book was based upon interviews with Andrew Carnegie, J.P. Morgan and other titans. Could this have been at least part of what these industrial titans believed was behind their successes?

Service develops conscious agility
Serving others will keep you present to the needs of those around you as well as keep you from becoming the center of attention. Test and see if the more you

disappear into service, the more you enter an eternal flow that correctly guides you to the next step. What if it is only when you try to stand out that you become noticed. This may be important when managing others, but can cause problems when serving them. When serving others correctly, the focus of those you are serving will be on their own satisfaction and accomplishment. You become background. This allows them to focus on their agenda. More will get done and the positive experience enjoyed by your customer will increase their loyalty and *your future business*.

Expertise versus Mastery
The difference in these words may appear as just semantics, but there are some deeply important points distinguishing these two states from each other. As we are continually talking about *Mastering Agility* in this book, it is important to understand the depth and power experienced on this longer, more challenging *path of mastery*. The following distinctions do not currently exist in the "real world." They are offered as suggestions to make it perfectly *and painfully* clear how you choose to use your hard-won knowledge. With this in mind, picture now having two very well-versed people in front of you; both are highly capable of, for instance, leading others.

Imagine further that they are twins. They have grown up together, attended the same schools and followed the same career path. Still, there is one major difference that distinguishes these two leaders. One considers himself an *expert* and tends to constantly justify and defend his decisions. The other chooses to *master* the art of leadership by asking followers curious questions, listening closely to the answers, then guiding listeners towards the agreed upon goal. Surely, many who probably consider themselves experts today would better fit the following suggested profile of a master. *What about you?*

Expert *(a humbly suggested distinction)*
Experts are very good at what they do, having studied a certain field for most of their adult lives (at least ten thousand hours on average, *according to, you guessed it, other experts*). They have built a reputation for having all the answers. *They know a lot* and take pride in highlighting and justifying that knowledge to you at every opportunity. Yet they have (consciously or unconsciously) chosen to cross a fine line with this amazing amount of knowledge.

Instead of using it primarily to enrich the lives and careers of those listening, they choose instead to exploit this knowledge as a means of bringing more attention, fame, and fortune *to themselves*. Not only that, if challenged, experts will often do what is necessary to prove and defend their point, sometimes shutting down and even humiliating a curious or inquisitive listener in the process.

Experts love to debate and to use their *knowledge as a weapon* to defend their reputation, the institution or the idea they represent. It becomes their identity and pride takes over. *Expertise is more goal than path.* Once reached, it becomes a badge to show off and defend. Even the expert's body language, stiff and defensive, often looks very much like an exclamation point (!).

Master *(another humbly suggested distinction)*
Masters are also experts at what they do. They too studied their specific area for most of their lives. They have also become the vortex of increasing knowledge in their chosen field. Masters also know as much as experts, but here is where the similarities end. Unlike experts, masters are usually thrilled and honored to share this knowledge with others in a way that it can be used and developed further. Masters love and seek chances to *serve their listeners* and to increase everyone's understanding. This is done through open and thought-provoking dialogue, where everyone's point of view is welcome and encouraged. *A reflective question (instead of a bullet-proof statement) is one of a master's most valuable tools.* They fully understand that by sharing their knowledge and being open to learn more, they will also continuously *expand their own expertise* as well as their ability to deliver and teach it. Everyone wins with a true master. A master is a true leader, as people naturally want to follow them.

Although fame and fortune can and often does follow, personal recognition is not the primary goal. In fact, when challenged, a true master will respectfully ask the challenger to explain his or her point to see if there is something new for all to discover. Debate is seen, by the master, as entertainment (at best) or a waste of time (at worst). The true master will continually seek to *create an open, curious, and collaborative dialogue* in which differences can be aired and discussed and where even more possibilities can be discovered and integrated. *The Master's calling card is your "Aha!" experience.*

Mastering anything requires openness, curiosity and an inherent appreciation of the value and attractiveness of serving others. They constantly practice and test their ability to teach, plus actively demonstrate their will and willingness to constantly learn and improve. Most of us will automatically answer we have these properties, wouldn't you?

Yet how many of us will continue to apply them in our lives, especially when we uncover a contradictory behavior pattern? This is, of course, where exercising these properties and qualities can drastically and truly make a difference in your behavior and your future. That's what makes a discovery like this so challenging. Keep in mind that this discovery probably means that you have been totally wrong, so far....

A Master's body language is usually soft, attractive and often resembles a supple, yet grounded question mark (?). *Through selfless service,* everyone benefits from a master. *Mastery is more path than goal.* This is truly where the master differs from the expert. The master openly admits his or her shortcomings, learns something, adjusts defective behavior and continues on the path. The expert often defends his hard won goal. Which behavior would you choose to follow?[xliv] Which behavior is more agile?

The Practice of Mastery: If this suggested distinction between expert and master inspires you to begin walking the path of mastery, the following points are offered to help you walk that path more effectively. These points can be used in all parts of your life. Keep in mind that a good skipper is often called the Master, a professional craftsman is called a Master and in business, an MBA is a badge of achievement. Below are some tools to help keep you on your path of mastery.

- **Remain curious** and remain young. Take every opportunity to ask questions and find out more about what interests you. Be curious and demonstrate curiosity and wonder to everyone with whom you come into contact.
- **Learn from everything**. Does that scrap of newspaper blowing down the street actually contain an eureka moment for you?
  How will you ever find out if you have shut down your curiosity and permitted the expertise of *what you already know* dictate the wind's and the paper's truth? For that matter, you may find it interesting to observe how often you find yourself dictating other people's truths too. Remember, the best *AHA* usually starts as an *"Oh Shit!!!"*
- **Learn, do, and then teach**. Taught in the best medical schools, this is a powerful three-step process to encourage you to become proficient enough so that by the third time you do something you should be proficient enough to teach it. If this is so, then what will you need to pay more attention to the first two rounds to accomplish this?

"There is no education from the second kick of a mule."
- James Dale Davidson's father

The world has changed and the more you can set your corporate ship and its crew on a path of mastery, the easier it will be to stay agile.

Mastering soft-skills, the journey

There are many other tools and tips to help you and your process. These should be enough to give you some concrete skills to begin using directly. The most important and most useable point you are welcome to learn from this discussion is that it is *your conscious choice* when you choose to expand beyond being an expert and begin walking your path of mastery.

26. Agility and What You Can Do

We keep coming back to the metaphor of a sailing ship and how its crew members, using effective navigation tools, can help the captain to navigate uncertainty. The skipper is the CEO, the crew are all the departments and the technologies are there to enable the CEO to plan and execute a successful strategy. All these resources, brainpower, energy and teamwork must be focused upon satisfying individual customer needs, wants and wishes as expressed through your team's clear understanding of their demands.

Focusing on your customers and what each one says eliminates much of the subjective opinions and isolated internal debates that can cause inaction. Many factors are never under the control of the captain, but *eliminating friction caused by other points of view than those of your customers* will unleash more focus and energy to better satisfy them.

Your captain must always remain very alert and clearly be able to understand and respond to the following factors:

- His own ship's (company's) capabilities
- Specific customer's situation and demands
- Customer alternatives
- Company ability to surpass customer demands vis à vis these alternatives

Your first step, preparing for your Dynamic Navigational System
It is our experience that even large successful companies can still solve their big structural problems, even those endemic to their industries. In order to thrive, let alone survive, breaking through these bottlenecks is now a necessity. To initiate this on your ship we recommend that you employ the following actions simultaneously:

- Effectively and passionately understand that your customers' experience is key
- Find and discontinue unnecessary expense categories. Do away with those *feel good* categories of expenses that no one understands.
- Eliminate or neutralize the financial risk of your customers as well as your own. Make what you sell a secure, comfortable and inviting proposition.
- Utilize more contract personnel and work more closely with them.
- Mitigate problems, inhibitors and bottlenecks by creating forward-looking information and action using the Dynamic Navigational System (DNS).

27. DNS Tools and Modules

This book is an invitation to begin building your own *DNS* by incorporating the following simple, proven tools and methods. Their use will drastically improve your *ability to respond* to an increasingly turbulent environment. Your ability to consciously steer your organization faster, more nimbly and effectively will become the difference between success and failure. Below are some of the effective tools you will need to accomplish this increasingly vital task. They will help you to identify old fashioned, slow and ultimately destructive management practices and navigate through or around them. Many of them have their roots in either the agricultural or early industrial society. Each of the tools below can be implemented via workshops, blended learning, train the trainers, coaching or as a pure contracted service. See the end of the book for more details.

Requirements
To drive your own *DNS* you will need:

- All current knowledge of your product, your customer and your competition
- A simple and extremely powerful *fact and perception based system* for analytics and effective marketing.
- Sales, marketing and management teams specifically trained to gather appropriate information and feed and constantly update your new system.
- An agile vigilance coupled to an active willingness and ability to respond quickly to changes in the competitive landscape
- An open mind and a willingness to commit to testing and measuring; in order to keep learning and improving (*upon what we suggest below*)

If this sounds highly sophisticated as well as expensive to implement, it's not. Keep reading to get a taste of all the changes that you can initiate yourself, NOW!

Distinct types of agility

We cannot stress enough the following *fundamental principle of agility*.

Agility is not just about the decision process. It's magic comes alive in the execution and implementation of those decisions you make!

You will also quickly begin to realize that all major inhibitors of change are found in the EXECUTION of change, rather than in the DECISION-MAKING process itself.

Deciding is relatively easy. Transforming those good decisions into practical change *that you dare to measure* is the key. The accuracy in decision-making is improving considerably with modern tools such as Big Data analytics. The issue becomes your agility in the *mastery of each execution.*

Many types of agility are now discussed and many definitions are given. We have chosen to focus upon the two shown below in this book, as *these have provided the most leverage* when it comes to delivering measurable results. We have successfully used the following two types of agility to help companies navigate current turbulent waters. Most of the tools below have traits from both:

Strategic

Spotting and seizing game changing opportunities. These tools focus on better strategic definition by describing in measurable detail the *Where, Why and What.*

Operational

Exploiting opportunities within a focused business model and helping to better define the *How, Who and When.*

The primary type of agility each tool below enhances is shown in the parentheses following its name. Most demonstrate a combination of Strategic and Operational properties with the one named being dominant.

28. The Agility Toolbox

Below are some of the effective tools we use that are immediately available and will make your organization more *AGILE*:

1. **Understanding Transformation and Agility** (Strategic)
2. **Forward Decision Drivers (FDDs)** (Operational)
3. **7S Framework (C7S)** (Strategic)
4. **Inclusiveness Funnel (IFS)** (Operational)
5. **Rolling Budget System (RBS)** (Operational)
6. **Marketing Responsibility Assessment (MRA)** (Strategic)
7. **Overhead Value Analysis (OVA)** (Operational)
8. **Leadership Assessment** (Strategic)
9. **Carve-Outsourcing Services (CORE)** (Operational)
10. **Injecting Entrepreneurship into your organization** (Strategic)
11. **Setting up a virtual or physical DNC** (Operational)
12. **Evaluating direction with the Strategic Triangle** (Strategic)
13. **STA+R** (Operational)

29. Tool One: Understanding Transformation and Agility

*T*his first tool is a process of discussion and dialogue where the need for and benefit of agility is thoroughly explained, discussed and anchored throughout your organization.

Recognize any of these companies or recognize their products?

- Digital Equipment Corporation and mini-computers
- WANG Corporation and word processing
- American Motors, Plymouth, Hudson, etc. and the auto business
- Eastern, Pan Am, TWA, Sabena and the airline business
- Nokia, Blackberry, ITT, Motorola and telephone terminals

Once upon a time these were merely *some* of the best and largest companies in their field. What happened?

One way or another, they all got stuck in *business as usual*. In their day these were some of the biggest names in the Computer/Telecomm, Automotive and Travel Industries. Each had a pedigree that they had built up and refined over a long period of time. In each case their industry changed so much *and so quickly*, that they were forced out of business or had to reorganize under stressful conditions. *Resting on their laurels* wasn't enough to keep them at the top of their game, especially when the rules changed.

Here we have proof that steering from the rearview mirror is a fool's game, especially if you add a bit of hubris to the mix. Tragically, displaying hubris is how many very talented executives were trained to behave and very often this ends up a habit to which they become blind to and ultimately contributes to their increased arrogance. In the current cult of star executives, many have actually been marketing themselves, using their bragging rights to garner bigger and bigger compensation packages, often at larger and larger firms. They often do this while nonchalantly brushing aside the fundamentals and humility that made them successful in the first place. Most seem unaware that they have unconsciously fallen into this trap and often will viciously defend their new expertise and *improved* behavior. Could the intensity and *expertise* of their defense actually indicate how much agility they have lost, suppressed or forgotten?

> *"Whatever you think it is, it's not"*
> - Ancient Chinese proverb

Many current executives cut their teeth in a much more predictable time, when past performance *could be* used as a reliable performance measurement. As the pace of events accelerate many of these current leadership icons have become unconscious slaves to old-fashioned tools that often become the ultimate cause of their destruction.

If you are wondering over what we mean, just remember one of our world's most tragic and destructive clichés, "*Our generals are still fighting the last war.*" How many brave, good-hearted young men and women have lost their lives because these "*heroes*" were not agile enough to put down their textbooks, become present to and handle the current reality in real-time?

Future success will require a whole new set of forward-looking tools to steer your company. With accelerating megatrends and big storms on the horizon, a whole new way of behaving is no longer an option. One thing is becoming more certain; what was true before will most probably *not* remain true in the future. Any effective change usually requires a process. To help you cultivate an effective way of enrolling others in your organization to understand and begin applying agility skills, we offer the following process. This process can be done best by a savvy facilitator in a workshop format with the specific purpose of creating a more agile business atmosphere.

A. Establish Urgency
Free thinking, responsible and potentially agile people will not blindly accept yet another transformation process. They need to understand *and sense* the reasoning behind it. Only your organizational *sheep* will offer blind acceptance, and they are exactly the people that most need to understand their part in *consciously* behaving with more agility. Remember, agility *does not* mean giving up your curiosity, skepticism or your ability to express it.

At this early point, the risks of why agility is important for the survival of the company and (each participant's job) need to be defined, expressed and *rubbed in till they hurt.* Every employee needs to be made keenly aware that more *business as usual* at this late date is just as dangerous as making a strategic mistake. Make your message simple and make it *sting!* Again, the best "Aha" experience usually starts as an (pardon the expression) "OH SHIT" experience. Why?

Up until this point, your listener has not *felt* the connection between his/her *business as usual* behavior, its growing and aggregated consequence. Bring up the Megatrends; hit them over the head with Perfect Storm anecdotes. Do it until they GET IT! Once that risk is defined, understood and becomes personal, they will begin to *sense* the gap between where their current behavior is taking them and the agility needed to change it. Only then is there room for change. Just as you cannot treat an alcoholic's need for liquor until they realize the emergency, neither will your crew spring into action just because you say they must. If that feeling of urgency is not expressed and experienced in a way that *emotionally moves* them, then your message will remain an abstraction and therefore, *someone else's problem.*

Once your reasoning is presented in an understandable and undeniable format, your listeners can then respond to it with personal and conscious choice. Therefore, make sure that all your stakeholders are equipped to answer the question, "*Why?*"

The more you can provide the understanding for *why* the change to agility is necessary, the faster you will get others to jump onboard. Make sure you advance beyond just *dumping more knowledge on them* and give them the information they need to *understand and experience* a personal and profound *AHA!* moment.

Remember, "*Knowledge leads to debate, understanding leads to action!*"

After this, if they understand the gravity of the situation, yet still choose not to accept it and begin changing behavior, then it's probably time for them to sign on to another boat.

B. Form a coalition of change agents

Find or create a trusted group who either inherently grasp what you are trying to accomplish or who are quick, curious and willing learners, *who possess a strong sense of personal integrity.* Arm them with your simple, emotional message, then get them out there as advocates. Have them explain *to everyone affected* why agility needs to be implemented. Have them read this book for instance, as we have tried to make our points as simple and as actionable as possible. Be sure each advocate can express a convincing and *moving* response to the question, "*What's In It For Me*" (WIIFM). The more quickly and powerfully this message begins to resonate throughout your company, the faster and more confident your collective jump to agile business will become.

C. Create a strong, simple vision and strategy for change

Ask anyone who has consciously given a successful speech; the key is the right balance of content and delivery. The more you design a simple, interesting and understandable story to support the change you want to affect, the faster you can powerfully convert people to your new program. The simpler and easier it is to understand, the less doubt and debate you will create.

The simpler and more *jingle-like* you can make your message, the fewer handles there will be to latch onto to start a debate. One of the reasons given that many great people have used simple parables to get their message across is that it addresses and satisfies the needs of both hemispheres of your brain equally. A simple message satisfies the practical, transactional, left hemisphere of your brain and its *jingle like, sing-songy* delivery will attract the more receptive, relational and artsy, right side of your brain. This is no time to get smart! Creating a complex, intelligent and often aloof argument will only succeed in confusing and shutting down your listeners' curiosity. To get things done quickly, you need both understanding and engagement. A simple, catchy and *actionable* message is the most efficient way to achieve this.

The key to this whole vision conversation is to distill your message down to its essence. Discovering those critical keywords and phrases needed to anchor listener understanding will encourage them to act. The clearer path your words and gestures create, the more clearly your milestones can be laid out and measured, the easier it will become to get others to sign on and support them.

D. Communicate direction/vision vigorously

Overdo it, constantly and creatively! It is better your people get tired of hearing your message than not to hear it enough. Keeping it top of mind with reminders will also boost integration. Make your message visible! Put it on posters, place it on everyone's email signatures and put it on everyone's screen-saver. Don't forget, one of the most powerful change agents is *nagging*. The trick is to enroll as many *co-naggers* as possible. Sooner or later with the help of a constant chorus of nagging, resistance usually gives way. Even those with darker intentions understand the power of repetition. For instance, Hitler, Goebbels and even Lenin have all been credited with saying something to the effect that if you, *"tell a lie often enough it becomes the truth."*

Want more proof of the power of repetition? Just raise some children! Persistence and determination bordering on stubbornness are the keys. Become relentless in broadcasting your message as often and as convincingly as possible. Encourage your agents, as well as everyone else with influence, to do the same. Mix in a little heartfelt passion and childlike curiosity with your professional determination and *don't ever give up!*

E. Empower others to act
Invite and encourage participation. Get everyone involved. A textbook example is Jan Carlzon's transformation of Scandinavian Airlines System. When he took over, his first task was to empower his front line staff to service each customer better. He talked relentlessly about the SAS employee team's "*fifty thousand moments of truth per day.*" This was an approximate number of daily contacts and opportunities the SAS team had to make a positive customer impression. The best way to get the ripple effect going is to delegate responsibility with others so they feel directly involved. The more you empower others, the more they will help shoulder your burden and the more this will positively ripple out into your market.

One of my first AHA's about service was working selling tires. For most people, buying tires rates right up there with going to the dentist. It's no fun. Yet the CEO, Tom Pumpelly's idea of the *Crescendo Effect* of a string of positive service impressions, from initial phone contact right through to leaving the mounting bay, allowed the company to grow from a local Washington D.C. phenomenon to one that stretched to the Mississippi River. In the 1980's it was very common to see a "*Tires by NTW*" bumper sticker on cars all over the Eastern United States. Think about the kind of experience it would take to get *you* to put a bumper sticker on *your car, advertising where you bought your tires...* As everyone in the company was on board to perform this kind of service, they felt empowered to deliver. Our customers responded!

Above all, the most important point in this whole empowerment process is to *make knowledge personal.* Engagement demands a *personal feeling of involvement.* Otherwise, it becomes just another abstraction. *There is no empowerment in abstraction.* No matter how intellectual and logical your message is, if you can just sightsee without direct involvement, it becomes about as motivating as watching TV. The moment of truth is when you and what you personally engage in are in play. It's riskier, but that's empowerment; i.e. "*No guts, No glory!*"

F. Create short-term wins
We have now developed a culture of all or nothing. You are either a superstar or a zero. Recognition may be making a bit of a comeback, but it is still rare enough to stand out. *Use this important tool to motivate and empower!*

Practice announcing small wins. Make a hero out of each winner. It does not have to be much in terms of what has happened or what is won. The main criteria are that it is measurable and indisputable. A simple mention in the company blog or in the newsletter is normally enough. A dinner or theater tickets is also an inexpensive way to get most people interested and engaged. We humans love to compete. Use this trait to leverage your message.

Break up each important process into small, measurable goals and milestones. Reward the steps in a visible way. It may just be that mention in your company newsletter, but *mark it nonetheless*. People love being acknowledged. Acknowledgement encourages involvement, especially when your peers recognize it.

G. Consolidate/cement and broaden effort

Implementing the above steps will both anchor the need for change and get your agility ball rolling. Once you start getting traction, keep it up. Be very careful that you don't fall into the same old ruts from which you have just escaped. Cement the changes into your **Rolling Budget System,** *Tool Number 5* and your **7S program,** *Tool Number 3*. It is even better if you can get each employee to willingly and physically stand for change and sign off on it.

Cement and acknowledge the progress you make and then allow it to bloom throughout your company. Again, *agility is not so much a process as it is a lifestyle*. Therefore, until it permeates your entire organization, there is still more to do. Agility needs to become viral. The more contagious you make your agility program, the more people both within and surrounding your organization will be positively smitten. This requires constant reminding, encouraging and acknowledging to a broader circle of listeners.

H. Institutionalize new approaches/products/services

As oxymoronic as *Institutionalizing Agility* sounds, your goal is to integrate these new agile wins into your company behavior. You want agility to become part of your new cultural DNA and this is what is meant here by our use of the word *institutionalize*. Probably the best way to describe this process (still no pun intended) is to *incorporate* it.

Separate or distinguish new groups and create new **7s systems** for them. Installing a **Rolling Budget** is another great example. These changes will promote and cement more organizational agility. They will feel superior to the static "*business as usual*" processes and traditional legacies that you replace. Count on them causing some friction, as friction is a sign of progress. Create a new agile "*standard*" in the company. Then measure it and observe how what you now institutionalize, begins to improve the spirit within your whole company.

Agility is about being flexible, powerful and conscious enough to avoid potential traps. Its realigning everyone's focus forward, to take advantage of the opportunities *ahead of your boat*. It is all about looking forward instead of groveling or grinning over those experiences now in your wake. This requires a distinct shift in your behavior coupled with a broader and deeper understanding of your customers' behavior. To improve on your forward vision, you need to set your sights on fully understanding why your customer does what he/she does. This helps train you and your crew to sense and anticipate your customer's next move.

Practice makes perfect
The practicalities of looking forward should be practiced in combination with understanding what consequences new technologies will have on your business. Also, remember to pay close attention to what effect the constant bombardment of new laws and regulations will have. Try to develop a feel for which direction they are headed. For instance, are lawmakers opening up new possibilities and deregulating aspects of your business? Or are they tightening down on opportunities to protect the current TBTF players and their now well established version of *business as usual*? The answer could well be found in the interplay between geopolitical upheavals that seem to currently be running amok everywhere. Missing just one of these important areas of agility can cause major damage to an otherwise foolproof plan. Getting them all correct will help put you and your company in a sustainable and profitable class by itself!

The growing importance of soft-skills
To accomplish this transformation requires strong doses of curiosity, compassion and empathy. These are three *relationship qualities* that have been sorely lacking in the *transactional culture* that has developed in business over the past thirty years. In fact they have often been interpreted as weaknesses on the executive floor where more robotic and *often sociopathic traits* have often been rewarded. Just think about some of the popular terms used to describe successful business leaders such as, "Calculating," "Sharp," and "Ruthless." Have *you* ever worked for someone like that and been motivated to enjoy doing your best? Authentic respect comes from admiration, not fear.

Balancing these soft relation building skills with technology and all those easily measurable hard skills that you either learned in business school or acquired from experience, will set you on the path towards mastering agility. *Balance is key.* The pressures from increasing competition, regulation and technology are becoming relentless. This is creating an unbearable level of stress for those still lucky enough to have a job. For instance, overlooking the symptoms that one of your key players is at risk of overworking her/himself can cause major health problems for her/him. It can also cause a logistical and business nightmare for you and the others who are left to pick up the pieces. Adding this extra stress on the rest of your already overworked team is not a winning formula. Therefore, be vigilant, encourage good performance and monitor your team's well-being and workload. A rejuvenated and restructured HR department can help.

30. Tool Two: Forward Decision Drivers: Constant Monitoring (FDDs)

*T*his tool is a powerful way to continually gain important sales, marketing, competitor and product development information from its source without pestering anyone with another survey.

But first, would you please take a moment and fill in the following questionnaire? Just kidding...

If you are sick and tired of being badgered to fill in yet another survey, do you think those with whom you do business are any different? Of course not! Current *business as usual* practices still dictate that this is the best way to gather important information. What if this practice is now actually alienating you further from your customers' loyalty?

Most decision makers now agree upon research that implies when all is said and done, you ultimately make your purchases based upon your perceptions and feelings. For instance, you may have all the facts and statistics showing that a product is either the same or technically better than another. Strangely enough, research finds that you still usually decide to buy, based upon your best friend's judgment and experience. *His/Her perception has now effectively become yours.* Importantly, we urge you to realize that in competitive product comparisons, the hard buying factors, *which are easily measured* e.g; Price, Delivery, Terms, Features and Performance, *are quickly becoming indistinguishable.* This is the *commodification factor* we discussed in the first section. Whereas, the *soft* and more *perception based* attributes are becoming more important; e.g. Personal Service, Trust, Design, Status. We further argue that *quality is also a soft buying factor.* In short, the warm and fuzzy factors are increasingly winning the day.

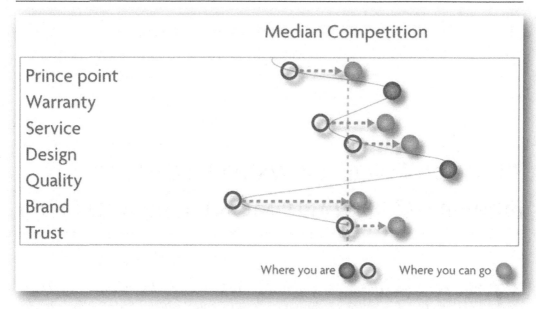

Figure 21 Forward Decision Drivers or FDDs

If you too agree with the concept that *in the end*, it is mostly perception, this realization opens the door to a very effective and *non-intrusive* feedback loop to determine what drives your customer's decisions. You can use this loop to:

- Show customers that you care
- Demonstrate your appreciation for their valuable time
- Get measurable information directly from the most qualified source
- Get a better handle on why your customers buy, *or not*
- Support and improve the perceptions of their reasons for buying
- Use it as a powerful closing tool
- Manage your sales team better
- Improve your competitive analysis
- Strengthen your buying trend analysis

The name of this Minerva Group tool is the **Forward Decision Drivers** or **FDD**. *FDDs* help you and your customer to locate and define their perceptive reasons for choosing (or not choosing) your product, together while painting them a more compelling reason to buy.

Just like the powerful ocean currents hidden under your boat, perceptions are subject to constant change. Therefore, with the power they exert, you need to continually monitor them as well as build up a database to measure changes in these critical trends. The process for identifying your customers' Forward Decision Drivers is a process combining technical tools with a number of practical workshops. It works best as follows:

- **Identify the Key Buying Factors** including the all-important Hard and Soft ones. This is most effectively accomplished via an open dialogue with those directly involved. This is often done best by in a workshop setting during a brainstorming session with your sales and service departments, plus other key players.
- **Arrange them** into an easily understood array and:
  - Build a data capture program or app which can quickly enter new data into your database.
  - Create a list of questions to quickly and accurately gather this information with the minimum amount of intrusion and irritation for your customer.
- **Ask each customer or contact in the company to rate them.** This can be done either on paper or *a simple app* and ideally shouldn't take longer than *sixty seconds to complete*. It can be an excellent and not-intrusive icebreaker or precursor to the business at hand or better yet, you can weave them into your typical sales or service conversation template. It is designed to be easy and our experience is that, when done correctly, it is always welcomed. It demonstrates quickly your interest in a non-intrusive and service minded way. It also provides you with a very high yield of answers due to its brevity and that it only asks for perceptions rather than facts.
- **Compile the data.** This can be done automatically in your back office.
- **Analyze the data** to determine your strengths and weaknesses in your market's eyes as well as from your competitors' standpoint. You can develop this system to automatically look for measurable statistical correlations and deviations.
- **Implement the needed changes**. Whether in your marketing, sales, or product development, adjust accordingly by taking the appropriate actions. Then measure the result from new data collected on your next visit.
- *Rinse and repeat.* This powerful tool will eventually become a behavior that you do automatically during each customer encounter. Your properly designed and implemented FDDs will minimize the risk of selling mediocrity; such as when salespeople blame their poor performances on bad pricing.

Expectations versus results

From the completion of your first survey, you will immediately begin building a database of those hard and soft perception factors that each of your customers *perceive* as most and least important. You will also create access to a number of other analysis opportunities such as:

A powerful, consequential sales tool

Sales people can immediately sell more in less time by using this information to better:

- Streamline your sales/service pitch by eliminating unwanted information
- Handle objections and build more value
- Focus on strengths
- Uncover and fix perceived weaknesses or learn to neutralize them better
- Float more trial closes with increasing confidence
- Deepen your competitive analysis by gathering unfiltered information about your customers' perception of your competitors
- Assess and offer a sharper (instead of deeper) discounts
- Adjust and ask for the close again
- Create better understanding, cooperation and more loyal relationships

Marketing can use it to:

- Strengthen your message and focus on those factors that *your customer values*
- Track trends in how changes in your message are being perceived
- Trigger and/or justify sought after features and developments
- Discover new objections and competitive threats
- Dial in more effective pricing strategies
- Choose the best, most efficient and appreciated distribution channels

Over time valuable data will be collected and compiled. Marketing will build a very detailed picture of how the product is currently and historically perceived. It will also provide valuable trend tracking, greater functional and qualitative information as well as statistical correlations throughout. *Effective FDDs can actually do away with the need for traditional and costly marketing research!* This information can now be continually updated directly from the best, most effective source available, your customer.

Management can use FDD for all of the above, plus you can:

- Eliminate excuses from sales people who are used to blaming price
- Bring new sales people up to speed quickly
- Support, train and encourage ineffective sales people
- Create a more powerful and effective sales and marketing message based upon what the market says it wants.
- Measure the effect of adjustments and tweaks with each new message iteration.

Thus, for about sixty seconds of your customer's precious time, you will have a tool that can support sales, marketing, management, quality control, logistics and service (to name just a few).

Keep in mind that empathy is different from market research, yet both are going to be needed in equal portions for sales success going forward. For example, knowing more about the customers than they know about themselves is the key to a powerful *Forward Decision Driver* (FDD) strategy. Loyalty improves further when you train to ask these simple questions with increased empathy and curiosity. This is a much better tactic than conducting the world's most effective interrogation or filling it the most beautiful and well thought out questionnaire. Master this tool and you can start anticipating future customer needs, wants and wishes better than they can. This kind of agility naturally leads to a sustainable win-win!

31. Tool Three: The Seven S Framework

*T**his proven tool is a process or framework with which to measure and adjust the balance, interplay and harmony of important hard and soft components your organization. It provides a practical picture and tools and tips of how effectively and successful your organization functions.*

Originally conceived by former McKinsey colleagues Bob Waterman, Tom Peters and Julien Philips in a White Paper called "*Structure is not organization*"[xlv], the Seven S's Framework presented there is said to have been the precursor to the 1982 worldwide best seller "*In Search of Excellence.*" The objective with this original analysis aims at a desire to understand why some companies seemed to be consistently more successful than others. The research done by the authors and their teams uncovered the following factors, which all conveniently started with an *S*.

The Seven S's

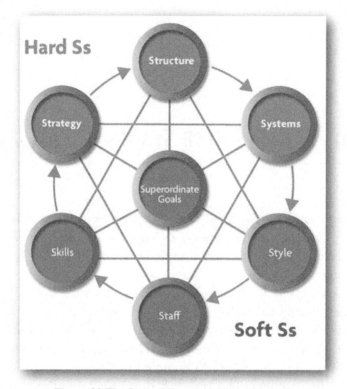

Figure 22 The Seven S Framework analysis tool

The findings uncovered in the initial research indicated that in successful companies, there was always a higher degree of harmony when comparing the interaction of these seven S's to those in a less successful company. In the thirty plus years since, we have uncovered more and more evidence that these important relationships are still constantly at work. Therefore, becoming more conscious of these factors and then deliberately balancing and harmonizing them have proven to be a valuable and on-going process. Now we have an environment of ever-shorter cycles and greater volatility. This puts tremendous pressure on your company's organization and systems. This forces you to become even more Agile. Paying close attention to the interaction of these seven properties that start with "S" is arguably more important now than when the book was first written.

For example, let's say that your company decides to expand aggressively. The *strategy* chosen is to grow its top line. This will be accomplished by increasing sales and capturing market share. In this scenario, this decision would create an obvious *disharmony* to continue systematically compensating the sales force based upon the bottom line. The profit numbers could increase radically, but the loss in top line revenue growth could kill not only the expansion plans, but also the entire company.

The 7S methodology, well understood and implemented, supports and helps your company work, metaphorically, as a well-oiled machine, a finely tuned orchestra or why not even a well-led crew on a sailing vessel. It is meant to be stable, as well as is in constant motion. This is very similar to the eastern Yin-Yang model. *The more everyone is anchored in a common understanding, the more they can work in a continuously evolving harmony towards well-defined and common objectives.*

Another example is where a company has decided to develop a new technology. Through the 7S prism they can easily discover that they might have everything else in place, but lack the appropriate skills or competencies. Armed with this insight, management can now invest in the correct staff, skills and resources to get it.

As a young McKinsey consultant, I had the challenge and pleasure of being in the group that provided the research from European corporations for this first 7s White Paper. What I learned about this methodology during this period I have continued to use and develop throughout my entire career. Even though the business environment has changed drastically since then, I have used this tool with practically every client since I learned of it. For analysis and managerial purposes, it is truly a useful and efficient tool.

This tool is best implemented in the form of a series of workshops focusing on defining, measuring and adjusting each of the seven Ss. The more the chosen group learns to measure and feel when the balance or interplay changes, the quicker they can respond and adjust the problem back into harmony. Thus, this is an ongoing process which should be effectively taught to and mastered by decision makers instead of creating a dependence upon outside consultation.

32. Tool Four: Inclusiveness Funnel (IFS)

*T*his tool can be employed as a powerful lever to increase personal engagement and motivation within a project, group or a whole organization. It is based upon that simple human behavioral fact that the more we feel included in a process or group, the more we will actively contribute and participate.

There is only so much you can do by persuasion, intimidation and ordering people around to reach a quick consensus. Not only that, these tools are becoming less potent as people become more educated and determined. With or without mandates, people instinctively *hate bullies.* This type of behavior fosters a feeling of helplessness. The more they feel that they have no say, the more they will actively resist whatever is being proposed or implemented, *regardless of its brilliance.* On the other hand, the more they feel included, the more they will willingly participate. These basic observations are the basis of our *Inclusive Funnel Process* or IFS.

IFS, a summary
This consists of a simple workshop based system with several brainstorming sessions that eventually funnel understandable results into a well thought out and mutually binding agreement.

The steps are as follows:

- Set clear objectives
- Agree with all stakeholders
- Brainstorm 1
- Homework
- Brainstorm 2
- Consensus workshop
- Homework
- Plan
- Execute

Figure 23 The Inclusiveness Funnel

The process works like this. Let's say your company has a big strategic decision to make. For example: Should we launch or not in the U.S.A.?

Your CEO doesn't have all the answers and is not yet comfortable enough to responsibly take this important decision. Instead of going with his/her usual small group of trusted and often "*HPPO*" based advisers, he/she instead *deliberately* seeks input from a broader group by conducting an *IFS process*.

Note: To ensure third party objectivity and efficiency our experience shows that, *the IFS system is best run using external or neutral facilitators and report writers.*

The IFS Process:

1. A list of relevant knowledge, opinions and ideas is compiled.

These come from the direct stakeholders whose judgment is already trusted, plus other important people involved in the process. In this first round a big group is sought, with varied but relevant backgrounds, taken from different levels of your entire organization.

2. **One or a series of workshops** is/are initiated.

All participants are encouraged to actively participate and the objective of the exercise is clearly defined and disclosed. The more everyone is comfortably on board with the task at hand, the more decisive the results will be. Each workshop ends with a *blind brainstorming* session where each participant is encouraged to anonymously write down his or her best ideas.

3. First Round Analysis.

The participants are sent home and the workshop leaders compile and analyze the ideas. They then prepare a report of their findings. They organize them, sift through commonalities uncovered and compile statistics. The result should be a simple three or four page report with a concise summary.

4. The Second Level of workshops is initiated

The most opinionated five participants from the original group, plus future project leader candidates and senior advisors are all invited back. Another round of brainstorming is initiated, but this time from the leadership perspective. Everyone will have prepared by studying the results of the first report.

A new report is then produced from this session. This report concentrates on leadership questions. Potential risks and opportunities are identified, analyzed and weighted.

5. The Third Level of the funnel

This latest report is distributed to the selected project leader candidates, one of whom will later be chosen to champion the final decision.

A new, even more intensive meeting is scheduled with these potential leaders. This meeting is facilitated all the way through to consensus. This simply means that *no one can leave until consensus is reached.* The focus here is purely on business issues. Personal concerns are deliberately omitted. The result of this meeting will be the creation and mutual agreement of a simple business plan.

The process is thus anchored broadly throughout the organization, providing a sense of attachment and inclusion for all. Then it is further narrowed down and polished until consensus is finally reached on how to implement it. The process can usually be accomplished within a month or two. Everybody feels attached and your CEO can sleep slightly better, as he or she has now collaborated with, and included the rest of the company in this important decision.

33. Tool Five: The Rolling Budget System (RBS)

This tool eliminates the frustrating "ketchup" effect of the traditional end-of-the-year "budget crunch" by finally disconnecting the process from its agricultural past and spreading it out over the life of the different products or services it serves.

"Can you call me after the budget is done?"

How many times have you heard this reply when contacting a decision-maker at the end of his or her fiscal year? If you think you are frustrated, listen closely to sense the frustration *in their voices*. That alone may make you feel better.

Creating more harmony and flow in your organization's financial process will not only ease tensions and tempers, it can also make it easier to quickly aim that flow away from financial traps and towards important and emerging opportunities.

The *Annual Budget* (most loved by accountants and Wall Street promoters) is actually an ancient anachronism, a relic from our agricultural past! It is possibly the most obvious part of this stubborn *business as usual* attitude that the world has accepted and has so far taken for granted. It actually may be one of the greatest remaining financial flaws in modern business. It truly is a holdover from a more rural society, where the weather and seasons steered our activities. The simplest, most agreeable cycle of comprehension was the yearly seasonal variations and their recurring weather patterns. The seasons thus became the basis for all major planning.

Think about it, the agricultural society has its basis in nature and is ruled by weather. Regardless of where you live, you have a natural cycle of seasonal activities to contend with. This in turn has had a profound impact on our calendar. We not only have the four seasons, but many holidays such as the American Thanksgiving, The Swedish Mid-Summer, The chosen dates for Christian Christmas and Jewish Hanukkah celebrations can arguably be traced back to the growing cycle. Many of the activities critical to our agricultural past were directly based upon the seasons. Therefore, major celebrations usually had to wait until all necessary farm work was complete.

Since Industrialization, we have increasingly learned to live using other cycles. For instance, products and services are now much more dependent upon their own cycles than upon the seasons. Despite this, almost all companies have doggedly maintained planning, reporting and compensation cycles based upon the planting and harvesting cycles of our food. Why? Now, that basis doesn't stand up to scrutiny, as we increasingly import seasonal foodstuffs from all over the world, year-round. Even though the origins are now totally irrelevant, the growing cycle still unconsciously and comprehensively influences the governance of corporate life. This anthropological fact now makes the annual budget an inhibitor of change and agility. For the biggest and most tragic example of this, look no further than your own annual budget process.

From roughly mid-October to the last day in December it is not uncommon for many large corporations (like yours perhaps?) to act like the approaching winter season and *freeze up*. Try calling a decision maker during this period and you will get that polite, but irritated, *"call me back after the budget is done."* During this time a disproportionate amount of time, energy and resources are spent on haggling over next year's budget. Often and tragically, *even the concerns of your customers* take a back seat to internal number crunching.

When this is agonizing process is finally complete what happens? All your other company systems hook up to what is decided. Financial decisions are now cemented in place *for at least one year forward.* Critical departments such as Marketing, Selling, Production, HR and the supporting compensation plans are now all anchored into it. Although quarterly tweaks can and often do take place, for the most part from now until the next budget crunch, anything that could change this budget, for better or worse, usually has to wait. Even desperately needed course changes, caused by a major disruptive events (e.g. leap-frogging technology that your competitor unexpectedly launches, or a surprising, game-changing geopolitical event), will often be dangerously delayed while waiting for the new cycle. Up to now, you may have been comfortably able to take credit for any windfall or blame any subsequent loss on the existing budget expectations. *How long will you continue to have this luxury* instead of just doing something about it immediately?

From the first day of the new budget cycle, executives and their wanna-bees now focus their time and energy on meeting or surpassing the agreed upon figures. They become heroes if they meet the budget and devils if they don't. The problem is that this hallowed budget is now cut off from the reality of your market and events in the world economy. All the while, changes in both of these realities continue to accelerate. Volatility and uncertainty are continue to increase. Despite this, most decision makers practice politely side-stepping critical budget issues instead, preferring to focus on the usual brush fires that litter their desks. Meanwhile, discrepancies begin to widen from the budget that most feared (but politely agreed to anyway) were optimistic, or just plain wrong, *before* the ink even dried back in December. "*Hockey stick*" reporting, based upon rosy "*guesstimates*," are becoming more common in this new era of great volatility with bigger, shorter cycles of new products and services.

As long as the economy is growing, this agricultural problem generates little concern. This is because budget goals are usually, easily met and surpassed. This makes those responsible look like gods. What we often forget that when things begin heading in the opposite direction, yesterday's corporate gods become slaves, handcuffed to the consequences of that same plan and risk becoming pariahs overnight. Their only respite is surviving until the situation comes up again on the next budget go-round. Then they have their once a year chance to change it. This of course, is if they are lucky enough to remember it and have also survived all the red ink and humiliation sustained during the most recent year.

Seasons or Cycles?
The vast majority of today's products and services have little or no direct connections to seasonal cycles or the calendar year. Yet to change this ingrained yearly cycle behavior to something newer will take a MAJOR effort. Remember, once the budget is decided upon, all other departments, especially support functions like HR and service, lock in to it and make any budget decisions taken *even harder to change.* Count on any attempt to be met with blind and unrelenting resistance.

Even so, the benefits of this large, but *one time change in behavior* may be very much worth the effort. For instance, you will quickly begin to realize:

- **Inefficient decisions can be adjusted** quickly, saving months of time and freeing up idle, often wasted resources for more important or promising projects.
- **Cycles can be given more time** to mature. They can now stretch over the hereto-sacred one-year boundary. This can prevent a premature decision to stop a promising project that has not yet blossomed into its long-term promise.
- **Biting off smaller bits** of the overall budget, over the entire year, eliminates the typical corporate year-end "budget crunch" that currently handicaps your crew's decision-making behavior and attitude for months.
- **Focus on the customer** and generating more business can again take precedence, even in the cold winter months when there is nothing else to do but spend, spend, spend...

For example, if you know that the natural cycle length of your product or service is one and one half years and you acknowledge your company's reaction time is 3 months, establishing a one and one half year cycle, with a quarterly review, will be a much more efficient alternative. This means that every quarter you now force your team to look a full *six quarters forward.* They can also adjust or tweak the current direction *every three months.* This means you gain at least three quarters time when compared to the traditional annual budgeting process. What would that extra time mean for your company's agility?

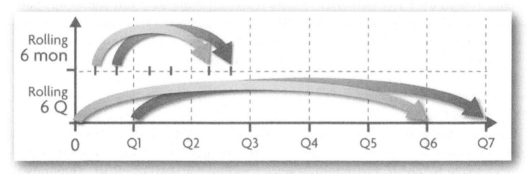

Figure 24 The Rolling Budget Process or RBS

The Rolling budget is a *major* tool that will help you adjust your firm to each of your product's *natural business cycles* and assist everyone in understanding and mastering your firm's financial reality. Moreover, implementing a rolling budget may really be cause for Thanksgiving! When November rolls around, it will feel more like a *normal* month, as you will already have next year's budget almost complete.

The Rolling Budget Process Steps:

Step One: Define the cycles
Assemble the responsible people to discuss and define the natural cycles for each group of products and services. Be sure to respect that different products have different life cycles and revenue streams. *Acknowledge and understand each* on its own terms.

Step Two: Plan
Create a holistic planning model that divides your product categories into distinct time cycles. For instance, Honeywell has products and categories ranging from home security to nuclear plant steering systems. Each one of these products has a different timeline and business cycle. You need to adjust and service each on its own merits. Remember that although all products are not the same, *when it comes to budgeting they are.* Now you are just recognizing them as having separate and unique cycles.

Step Three: Establish routines
Having budgets expire and renew at different times during the entire year will put increased strain on keeping track of them. This has to be consciously and firmly taken care of by finance and accounting. To help anchor these now individual processes, it is important to create a simple, graphical, holistic representation of all the varying budget cycles and place them *where everyone in a decision-making role can easily see them.*

It is also advisable to create a hybrid model for responsibility between marketing and finance. These financial cycles must be decided upon with the help of the eyes, ears and intuition of your marketing team for them to remain correct. If you truly want the complete picture, internal and departmental factors, as well as industry and global factors *must be taken into consideration.* Can you name a group of people who can contribute this type of up-to-date input better than marketing? (If you can, then you better, quickly take a closer look at what responsibilities and functions your marketing department currently has!)

Step Four: Align compensation
In the final analysis, a successful business is still based upon a satisfied team. Therefore, your bonus and compensation systems need to be updated to reflect these new rolling changes, *in a way that is acceptable to your employees.* As Geoff Colvin writes in the

November 1, 2015 issue of *Fortune Magazine*, "*In the 21st century Corporation, whether it is acknowledged or not, employees own most of the company assets because they are the assets*[xlvi]. Should you forget or avoid this crucial step, you may turn around and find your best and brightest people and assets working for the competition."

Step Five: Adjust all other systems

All elements of your entire business system, per category, *including your personnel and planning systems will also have to be realigned.* To really cement this, close cooperation with your HR people is highly recommended. This is so that work flow, including those actual seasonal adjustments that do remain, can be dealt with on a rolling basis. A good way to analyze and harmonize this whole process is doing it through the lens of your **7S system**. The result will be more cooperation and less hiccups once you are up and running. Review the impact and implement all potential actions for each 7S step *every time the plan is updated.*

A big help to anchor this change process will be to increase your use of automation. Use available technology to automate and accelerate accounting all processes necessary to enable closing your books more frequently. For instance, create or acquire a "*Virtual Close*" process.

Once all these systems are rolling along, they should also be graphically represented in your new *Dynamic Navigational Center*. Building your own DNC is described in detail later on.

You can count on that installing your Rolling Budget System will take more time than you think. Start with the understanding that the full implementation of your rolling budget will take *at least one year to complete.* As this is such a big project, the greater the support for it, the faster and smoother the change will become.

Therefore, make sure to mandate key players to spread the word. You want them to become your trusted agents of change. Mandate responsibility and get the action going. Create a story and make sure these players can verbalize it in a way that all their listeners can understand and can begin implementing effectively. Your agents *must be able to empower others* to create and announce progress, especially on the short-term wins. Make sure that this important change in course is observed and recognized by everyone.

Changing to a rolling system is a big change, *but the end result is worth it!*

Although the overall amount of energy will likely remain similar, spreading your budget process out over the entire year will help avoid all the pent-up frustration brought on by the shutting down of critical functions, sometimes for months at a time. Most important of all is that you and your company will definitely become more connected to your market's specific reality.

Implementation of the Rolling Budget Process usually takes the form of a series of workshops with the assistance of consultation, coaching plus technical support.

You will also become far more nimble and agile in running a profitable ship. Some agile corporations have already started this. For instance, here is what former chairman of EMC, **Michael Ruettgers,** had to say:

> *"You have to be nimble enough to respond quickly to unexpected changes. For example, our new six-quarter rolling budget process allows us to constantly adjust our budget allocations to meet changes in the market [and]... the regular and detailed sharing of information allows us to effectively look at our P&Ls on a monthly basis and make business decisions on the fly."*

34. Tool Six: Marketing Responsibility Assessment (MRA)

This tool literally refocuses your corporate ship towards the horizon and success by re-invigorating your marketing people to work with what they were trained to and love to do.

With the focus on sales and finance during the last few decades, the power of pure, old-fashioned marketing has been diluted to become a stepchild of sales. *This makes total sense*, especially lately, when so much money has been sloshing around that many well-off people buy almost by habit. After a quick Google search, we are off to the store or into a bookmarked web-shop and either way, the shopping carts start filling up. Who needs powerful marketing in this environment?

To answer this, just put your ship's helm in the boiler room. Notice how easy it becomes to avoid the larger icebergs of today's increased global competition, the rocks made up of *The Next Big Things* and the Storms of sudden global financial up- and downdrafts, to name a few? Sadly, our experience confirms this trend of weak and undefined marketing as being an increasing problem for companies striving towards better and more agile navigation.

For the agile amongst you, this also opens up an opportunity! An opportunity which most companies have forgotten about or have chosen to avoid. Marketing is one of the best and most critical functions for increased agility. Just like HR, it is currently misunderstood, mistreated or positioned *tragically wrong*. This is most obvious in industrial companies, but to a lesser extent even shows up in the *Fast Moving Goods or* FMG sector.

In a recent C-Level survey performed in medium to heavy industrial companies, it was discovered **that 80% of** the CEOs who were interviewed could not even correctly define what marketing was. Most definitions explained it as, *"marketing was equal to sales plus advertising."* Again, if everything is going according to plan and your corporate boat is also rising in a sea of newly borrowed and printed money, this kind of definition will make sense. You are also warmly reminded again of what the mythical person jumping out of the Empire State building was heard to say as he passed the fifth floor towards the rapidly approaching pavement, "Everything is just fine, so far"… With the trends and storm warnings we have discussed that are whipping up an already uncertain sea, it may be worthwhile taking out your Marketing 101 book and give it another, closer read. There is no better way to ground yourself and your business than with the fundamentals.

This book is written to remind you that your marketing department should spend its time and resources observing and understanding what is ahead, rather than behind it. Your marketing people should thoroughly understand their customer as well as the current and future competitive environment, or *quickly find another profession.*

Sales is not marketing!
Correctly defined, your marketing organization has very little to do with sales. To be truly agile, marketing's true focus, interest and responsibility must be firmly fixed on the classic 4 Ps. The job of selling gets much easier when this is successfully accomplished!

As a reminder, the traditional 4 Ps are:

- Price
- Place
- Promotion
- Product

Out of these four, most respondents in the above surveys usually managed to get one area out of four correct. The conclusion here is that *many industrial multinationals are handicapped by not appreciating marketing's capabilities or its real responsibility.* In a truly agile environment there should be heightened marketing input and influence rather than less. When used correctly, Marketing is the center of your organization's sensory mechanism! A well-defined marketing department with a strong Chief Marketing Officer or CMO is, or shortly will be, the natural navigational hub in an agile, sustainable and *profitable company.*

In well-developed, marketing-centric corporations such as P&G (Procter & Gamble), the establishment of strong program managers, who are fully line-responsible for all Four Ps, is standard practice. Compare this to other more industry-centric corporations and there you will see that *make/buy, pricing and launch decisions* can often be the responsibility of everyone from R&D to sales, production and *even finance!* Take a step back and ask yourself, "*What are these departments doing making marketing decisions?*"

When these critical marketing functions are downgraded and parceled out to others, your marketing people are robbed of their dignity and ultimately, their reason for existing. To add insult to injury, the general attitude often expressed by those inappropriately charged with these important decisions is something like, "*Well, we price it at what the market can bear.*" Try and get a sense of how capricious this *seat-of-the-pants* attitude sounds! This usually shuts down any budding ability or *will* for good marketing people to engage and look forward. Get a sense of how helpless it sounds. If you get any sense of this being the situation onboard your corporate ship, *consider yourself blind* to what is now rapidly floating towards you.

Inefficient marketing = Inefficient business
This nonchalant attitude creates a dangerous add-on effect. It can weaken your sales effort by allowing some *much too comfortable* sales people to ride around on their high horses and blame *bad pricing* decisions for everything, especially their missed sales numbers. Ironically, there may be some twisted truth to this claim, especially if your marketing people have unwittingly been stripped of their ability to do their job. Wouldn't this also further disrupt and inhibit their ability and motivation to help fix the situation?

Leaders, who are *sold* into believing that bad pricing is indeed the problem, often irritate the problem by spending a disproportional and unnecessary amount of precious energy and resources on even more cost-cutting efficiencies. This is instead of improving pricing, where they would benefit most. Revenues usually fall, as ineffective salespeople feel further justified in their poor performances. Ironically, marketing may *also suffer further budget and personnel cuts* due to this totally misguided exercise!

Anyone that understands the power and simplicity of basic marketing, as it is supposed to be implemented, will also understand that effective pricing models will *always* have a vastly higher impact on the bottom line than cost models. Why?

If you have allowed your marketing people to do their homework on cost and have a competitive product, *every price increase, and every extra penny generated from them, contributes unfettered to a more robust company bottom line.*

The 4 Ps, a review
A simple solution is to prepare a *Four P Marketing Review,* based upon the suggestions below and assess your marketing muscle. This can easily take the form of a simple internal survey-based analysis. This can be enhanced by some personal, objective interviews. Done effectively, the whole process should take only one day to execute.

Price

Pricing creates so much more positive leverage than cost cutting does, but that power often goes unnoticed. Company focus is normally put on cost cutting. More often than not, the marketing department is not even responsible for pricing! *This is plain wrong.*

Question One: *Who is responsible for pricing decisions in your company and why?*

Place

Distribution channels and all clusters of employment and contracting must be regarded vis-à-vis current and future customer needs, wants and wishes. The process of bringing a product or service to the market place, as efficiently as possible, is central to any true marketing department. This is more often than not handled on an ad-hoc basis and often triggered by the sales manager. *This is also wrong!*

Question Two: *Who is in charge of the process of bringing a new product or service to market in your company?*

Promotion

Possibly the best understood part of marketing is promotion. But even here this understanding is curtailed by marketing only being fully responsible for external promotion and advertising issues. Effective internal communication is often forgotten.

We have further argued that both external and internal corporate training should also be part of the marketing department rather than the HR department, where it often resides. The skills needed for effective behavioral change are much more akin to the skills in communication rather than the typical skills used in HR, e.g. hiring/firing, personnel evaluations, payroll, pensions, etc. As product cycles continue to shorten, corporate training increasingly becomes a bottleneck for new launches. An efficient training function needs to be incorporated into the eyes and ears of the front-line *more effectively*, so the internal training offered strengthens and compliments the anticipated needs for success.

Effective promotion requires communicating effectively to the listening that already exists or new listening you choose to encourage in the market. Obviously, the department responsible for seeing, hearing and feeling the market pulse for your products can only function effectively by sensing proper and timely *forward looking input*. Therefore, all internal and external communication should flow through marketing. This gives those who are specifically trained to understand and communicate the interaction between your market and your message the best chance to function effectively. Optimally, Marketing should have all internal and external communications, *including Corporate Training*, reporting into its function.

Question Three: *Where does the responsibility for all your different company communication and training functions lie?*

Product
All aspects of product features, benefits and new product development must be accepted and triggered by a marketing decision. In an agile company marketing triggers R&D. Our experience has shown that most often R&D triggers R&D. When this is the case, R&D becomes more of an insulated and costly playground for pampered geniuses rather than your company's creative arm. This further disconnects marketing's eyes, ears, nose and intuition from what is being created in the mind of R&D. R&D disconnected from Marketing's keen senses is wrong!

Question Four: *Who is responsible for and triggers R&D decisions in your company?*

Up the Down R&D Escalator Revisited
Let's take another look at the metaphor for the current challenge facing your Research and Development department; climbing up the downward Research and Development Escalator. This metaphor is used by among others, the Swedish telecom giant, Ericsson AB. Compare the inevitable forward progress of new inventions and products to an escalator that is headed downward. Picture your R&D people walking up that downward moving escalator. The faster they work, the higher they climb on it in relation to the market and their competitor's capacity to innovate. What happens, though, if they stop, even for a moment's rest?

Just to keep up with the market changes *they have to keep climbing*. To get further ahead, they have to climb up the down escalator at an even faster rate. Now what happens when more competitors *from all over the world* enter your market?

That escalator begins to move faster and there are more people, bags and obstacles to avoid during their ever more frantic climb. What if this is metaphorically the situation facing you and your R&D crew today? If they are now focusing on carrying their latest developments up that escalator, do you think they would appreciate a bit of help in finding the most efficient path up that cluttered, moving staircase?

Time to let your more agile and 4P focused marketing department lead the way!

***World-class agility* will transform research and development**
Another related situation is that, for too long a time, tradition has dictated that R&D needed to be done by highly trained and *responsible* people in the developed western countries. Once upon a time, *only* after a high-end version of your new product was ready, a watered down and cheaper version would then be synthesized for smaller, *developing* markets. The selling to these *inferior markets* would then commence. What has now happened to this time honored, traditional way of handling product development and *what does this twist have to do with agility?*

For anyone who has traveled to most developing countries recently, you cannot miss that there are now very many well-educated, relatively well-paid and communicative people virtually everywhere you go! Many are as good, if not better engineers and technicians than those back at your own headquarters. More importantly, *they are also still more cost effective to use!*

This development has opened a brand new door for the agile. You can now literally turn your insulated R&D process on its hitherto comfortable head! From this point on, instead of developing a high end product in a high cost location first, then taking the bells and whistles off to sell it in a lower cost market, it is now possible *and much more profitable* to do the exact opposite!

Right NOW, by developing a low cost alternative of your product in a highly qualified, but low cost location first, you immediately shorten and cheapen the traditional development cycle. With this new approach there is obviously *less time, energy and investment needed to research and develop!* You lower the cost of the work performed by an order of magnitude *directly*; since those local labor costs *sink dramatically* compared to your "*normal*" process. Not only that, you can now begin recouping your costs faster by releasing the new product directly into these local markets, long before you normally would. Only then do you take this simplified and now tested model back home. There you finish the development process in the high cost location. Now you can even afford to develop more high-end, high-margin gizmos, as you can finance them from a present and growing, *rather than future* revenue stream! This will help you maintain and enhance your competitive lead.

Agile marketing generates agile business
In a truly agile organization, your *Chief Marketing Officer* or CMO should enjoy the same listening and respect as the *Chief Financial Officer*, CFO.

When this first critical step in balancing corporate influence is complete, then a powerful and agile triangle of CMO, CFO and CHRO (Chief Human Resources Officer) can begin to function as a well-oiled team. Your forward-looking team, the one needed to run your *Dynamic Navigational System*, will now be in place. As you will soon see, this *DNS Troika* is enormously important for future success!

First, make sure you install some marketing muscle. *Reintroduce* true marketing, *based upon the 4Ps* into all your companies and segments. Then let Marketing, HR and Finance eventually "run" your *Dynamic Navigational Center* or DNC together as described below. The very first thing to do when addressing marketing is to understand the current state of affairs by analyzing the marketing muscle in the group. The four questions above will be a powerful start to this process. There are, of course, much more specialized methodologies available to accomplish this analysis. Never forget and let both sales and marketing constantly nag you that in the end, your customer comes **first, last and always**.

35. Tool Seven: Overhead Value Analysis (OVA)

This is a powerful and very objective analysis tool that can help you to evaluate where there may be extra fat to trim from your organization, without the complication of human emotion. Although this sounds counter to our book's overall message of bringing emotion back into your organization, there are nevertheless some places that emotion will remain counterproductive to the intended goal. Eliminating overhead is just such an area.

Cost cutting is always inferior to efficient pricing.
One of the most dominant beliefs governing today's *business as usual* mindset is that improving efficiency (i.e. cutting costs) is the most reliable way to increase profits. This thinking is especially true in an environment where market requirements change only gradually; one where companies have the luxury of plenty of time to minimize existing product production costs. *When was the last time your market looked like that?*

Today of course, constant efficiency improvements are a prerequisite for a healthy and sustainable bottom line. They are now almost a requirement and soon actually will be. Even so, they're no longer sufficient by themselves. To be agile you need tools for both sides of the coin. Only then can you use them all to go deeper into the *entire valuation process.*

OVA is also a proven McKinsey cost cutting methodology that is both simple and brilliant, as well as effective. This tool was invented by Jon L. Neuman from the New York Office of McKinsey in 1975 and subsequently published in the Harvard Business Review[xlvii]. The ideal organization, department or group with which to perform this process contains ten to 200 people. In our experience, overhead organizations such as Human Resources, Finance, Accounting, Reporting and *other support functions* represent your first, best candidates. Surprisingly, these support functions have so far escaped many previous downsizing efforts. *Could this have to do with that they were often the ones usually charged with performing the downsizing on the other departments?* Regardless, we find these groups can have considerable fat left when put under the OVA microscope.

Absent this methodology, companies still routinely take a *twenty percent chop* right across the organizational chart. The natural consequence of this slash and burn policy is that cuts are made in areas that currently show promise, thus inhibiting areas that are currently being promoted and invested in for the future. In contrast, relatively little is cut in groups where there is still massive waste and redundancy.

"*Don't go away mad, just go away*" - Charles Schultz

The reason OVA is so effective is that it is extraordinarily objective and *selective*. Therefore, it can be used with *surgically selective efficiency*. When performing an efficient overhead value analysis, emotions cannot cloud the issue. They will influence your view of that which needs to be objectively addressed to maintain forward motion. It literally boils down to this; face a smaller amount of emotional blowback now or face organization-wide blowback in a rapidly approaching, increasingly uncertain future. Your choice Captain. Again, a good amount of the inevitable emotional damage you will encounter can be further limited using a bit of empathy. Have your crew practice being more conscious of the content and delivery of potentially career threatening messages. This absolutely includes your own presentation.

Overhead Value Analysis in practice
Once again, OVA works best on support functions. This methodology is not as effective on forward-looking departments such as sales and marketing. Forward-looking groups *can also be potential candidates* for this analysis, but they must be subject to special treatment since they are, directly or indirectly, revenue-producing entities. Their leveraging effect on your bottom line is *the key issue*. Get it right and it will work. Get it wrong and it will not only wreck your bottom line, it will also directly *crush any team-spirit you have previously built up.*

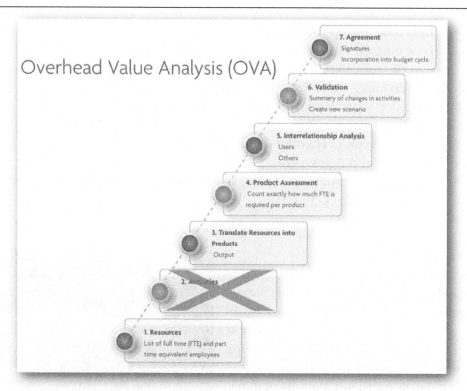

Figure 25 Overhead Value Analysis or OVA, Originally from McKinsey

The OVA process is fairly simple and effective. It can be done as a project, implemented from inside, but usually better from outside, or by using workshops with key internal people. We strongly recommend facilitation from a third party. The key points are.

1. **List all functions** (the responsible people) and all other non-personnel resources. Redefine them in terms of Full Time Equivalent Units, or **FTEs**.
2. **Translate their output** (services, reports, etc.) into Product/Service FTE units.
3. **Skip defining and evaluating each activity** and focus on the results produced. *Who does what* is not important here, only accurately and objectively measuring the resulting output of those efforts.
4. **Define and analyze the output**
   Where does it come from? What is its frequency?
   How many FTEs does each output require?
5. **Assess the output**
   Where do these results end up, who uses them and how much are they used?

6. **Interrelationship Analysis**
   How much is each specific output valued and used?
   Can this information be sourced elsewhere, or used with something else?
   Can certain groups share the output more efficiently?
   If we stop sourcing it, will it *pop up* somewhere else?
7. **Validation**
   Perform a comprehensive "*What if?*" analysis on the output.
8. **Summary and Agreement**
   Get all stakeholders to *sign off* on the findings and then integrate them within the budget cycle.

Selectiveness is key
Start with well-defined overhead cost centers. This is irrespective of whether or not they have been affected in previous downsizing attempts. Who does what, and for how long they have been doing it, is becoming *precariously* inconsequential. This may sound very cold in its execution, but what if it may increasingly be the key to your organization's survival and subsequent success? This is again where your redefined *HR angels* will play an increasingly vital and empathic role in motivating everyone affected, by:

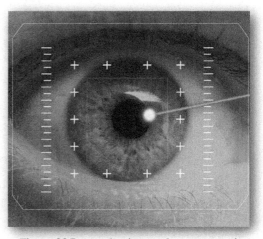

Figure 26 Be as selective as a laser surgeon!

- Encouraging and training them to increase their *measurable value* to the group
- Effectively express the value with conversational and presentational mastery
- Better handle finding other income sources, should this OVA analysis affect them personally and *precariously*

On the brighter side, you may become keenly aware that some departments may actually need to be boosted rather than cut.

Objectivity is crucial! With the possible exception of the first step, the rest of the OVA process is focused upon the effectiveness and measurable value of each specific output. This literally means focusing closely on the following:

- Who reads which reports?
- How powerfully does what they contain affect the reader's ability to perform?

- How can this information be shared more effectively?
- Is there better information available faster, from other sources, and *at a cheaper price?*

Other streamlining tips
In today's rapidly changing markets, many products become obsolete before they have been "*leaned out,*" so managers get less time to optimize their production processes fully. Companies are now implementing two new strategies:

- Increasing flexibility and embedded intelligence going directly into the production process
- Integrating Research and Development with Operations creating what is now called *DevOps*

Building flexibility and embedding intelligence
Embedded intelligence can, over time, help companies to improve both the performance and the *value-in-use* of products and services, thus improving their pricing efficiency. In a sense, digitization is empowering businesses to go *beyond efficiency*, to create effective learning systems that work *harder and smarter*. Doing this helps to adapt even quicker to changing conditions and needs.

For instance, a certain web-based global hotel-booking platform began using quicker feedback cycles to reframe the focus of its business model from the standard one at the time, to a new user based satisfaction model. By pioneering this they succeeded in creating brand new revenue opportunities. Until this particular project was undertaken, the hotel-booking industry's central belief had been that online success depended on two things: negotiating power with hotels through measurable traffic statistics and a reliable web interface for customers.

One company was one of the first to rethink the established belief that when customers booked a hotel room they were only interested in convenience, speed, and cost. They tested different models with small improvements over a longer time. For instance, they tested warmer and cooler tones on website graphics. They added testimonials from satisfied customers. Their testing confirmed that their site had transformed into more than just a typical hotel booking service; it now engaged the customer's interest. They also integrated feedback effectively and began testing experiments into key activities on a daily basis. They ended up creating a true *online learning organization.* They were learning and adjusting as they went. Just like

Amazon, it now adjusts and tweaks its site daily to boost customer engagement and increase revenue. For anyone who has booked a hotel online recently, this type of *online experience* approach is now being adapted as the prevalent one.

Creating DevOps

In the same vein and also to develop more of an edge in software development, successful companies as diverse as Red Hat, IBM and Amazon are speeding things up by integrating their R&D department with operations. As we previously mentioned, Amazon is rumored to have on average one hundred development projects deployed on their site at any given moment. This allows them to get real-time performance measurements and feedback, directly from customers who are actively shopping in real-time. They then tweak these developments from these live measurements, which are taken directly from current customer experiences.

As this goes to print, we came across another wonderful, out-of-the-box application of technology. According to *Fortune Magazine's* November 1, 2015 article "*Burning cars are never a good thing,*" Tesla had a problem with its batteries bursting into flames. The cause was finally identified as stemming from the batteries being mounted too close to the ground. According to this incredible article, instead of a massive recall, "*Tesla beamed an update of the software to the affected cars, raising their ground clearance at highway speed by one inch. The problem went away.*" Simple? Maybe… Agile? Definitely!

36. Tool Eight: Simple, Effective Leadership Assessment

This tool simplifies and lowers the cost of leadership recruitment with no compromise in quality. This is accomplished simply by focusing more on the traditionally immeasurable soft-skills that a leader (as distinct from a manager) needs to succeed.

A lot of effort and huge amounts of money go into analyzing and choosing organizational leaders. In the last few decades, the Evaluation and Headhunting Professions have become big business. Many headhunters charge enormous amounts for evaluating candidates. Now, what if their primary analytical methods still miss the most important points of leadership?

Managing is usually about measuring and allocation, whereas *leadership is about passion.* Express your passion in a way that (emotionally) "*moves*" people to action and watch them become inspired to cooperate and succeed. To paraphrase Rear Admiral Grace Hopper, you manage finance, products, and even services, *but you lead people!* If you want a good manager, then by all means use all those expensive evaluation options; or *better yet buy a software program.* If you want a leader though, you may want to read further and begin using our simple four-point test. A major difference is that in our version of the process you will *save a huge amount of money.*

Unfortunately, we often see that with the current *academic approach* to leadership testing, the important and *emotionally based* leadership *soft-skills* often get lost in the evaluation process. Millions are spent on all kinds of behavioral profiles and leadership assessments. Popular examples include, 360, Myers-Briggs and DISC, to name a few. They absolutely do produce important profile information that can be used in many creative ways. Yet they all have two things in common:

- They all rely upon measuring from a strict battery of questions
- They often cost enormous amounts of money, especially when an executive position is in question.

Our experience is that when judging current management teams, we see a lot of unfortunate hiring, firing and promotions that took place, didn't take place or which shouldn't have taken place. These are all partly due to trying hard to put a soft, round leadership peg into a hard, square management hole.

Remember, there are *at least two* distinct ways you can use the word *sense*. One is to measure various degrees: as in hot/cold, hard/soft, dark/light, on/off, etc. More to the point is the expression, "*If you can measure it, then you can manage it*" or at least make a decision regarding it. The other is *sensing* as in *feeling*. This is where you learn to sense or feel what is happening around you. You can also practice *emoting* a certain sense of your *feelings* in order to inspire and engage others. Which of these descriptions do you think works better when your goal is to inspire others to follow?

More importantly, how *does it feel* when you are forced to take a battery of tests with questions that you *sense* were written, "*long ago in a universe far, far away?*" While completing what often feels like a long and totally irrelevant questionnaire, you discover that what you really burn for was either reduced to one multiple-choice question, or forgotten completely!

To assess *leadership potential* correctly and distinguish it from common *management skills*, the following properties, qualities and your relationship to them need to be addressed:

- People/Partners
- Customers
- Competitors
- Product/Services
- Economics, Mathematics and Analysis
- Strategy/Tactics/Structure

Strategy/Tactics/Structure are addressed throughout this book. So let's spend a few minutes on the other topics. Let's discuss them from the prospect of being a more agile leader, capable of using your senses to express your message effectively and guide your crew or company through uncertain waters. To do this you must be fairly balanced in four critical areas, three of which involve further *soft-skill development*. We strongly suggest you evaluate potential leadership candidates in the following four areas of human passion. See if you can get a sense of the power, simplicity and beauty in how the following areas can be focused upon and how they can contribute to being a respected leader.

- **Passion for People**: *How can you be a good leader if you don't like people?*

    To lead others, you must come across as empathetic, trustworthy and likeable. These traits will make you seem more authentic and attractive for others to follow your lead. There are many good analytical types out there, but what if they only have it half right? Remember the key to success is *good content* and *actionable delivery*. Leaders must have a high degree of passion and emotion with regard to relating to people as in the end, *it is always and only about people*. Are you attracted to this candidate? If so why?

- **Compassion for Customers**: *How can you be a good leader without being compassionate, curious and empathetic to each customer's **individual situation**?*

    You need to be interested both technically and emotionally in the people who are buying your services and products, *in a positively contagious way*. As a leader, the more your compassion ripples out to those who need to hear and feel it most, the more they will be *attracted to doing business* with you and your company. Do you feel that this candidate sees, hears and understands you?

- **Product/Service Fanatic**: *How can you be a good leader if you don't know your products and services inside and out?*

    A powerful leader must be curious, interested and passionate about the products and/or services your customers are buying, *as well as those your competitors are offering*. You need to be continuously curious, ask about, and engage in the following:
    - What are the future substitutes and/or technologies for your products and services?
    - How can you improve on what you provide?

- **Math Competence**: *Being a good leader means you can count!*

    Being good at math is one thing. Expressing *excitement* when analyzing those numbers is even better! How can you even consider yourself a leader if you cannot calculate whether or not (as well as when) your products will pay off?

    Leaders are employed *to get a team to produce measurable results*. To do this effectively, you must also enjoy being able to connect the numerical dots. How can you expect to navigate effectively unless you can sense (meaning both to *calculate and feel*) the consequences of your decisions and actions. It will be even easier to accomplish and you will produce better results *if you also enjoy the ride*.

In short, costly management assessment and analysis systems may be missing the leadership point. Assessments and evaluations cost both time and money. At this late date, even the most effective ones do not capture these four simple, but critical leadership traits. These traits can be effectively qualified by one person, well versed in them, who asks appropriate questions and *senses* (again using *a balance of both definitions*) the candidate's responses. Furthermore, to make this shift effective, those already in leadership positions in your company must start *singing from the same hymnal* by also praising and applying these four traits. Otherwise, forget about becoming more agile. Your efforts will wind up looking like more inconsequential *bling*. To get this whole process going takes a measurable and sincere effort to train everyone's power and effectiveness in oral, written and body language. This of course, means everyone, *including you*, needs to be more conscious of, and being able to adjust their own message *for maximum efficiency, understanding and action*.

In our fast moving, exciting and volatile world, it is natural that younger and inexperienced (as well as normal hard working) employees are forced to observe and respect the behavior of their leaders. As it is getting wilder out there every day, many "worker bees" *must* often put their *blind trust* in their skippers, because there is little *time for conscious reflection or thinking for yourself*. Therefore, your skipper better know how to navigate the ship and inspire the crew or, by the time the crew does begin questioning their behavior, everyone on board will *risk* going down with the ship!

This book is about the tools and methods needed to create an agile organization. What sets us and this book apart from a standard business book is that your authors heartily agree that, without being able to consciously experience and *genuinely express human emotion*, you *become increasingly disadvantaged*.

Without constant development of your soft-skills, you will lose your ability to engage others and get the results you desire. The days of command and control are rapidly coming to an end! Again, it is always and only about *people*. The more you practice understanding individuals, develop your respect and compassion for their individual emotions and behaviors, *and not just on an intellectual level*, the more powerful, agile *and attractive* you and your organization will become.

El Al provides one of the best examples we have come across of applying the above type of leadership thinking. Their safety success is now reflected in the long and uneventful flight record of Israel's national airline. With a tragic and bloody past, filled with too many hijacking attempts and terrorist attacks, they were forced to think *outside the box*. They instituted a series of simple questions, which enable their specially trained, *and body language conscious* security people to quickly and (as evidence suggests) effectively *sense* each individual passenger's behavior. Since they started this program, they have not had another tragic incident. This is the power and success of leadership by *sensing, using both measurement and feeling*.

37. Tool Nine: Carve-Outsourcing Services (CORE) for Specialized Functions

This tool is a high-level, corporate surgical tool that can be used to gain heightened efficiency through identifying and redeploying non-core operations, This is accomplished by sourcing them to more powerful, pure-play business allies. The result is a higher quality operation and product, with more satisfied and motivated workers, at a lower cost

One widespread premise in modern business has long been that companies increase their competitiveness by *owning the assets that matter most*, in their chosen strategy. Competitive advantage, according to this belief, comes directly from owning and controlling these valuable assets/resources. Historically, these resources have tended to be scarce and needed to be utilized efficiently over long periods of time. They normally used to be company and location specific. Ownership (rather than leasing, renting or outsourcing) frequently appeared (and often still does) to be the best way to ensure exclusivity. But what if now these costly assets are used infrequently or inconsistently?

The decreasing effectiveness of ownership
A powerful and timely discussion has arisen especially since the American Real Estate collapse of 2007. *Is it still better to own?*

Let's start with a house. You may have the title to it, but what good is that if you also have it mortgaged to the hilt *and fall behind on your payments?* What about if you fall behind in your property taxes? So, paper and ego aside, *who really owns your house?*

From a business standpoint, if you add together the accrued interest you pay on your mortgage plus what it costs in taxes and upkeep, *how much does that house really cost to own* compared to the value of its utility?

Could not owning it actually be a better deal?

The same holds true for most of the services you can now outsource. If we just focus on marketing you can now get good advertising copy, SEO optimizing and a professional layout starting from five dollars each on for example, Fiverr.com. Compare that to paying a full time staff and keeping their tools and resources up to date, is *it still better to have these functions in house?*

By increasing transparency and reducing search and transaction costs, digital technology is enabling new and better value-creating consumer models. As a result of this, ownership may have *already become* an inferior and *increasingly unprofitable way* to access and service key assets; and this doesn't include *steadily increasing tax burdens. The* traditional way of doing business is increasingly being replaced by flexible win-win commercial arrangements using partners with better, laser-specific skills and competence.

One of the most controversial examples of building a huge, multibillion-dollar business without owning the assets is Uber. It is basically a skeleton staff and some nifty software that *controls* a multitude of rolling assets and people, namely independent cab drivers. Its per-employee valuation is currently astronomical.

With all the opportunities to minimize cost in all of these areas, one of the most common and accepted solutions is to outsource. Surprisingly, this has become an almost catch-all solution. Yet all too often, it later fails.

From our experience, the most common reasons given for why a chosen outsourcing company ends up being fired always seems to focus on one or more of the following:

- *"They didn't understand the…*
    - *Customers*
    - *Technology*
    - *Products*
    - *Work Culture*
    - *Systems"*
- *"Their established routines took longer than our norms"*
- *"Cost analyses proved that we really could do it ourselves just as cheaply"*

Regardless of the reason for failure, statistics point to up to forty percent of all outsourcing deals currently wind up failing and *costing enormous amounts of time, frustration and money.* The unhappy client often decides to take a step backwards and *insource* the process again. The whole thing becomes at best, a costly embarrassment or at worst, the death of the company. Does this sound like an agile solution to you?

You become the risk
Most companies involved in the outsourcing business normally force their clients to use their proprietary systems and their own *"qualified personnel,"* to ensure that proven and well-defined procedures are precisely followed. Examples of this are SAP, IBM, and Accenture. This is fully understandable, as requiring strict adherence to the system is believed to ensure the project's success. Yet this obvious *covering of your "ass-ets"* approach also offers your chosen outsourcer a juicy opportunity. They can now easily blame any subsequent failures upon *your firm's* inability to grasp the brilliance and effectiveness of *their* system. In other words, you didn't follow their instructions correctly...

Your outsourcer is the hands-down expert at using her own system, but what about their ability to tailor it to meet *your specific needs?* Each point in every one of their suggested guidelines and procedures *can represent* an additional **possible point of failure,** should your way of doing things be found to be at odds with theirs. Also, can you think of any incentive for them *to adjust their system to your needs* compared to you being forced to *adjust your needs to their system?* Will these costs be equally divided? Tragically, most of these points of friction do not show up until long after the contract has been signed and your payments have started.

To effectively handle these concerns and create a win-win collaboration, our trademarked methodology called *Carve-Outsourcing*™ or CORE was developed at Catalyst Acquisition Group LLC and is now available through The Minerva Group. Its basic structure is easy to understand and the following explanation may help prevent you from choosing to outsource with the wrong partner or not fully appreciating the risks if you do.

CORE is particularly efficient in many specialized overhead service functions such as training, event management, conference management, training administration, etc. Companies like Cognizant and Minerva will take on your existing department or parts of it, as well as existing staff, system and products, *as is!* Then, as part of the service, they will upgrade their effectiveness and lease or sell this upgraded service back to you, at or below your current cost level. This ensures that your company can save money, get a much better service *and feel safer during the entire transition.* This also *eliminates much of the precariousness and worry* for those employees in the outsourced department. Also, you can now rest assured that your way of doing business will remain fully understood from day one. Finally, you will be guaranteed that the performance and result will never be worse or more expensive than it has been historically. This is the methodology behind, **Carve-Outsourcing™** or **CORE™**.

A hybrid of the best
CORE™ can be further described as an *optimized hybrid* of three different concepts:

- **Mergers and Acquisitions**, where you merge or purchase a company or group to expand into new territory or enhance what you already do well.
- **Outsourcing** where you farm out an existing task or process to another firm. They handle that responsibility more efficiently because that is where their competence excels.
- **Spin-Offs** where you create a specialized subsidiary that now has more freedom to excel at what it does best. There is also the enhanced opportunity for your former colleagues to test and evaluate new ideas and methods than they ever could have when they were part of your *parent* company.

To increase agility, constant focus needs to be upon the question of who can do each task, product and process faster, better and cheaper. Anchoring this concept in reality, it is important to understand the gravity of the following statement.

Everything we do by ourselves will be anchored in and influenced by our own inhibitors. These consist again of our own internal behaviors, systems, culture, organization and processes. These concerns naturally begin to fade as you enter into your own **CORE™** process.

Here's a quick lesson in how the process works.

Step One, the Audit:
To assure absolute success, you should first perform a specialized audit procedure in each area of interest. We, *of course*, recommend one based upon our Trade Marked **STA+R methodology**. Skip to tool 13 for details.

Step Two, Defining your company's primary role:
It is critical to understand what your company's essential role is in the world. In this step, you will become very clear as to whether your role is to build, implement, market or develop a product or service. Regardless of whether it is producing ball bearings, installing communication equipment, manufacturing bowling pins or

serving fast food, this process will get you and your team crystal clear on a powerful and useable definition of your core business.

Step Three, Efficiencies:
Once defining your role is complete, everything that is not directly related to your core skills and business becomes a candidate to outsource. Objectively, all of these non-essential roles now become potential areas for outsourcing, but due to their more general nature, most overhead functions are the prime candidates.

Thus, **CORE™** increases your agility in the following ways:

- **Pure-Play means increased competence.** Your old department has now become part of a group that has its core competence as its own specialized business model. It now becomes a congruent, *Pure-Play* company. Everyone involved will now get to develop their expertise in their chosen field. This model thus offers a more relevant, challenging and exciting home for your effective and responsible, former employees.
- **World-class Tools.** You can now be assured of up-to-date *Best Practices* and quicker implementation of next generation methodologies and technologies. This is an immediate requirement, as your former colleagues will now also sense their own burning need to *get agile or die*. They are no longer in a company backwater. They now need to actively compete for your business against *best in class* competition, or die trying.
- **Traditional ways of doing things are augmented** with best practices from industry leaders. Petty internal politics and bottlenecks that used to gum up the process have to be wiped away. The result is world-class efficiency, yet with a warm and familiar touch.
- **Conflicts of interest are reduced/eliminated**
  There can no longer be any question of a bureaucratic department head needing to protect pet projects or cover his/her *ass-ets*. Now there is no more dreaming up justifications and excuses for the failure of his/her own decisions.
- **Less overhead and more flexibility**
  The entire department now becomes a recurring expense from an independent company. You should immediately begin to see cost savings in the neighborhood of 25%. Should times get rough, you can scale down your costs or metaphorically "*trim the fat*" without carving into the bone.
- **Increased ability to switch outsourcers**
  You can now switch or alternatively, shut down the whole department or parts thereof, should this separate entity fail to satisfy your needs, wants and

wishes. When things are going well, response time to your requests should be much quicker.

Outsourcing still demands responsibility

It is very important to keep in mind that outsourcing *does not remove your responsibility* for making sure that each outsourced job gets done. For example, should you outsource your IT department to IBM, Cognizant or Minerva, you would be well advised and encouraged to retain an internal manager, a homegrown champion who can monitor and manage ongoing events and activities. This is important in order to guard your ongoing interests.

Some outsourcing examples

Siemens jumped early into the outsourcing boom by moving much of its software development to India. In the early days, this information was then transmitted by satellite at the end of each business day, back to Germany or in many cases directly out to the specific project site. This allowed the company to charge local rates for development services that actually cost much less. This process drastically improved their profits.

In recent software examples, Microsoft's Office 360 is a subscription-based application of its popular smorgasbord office suite of products such as Word, Excel, Publisher, and PowerPoint, with a dessert of free Skype usage. Adobe now offers its products such as Acrobat and Photoshop in a similar fashion. With your subscription, you will get the latest upgrades from these giants directly to your computer as soon as they are available. Google has a similar suite of products, but their price is even better... They are free!

More practically, in most every office, you now have a cleaning company that comes in to keep your office looking fresh and to replenish various consumables in the bathroom and pantry. Most coffee services and many other refreshment, fresh fruit and snack services are delivered on a regular basis from your chosen outsourcer.

Many companies, both large and small, use services like Dropbox and various secure, cloud-based services to handle their data. Basic bookkeeping to full blown cloud-based business systems can make keeping track of your money easier than ever. Computer based services, from having an on-call PC repair person to managing your entire data department, are now available. Need some office help and can't afford to hire someone? No problem. Google the phrase "*Virtual Assistant*" and you will be able to find the exact service you are looking for, often with both reviews, testimonials and a great price. Fiverr is a prime example of a site to find just about anything regarding getting your online message out in a fast, professional way.

Even in shipping, a great example is offered from a June 2015 McKinsey article called, "*Disrupting beliefs: A new approach to business-model innovation*[xlviii]" by Marc De Jong and Menno van Dijk. "*Consider how a big European maritime port embarked on a large scale land management program. The industry belief reframed by the port was that large liquid-bulk-load ships valued private access to storage tanks. The underlying assumption was that shipping companies wanted the ability to deliver their bulk loads anytime and therefore required entry to their tanks at close range.*"

"*In response to this perceived need, most maritime ports have developed jetties to which they provide individual shipping companies private access - essentially the equivalent of "ownership." As a result of each company's varying schedules and traffic, many jetties ended up being mostly unused, but others weren't sufficient for peak times. Seeing this problem, the port's management reframed the industry belief by asking if customers cared more about access on demand than exclusivity. The port now intends to help all customers use any jetty to access any fuel tank, by developing a common-carrier pipe connecting them.*"

Outsourcing is a trend that is just getting started. Finding the correct outsourcer for you first depends upon getting clear upon what you want. Accomplishing only this first, simple step, to get clear on your needs, will give you much more control over the rest of the process and your final result.

38. Tool Ten: Injecting Entrepreneurship

This tool will help you nurture a young, daring spirit of creativity and development even in a large and cautious company.

First, a very important disclaimer and red flag!
Many executives and "*talking heads*" argue that the entrepreneurial spirit is the one and only key to making your company more agile. *This could not be further from the truth!*

Just trying to define *entrepreneurship* correctly can make you dizzy. Some common denominators are: risking your own money, starting up something new, aggressive leadership, vision into action, etc.

Wikipedia states: "*Entrepreneurship is the process of starting a business, typically a start-up company offering an innovative product, process or service*[xlix] *The entrepreneur perceives an opportunity and often exhibits biases in taking the decision to exploit the opportunity. The exploitation of entrepreneurial opportunities includes design actions to develop a business plan, acquire the human, financial and other required resources, and to be responsible for its success or failure.*[2] *Entrepreneurship may operate within an entrepreneurship ecosystem which includes government programs and services that support entrepreneurs, entrepreneurship resources (e.g., business incubators and seed accelerators), entrepreneurship education and training and financing (e.g., loans, venture capital financing, and grants).*"

Does that simplify things for you?

However you define it, entrepreneurship is a powerful, creative force, if directed correctly. A brilliant application of entrepreneurship is, for example, launching a new product or service. Yet, it is not uncommon that an entrepreneur might also turn out to be the most single minded, money driven and inflexible person in the company! Many are later shown to have *no willingness whatsoever*, to move, adjust or accept any agility at all.

So let's define and distinguish the following terms more clearly:

a/ An *entrepreneurial company* is a company without legacy to hinder it in its quest for success

b/ *Business agility* is the ability to change or adjust direction quickly and effectively, *whether you are an entrepreneurial company or not.*

As the skipper, injecting entrepreneurship back into your established corporate structure may be one of your greatest challenges. It is also no wonder that most *successful entrepreneurial leaders* ultimately sell out or hire an agile leader to take over their successful enterprise, once it is up and running. This is usually a wise choice because the personality type that makes a good entrepreneur, more often than not, usually displays the exact opposite behavior needed to maintain growth and stability. At some point, the freedom in unfettered entrepreneurship naturally begins to complicate and conflict with the systems necessary to continue growing. That freedom to think outside the box is what often ignited the company's initial success. As the famous battle for control over Apple's future between founder-entrepreneur Steve Jobs and hired-in manager John Scully reminds us, there are exceptions to the rule and timing does matter. Ultimately, without a continuous, fresh stream of entrepreneurship, emphasis ends up being focused upon caution and maintaining a *business as usual* stance. This persists until the forces of legacy and bureaucratic momentum simply overwhelm yet another *once-successful* company.

Usually, the bigger the company, the larger the entrepreneurial challenge. Large corporations have been struggling for decades to inject entrepreneurship into their organizations. This problem is recognized and is nothing new. Still, many have experienced *the hard way* that newcomers to their market are more agile and much faster with innovation. The result has been that these wide-eyed *newbies* can (and often do) take big chunks of market share and attention quickly. They can introduce faster, better and cheaper products before established companies *even sense a threat.* What if other established industry leaders have so far just been lucky?

We have already talked about established and successful companies and their valiant efforts to become more flexible, many of which failed horribly. Their failures are usually due to ingrained traditions, legacy systems, cultures of mediocrity and processes that all support the *four big inhibitors of change:* IT, Systems and Processes, Organization and (not least) Culture

For anyone used to a large company, it is no secret that entrepreneurs find it difficult to work within the strict, monitored confines of a contemporary corporate structure. Just having to wear an ID badge drives many pure entrepreneurs mad! Yet don't shorter and shorter cycles now demand a more entrepreneurial approach? How can this dichotomy be resolved?

A solution?
Many companies have chosen to create distinct groups, projects and divisions that function separately, *at arm's length*. This deliberately puts distance between company imposed legacy systems and these new *cowboys* tasked by the "*Suits*" to achieve greatness. Sometimes totally separate subsidiaries and entities are created to actually wall off what, in the worst case, could be called *corporate rot*. These rebellious, yet productive groups have been called *Intrapreneurs or Skunk Works*.

The pitfalls of structured entrepreneurship
Having worked with a project orientation all our lives, we see this unshackling and selection of *appropriate individuals* who seem to have the *Right Stuff* as your key to success. Giving them room to run directly contributes to creating profitable entrepreneurship or intrapreneurship.

Having made this point, the question then naturally arises, "*Is entrepreneurship a gift with which you are born, or a trait you can develop through training?*" With practice, determination and the right environment, *anything is possible*. What we have discovered though is that it is much more effective to find those special people who already have that free thinking entrepreneurial spirit. They can usually get up and running in these companies and subsidiaries to produce miracles *at a much quicker pace*. In other words, practice noticing those who are naturally *agile*.

We have also observed that countries, cultures and organizations *blessed* with high levels of entitlement are often *cursed* when it comes to entrepreneurship. In these cultures those naturally gifted entrepreneurs can become uncomfortable and even resist being unleashed. Due to the gravity inherent in oppressive peer pressure, they usually will try to avoid letting go of structure and inhibit the qualities necessary for real entrepreneurship. Unfortunately, acceptance by the crowd usually overwhelms most everyone's spirit for adventure, except for those with the most obsessive and compulsive entrepreneurial behavior.

This reality can further aggravate any future hopes of being both agile and entrepreneurial. How? Easy, the only entrepreneurs who make it through this gauntlet of conformity often become fanatics with tough skin and hardened views of how *entrepreneurship "should be"*. Once they make into a position of power, they have usually trained or been forced to become less agile just to survive without going crazy. Think about it. If you constantly had to argue that your way was the right one, how agile would you still be?

We have mentioned entitlement in a number of situations, but there is still one more. What if it can take the form of a highly unionized environment (France and Sweden are good examples) or highly structured or hierarchical cultures such as Finland and Japan? If everyone in a culture has been brought up doing everything equally or knowing and sticking to their assigned place, how much of a need still exists for free thinking or acting creatively?

Yes, there are always exceptional examples of people who come from these places and thrive on going directly against their societal grain. For instance, some Swedish rebels like Alfred Nobel and one of Skype's founders Niklas Zennstrom became fabulously rich and successful in spite of their environment. Keep in mind though that their entrepreneurial behavior is far from that of the normal Swedish worker attitude. Yet, even this well-established norm of mediocrity could be changing,

Younger Swedes are beginning to sense how precarious their chances actually are of getting and holding a "real job." They are beginning to sense that they will probably not be benefiting from the established (and deteriorating) welfare system in a way that equals to what they are currently forced to contribute.

Entrepreneurship in these rigid or traditional environments is often viewed as a threat to the status quo and quite rightly so! Sweden's social cost structure is still primarily set up to handle the decreasing Salariat. For instance, one of your authors has learned *the hard way* that an entrepreneur that has a run of bad luck for more than one year can be ostracized from standard unemployment and sick leave benefits. In this case, both Swedish Unemployment and Sick Leave System payments are directly based upon what you made in the past year. If you have a rough year or two you often wind up having paid into a pool of funds that you will now find impossible to access. Even in the most effective welfare system on the planet you can still fall through the cracks, especially if you have an entrepreneurial bent.

Therefore, it often takes either lots of guts, blind luck, a bit of stubborn stupidity, or a mixture thereof to dare to start your own company. This is especially foolish if you have a weak business plan or find it tough to articulate why people should buy your product. Still, for an increasing number of us, the taste of freedom that entrepreneurship provides is still too tempting to go back to a standard nine-to-five job or, many (who have been laid off or unemployed for a while) *simply have no other choice.*

Brainstorming the Intrapreneurial Process:
Starting this process is best accomplished through a series of workshops followed by an action plan, implementation and follow up, which includes coaching or mentoring to make sure your plan sticks.

Workshop 1. *Uncovering Entrepreneurial Potential*
This is a workshop designed to uncover entrepreneurial talents, brainstorm on how to optimize them, to further open up and allow for entrepreneurial practices into your organization. This is a brainstorming *free for all*, where everyone can contribute to a "*Christmas wish list*" of:

- what is needed
- what they are able to contribute
- what they would like to do
- what they see as possible/impossible and why?

Workshop 2. *Identify, Agree and Implement*
This second workshop takes the next practical step. Its purpose is to identify candidate areas, to agree upon which of them offer the most potential and would be easiest to implement into this new way of working. The workshop then winds up with participants mapping out the steps of a realistic implementation plan.

Once you have decided and agreed upon where entrepreneurial practices would be most effective and welcome, it is time to create your action plan. This is where you specify what the real goals will look like. You will now endeavor to find someone who will not only be personally responsible for this achievement, but burns to champion the process. The final piece of the puzzle is setting up and agreeing upon measurable, manageable deadlines with this champion.

Its implementation:
Implementing a solid strategic, entrepreneurial plan can help energize and optimize those newly discovered people and resources. It will point them directly towards your customers' needs, wants and wishes, as well as how to better highlight deficiencies in the organization. Once an action plan is agreed upon it is time to break the deadlines down into a timetable and assign a tight budget to these "*Intrapreneurs*" and "*Skunk Workers*." Then and MOST IMPORTANTLY, take a

conscious and visible *managerial* step back and allow these now officially sanctioned *rebels* the freedom to do what they love.

Coaching entrepreneurship to success

Remember, "*You manage things and you lead people.*" – Grace Hopper (again). Good leadership often has as much to do with being the silent *space* (where others can boldly create) as it does actively encouraging others with what to do. Although there is a critical need for a clear strategy and measurable objectives, once they are established it is time to let go and trust these creative individuals. *Dare yourself* to allow *their* process to unfold *in their chosen way*. Keep your eye on agreed upon goals and their timetables.

Trying to babysit this group of unleashed entrepreneurial cowboys will compress that freedom that you have just committed to sanctioning. This will be seen as raw betrayal and will succed in killing any future trust in the value of your word. To help anchor and cultivate this new, entrepreneurial way of thinking you now need to back off and coach them instead. The more you give them the trust, responsibility and freedom they desire, the quicker you will receive back the result *everyone wants*.

Learn to coach.

- Practice asking reflective questions
- Listen with all your senses to what is said and not said
- Encourage them to think for themselves
- Complement good ideas
- Openly acknowledge all milestones that are achieved.
- Reward good results

Then watch your team become more self-inspired and engaged to achieve greatness!

A sneaky, but effective tip in the accompanying managerial process to minimize internal resistance is to call these entrepreneurial undertakings *projects*. This is in lieu of going full out and starting other departments or creating separate companies. Calling them projects makes it much easier for those cautious peoplein your organization (who have invested a lot of their career in your company's traditions and legacies) to more easily swallow this new way of working.

Using this little trick, these dedicated yet conservative team members can then relax their guard and let these new projects do their thing, on a longer, but still visible leash. The trick here is that it is often easier for those in your organization, who are used to structure and limits, to *accept a project* instead of just letting go of it completely. By definition, time and resources are always limited in a project. Therefore, these cautious decision makers can now feel a bit more comfortable. This way they still feel they retain some practical means to *pull the plug, if needed*. Chances are though that they probably wouldn't dare.

The pitfalls of entrepreneurship/intrapreneurship

Yet beware! Should your company try populating these new, faster, more creative ventures with legacy prone employees, they can quickly strangle any entrepreneurial spirit that may have begun to blossom. Experience teaches that freedom, *combined with responsibility*, encourages powerful entrepreneurship. The more you try and shackle your workers, *even with accepted and popular programs such as TQM or Lean*, the more you will ultimately force them a into process that they consider constraining, irrelevant and sometimes plain silly. If you do, count on them leaving!

Entrepreneurial success

Look no further than Google to see a brilliant implementation of intrapreneurship. Somehow, they have managed to grow into a major corporation without losing their corporate ability to think like entrepreneurs. Hewlett Packard was another success story, which was started in a garage by two entrepreneurs. Over time, this once great company seems to have lost touch with its entrepreneurial roots.

Apple is a microcosm of the pluses and minuses of this whole discussion. This company started as an entrepreneurial success story with Steve Jobs and Steve Wozniak at the helm. It began to grow faster than they could "manage." To their initial credit, a successful and *traditional manager*, John Scully from Pepsi was then called in to run it. A titanic clash of cultures and egos developed, pitting entrepreneurship against *business as usual*. It almost crushed the company. *Business as usual* won out for a time, when Scully successfully engineered a coup and threw Jobs out. Just a few years later, Scully's strategy was found wanting, then it faltered completely. An older and more experienced Jobs was then called back in, With his entrepreneurial genius now seasoned with better management skills, the rush to current Apple greatness began. It will be interesting to see how Tim Rice fares in Apple's next chapter, which is unfolding as this is written.

These stories are not as unique as you would think. An entrepreneurial visionary has started many successful companies. The biggest difference between Hewlett and Packard, Jobs and Wozniak and today's entrepreneurs is the pace of their success. Zuckerberg's Facebook, Zennerströms Skype achieved billion-dollar success and these individuals achieved heroic celebrity *in less than ten years*! That blistering pace is on track to increase even more quickly, going forward.

Entrepreneurship's missing link; passion

The most important lubricant in creating a well-oiled and outstanding team of Entre- or Intrapreneurs is *passion*. The ability to express and bring alive that for which you *burn*. The more you encourage them to let their passion loose, the more they can put that exciting and contagious feeling into their work. The best way to encourage others to unleash their passion is to relax, then constantly and contagiously *practice unleashing your own.*

Expansion versus compression

An important key to uncovering how much of this entrepreneurial lubricant can be found is by observing behavior. Is your team's behavior relaxed and expansive or tense and compressed? The freer and more expansively the team moves and communicates, the more room they usually sense to express themselves. The more room they have to express themselves, the more fun they can have while successfully solving the challenges at hand.

The opposite is true also. If you observe your team of entrepreneurs looking tense or you sense a feeling of compression, it is high time to act! If you notice them just doing their jobs, with little or no self-expression or walking around with their heads down, locate the source of their resignation immediately. Be aware, it can and often is you! Hesitate, *even for a moment*, and you may end up with sub-par results, lose your best cowboys to the competition and often both.

Entrepreneurial mergers and acquisitions

As we mentioned in part two, we see a rise in mergers and acquisitions going forward, *but not in the traditional sense.* The new M&A model will be much quicker and more entrepreneurial. Many enabling tools have been developed to enhance agility such as DDR (Digital Data Rooms). Another good example of such a service is DataSite.

Motivations for quick M&A

This new era of agility will push corporations and institutions to further consider M&A as a primary area for growth. This trend actually started long ago. Many people do not know that most of Microsoft's incredible growth has been made via M&A. Their strategy, sometimes referred to as *embrace and devour,* pretty much sums up finding something good and acquiring it. In Sweden, the Electrolux Group was more or less re-created by Hans Werthen as an M&A growth machine. In the future, many companies will look to an M&A solution instead of trying to be agile enough in their own so-called *core business*. In its extreme, this strategy will make many corporations look more like some agile and effective Private Equity (PE) firms like *Platinum Equity Holdings*. They may even come to resemble traditional conglomerates. Many will focus on synergies in *distribution and branding* rather than in the traditional cost area of *scale, technology and production*. This in turn, will also require equal agility in being able to identify and divest slow moving portfolio companies. Stragglers that drag down the average growth of the whole group.

As with all other non-core functions, internal M&A departments are also the victims of the *Big Four inhibitors of change*. We therefore envision an increased move towards outsourcing even for these internal M&A departments to specialized providers. There they can be much more cost and time effective. For companies faced with M&A opportunities, many factors need to be considered, including:

- Finding candidates with adequate compatibility to merge with or acquire
- The global impact of the arrangement
- The likelihood of a quick and painless negotiation process

The dealmakers – those entrepreneurial front-line workers, who spearhead these deals – must address all of these factors and others in order to successfully broker these M&As.

Decision makers, prospective investors and investment banks currently have a very few tools to provide a quick assessment of a proposed deal. That is without spending (or wasting) too much time and energy on minutia. To help, we offer the *accretion / dilution analysis*.

What is Accretion / Dilution analysis and its value?

The answer to this question is the following question: "*Does the proposed deal increase or decrease the post-transaction earnings per share (EPS)?*"

This fairly simple analysis determines the justification for the deal. The steps are:

- Estimate a pro forma net income for the combined entities
- Calculate the combined company's new share count
- Divide pro forma net income by pro forma shares to arrive at a pro forma Earnings Per Share or EPS.
- Double-check the accuracy of your numbers

Is the calculated pro forma EPS higher than the original EPS?

An increase to EPS is regarded as *accretion*, while a decrease is regarded as *dilution*. Many on Wall Street typically frown at dilutive transactions. If the deal has a reasonable likelihood of turning accretive from the second year onwards, the proposed business combination may be more palatable.

Accretion / dilution analysis is often seen as a proxy for whether or not a contemplated deal creates or destroys shareholder value. It is a very simple, but practical tool to have handy.

Is there vulnerability in agility?

In western culture the word *vulnerability* is often associated with being weak. Many also see it as a negative personality trait. We have sometimes even used this generally accepted way of defining it in this very book!

What if this is not the whole story either? What if vulnerability actually demonstrates your capacity to relax and be ready for everything? What if it defines your ability to have all your physical and mental resources ready, willing and able to handle whatever threat or opportunity presents itself, here and now?

This is how a true master of martial arts treats vulnerability. Just as you can catch more money in an open and relaxed palm compared to a tight and straining fist, so can you increase your chances to be agile, if you stay vulnerable and keep all your resources at the ready! How many more threats and opportunities will you be able to see and respond to *with increased agility* if you practice being vulnerable?

Why is this fuzzy-sounding soft-skill so important in this age of agility? Because the more energy you use, straining to prevent or anticipate threats and opportunities, the higher the risk becomes that you may get tired and miss an important cue. You need to be able to focus on or avoid the less important ones. This can be on a personal as well as corporate level. One wise man who also happened to be my father, Birger Amell, once said, "The size of a man is often shown by the size of the things that upset him." The Point he was making was that too much energy is spent getting upset over or worrying aboutthe wrong or petty things.

Lean Startup

What is Lean Startup?
Below is another angle to encourage agility and entrepreneurship and is penned by friend and colleague, **Andy Cars,** founder of Lean Ventures and Seedcap.

"As a term, *lean startup* was first used in 2008. It was coined by Eric Ries on his blog *Startup Lessons Learned*, in a post titled *The lean startup*. Lean startup has its roots amongst high-tech start-ups in Silicon Valley, but has since been adopted by start-ups worldwide, and has also won great acclaim amongst large established companies and organizations such as General Electric, Telefonica, BBC and even the United States Government, to name a few.

But before we get ahead of ourselves, let us start by defining the meaning of *lean* and *startup*. All too often we talk past each other without understanding the meaning of the words we use. For example, have you ever stopped to ask yourself and your colleagues how they interpret the words *lean, startup* or *innovation* - words often used but seldom understood?

Traditionally *lean* is associated with the Toyota Production System, Total Quality Control and Six Sigma, where the focus is on reducing waste and the number of errors that occur during manufacturing. However in *lean startup*, being *lean* means to use the least amount of resources whilst iterating towards a solution that addresses the customer's most pressing problems significantly better than competing alternatives. It is not about streamlining or incrementally improving the existing production system; it is about finding out what to build in the first place.

When it comes to the often misused word *startup*, the accepted definition in the startup community, comes from Stanford Professor Steve Blank, and reads as follows:

> "*A startup is a temporary organization designed to search for a scalable and repeatable business model.*"

What this means is that a *startup* does not know *who* the customer will be, *what* the final product or service will look like, *how* to price the offering, or *how* to best reach their customers. What *startups* have are a bunch of assumptions.

While a startup is *searching* for a business model that works, an established company is fully occupied with *executing* on a finely tuned business model that figuratively speaking generates $ 2 for every $ 1 that is put in. Yes, we are talking about the golden cash cow that established companies tend to protect until their dying days.

The differences between *searching for a business model* and *executing on a business model* are as significant as night and day and affect everything from metrics, methods and tools to recruitment, incentives, leadership and definition of risk. And this is where *lean startup* comes into the picture. *Lean startup* is both a methodology (or set or methods) and a mind-set that fundamentally differs from "business as usual."

The overall process is often illustrated in its most basic form as shown here (borrowed from Eric Ries book *The Lean Startup*, published in September of 2011.)

Lean startup is data- and experiments driven, where the aim is to turn assumptions into validated learnings as fast and efficiently as possible.

Lean startup advocates a *fail fast - fail often* mind-set in order to gradually learn and understand more about the pain points and constraints that the customer is experiencing.

The goal is to achieve a so-called *problem/solution fit*, i.e. we have something that the customer wants, and ultimately *product/market fit*, i.e. we have something that the customer is willing to pay for and where the cost of recruiting a new customer is significantly lower than what we can earn from that customer. Or put differently, to build a sustainable business, Customer Acquisition Costs have to be significantly lower than Customer Lifetime Value (CAC < CLV).

The key is to learn what works and what does not, as opposed to prematurely executing on the wrong business model. According to the data scientists at *The Start-up Genome Project*[i], the number one reason why start-ups fail is because they scale-up too early. Since scaling burns money like nothing else, scaling before reaching *product/market fit*, only results in a deeper hole in someone's pocket. While sales may very well increase, profitability will remain elusive.

Fundraising to promote something that the market does not want is a sure recipe for disaster. Boo.com, Webvan, Better Place and Pets.com[li], are only a few examples of failed start-ups that chose scaling to capture market share over providing customer value. They ended up burning hundreds of millions of dollars of other people's money in the process.

As always, the devil is in the details. Doing customer interviews in a way that introduces large amounts of biased data, or only relying on quantitative data while ignoring qualitative data, will only cloud judgement and increase the chance of failure. Since the most likely scenario is for the initial business idea or model not to rhyme with the market, *lean startup* practitioners do not spend valuable time writing thirty-page business plans with five-year Excel projections to boot.

Instead we quickly list our assumptions about the market on a *business model canvas* [lii]. Then we identify the riskiest assumption that if it were not to hold true, would kill the business idea. Next, the focus shifts to turning the assumption to be tested into a measurable hypothesis. We design our experiment and set a target for what we hope to achieve. Then we "*get out of the building*" and run the experiment. Based on what we learn, we update our business model canvas. All of which can be done within one week. Compare that to most large companies that take several weeks just to call a meeting in which the HPPO (The Highest Paid Person's Opinion) often prevails over a data-driven approach.

If the assumption is not verified (which is the most likely scenario) we start from scratch with a new experiment - and keep at it until slowly but surely (or as long as the funding will take us) we crawl towards something that the market wants and is prepared to pay for.

The experiments are often referred to as *MVPs (Minimum Viable Products)* or *MVEs (Minimum Viable Experiments)*. MVPs are used to test for *user engagement* and MVEs for *initial user interest*. Similarly, prototypes are used to answer the question "Can we build it," while *pretotypes*[liii] are used to answer the question "Should we build it." By putting a pretotype in front of customers, e.g. paper sketches, explainer videos or landing pages that communicate the value proposition, we can test for and measure initial user interest. Since the aim is to use the minimum amount of resources possible to maximize learning about the most risky assumptions, the pecking order should be *pretotypes* and *MVEs* followed by *prototypes* and *MVPs*.

There are many who have helped to develop *lean startup* to where it is today. The *Business Model Canvas*, which has become a key element of *lean startup*, was first presented by *Alexander Osterwalder* and *Yves Pigneur* in their book *Business Model Generation*, published in 2010.

Ash Maurya introduced his own version of the *Business Model Canvas*, which he calls the *Lean Canvas* in his book *Running Lean*, published in 2012. Another *Business Model Canvas* variation is the so-called *Javelin*, also known as the *Validation or Experiment board*, developed by Trevor Owens, founder of the Lean Startup Machine.

On the metrics side, Dave McClure, founder of the *500 Start-ups* accelerator program has contributed to the ever-growing *lean startup* toolbox with his *Startup Metrics for Pirates*, which Alistair Croll and Benjamin Yoskovitz then elaborated on in their book *Lean Analytics*, published in 2013.

The above examples show that *lean startup* is a set of methods and tools under constant development, but with the distinction that they all share one common mind-set, namely that of disciplined data-driven experimentation in direct contact with the customer to quickly and economically find a business model worth scaling.

Those who are the most creative in designing and running experiments to obtain validated learning, will be those who are the most likely to succeed. Remember, everything is an experiment.[16]

---

16 Find Andy at: www.andycars.branded.me

39. Tool Eleven: DNS and the Strategic Triangle

*T*his is another simple balancing tool, which is an easy and effective reminder to aim your sights on the forward horizon, instead of in the rear-view mirror as you sail.

Strategic plans are very often overdeveloped in some areas and underdeveloped in others. This phenomenon can easily be traced to Globalization. Globalization increases the pressures resulting from greater competition and thus *increases the subsequent focus on cutting costs*. This phenomenon has drastically expanded over the last few decades in lock step with the explosion of global competition. In many cases, costs have been cut way past the fat, through the muscle and deep into the bones of many companies. This directly limits their capacity, resources and ability to plan ahead at all. *How can you expect a company to become or remain agile in this weak and emaciated situation?*

To regain a balanced planning perspective, we offer you our *Strategic Triangle*. From the three rings of *customer, company and competitors* you can create a clearer and more balanced path towards your stated objectives.

From now on, your strategy should equal the harmony of your own:

- **Optimized Company resources** to efficiently meet...
- **Customer demand** vis-a-vis customer alternatives, the...
- **Competition** using...
- **Strategy** and tactics to describe how to handle it

When this formula is accepted and implemented, you can begin placing relatively equal amounts of energy into these distinct areas. Once again it is our experience, drawn from analyzing strategic reports and plans offered from most of our clients, that there is a chronic imbalance between these four factors. In fact, it is not uncommon to see eighty percent of management's time, energy and resources spent on internal issues, ten percent customer concerns, one percent on the competitive environment and, the remaining just 9% on directional or strategic decisions.

Our experience suggests that optimal agility is attained when this situation is rebalanced closer to a thirty, thirty, thirty and ten percent split. Metaphorically, this is in terms of total calories burnt in the different areas (See figure below)

Figure 27 The Strategic Triangle

The Test
The quickest and most effective test to measure the weighting of these areas in your current plan is simple. Just take a printed copy of your current business plan,

separate these three sections from each other and then simply weigh the paper contents of each. Each section's comparative physical weight will provide a quick, but reliable indication of the *weighting* you have placed on each of these important strategic components in your current plan. In fact, most CEO's find this simple test both refreshing and appreciated. It demonstrates a classic, visible case of "*not seeing the trees because of the forest.*"

This simple test makes it obvious, even to the *Highest Paid People's Opinions*, that unless you have a balanced plan, it is virtually impossible to focus on thinking forward. It is also important to note that once this rebalancing is complete, up to 70% of company energy will now be used to *make your strategic report more forward looking.*

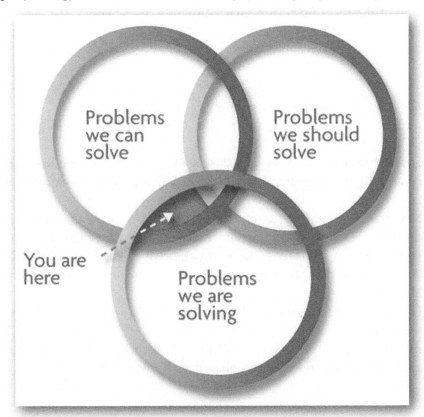

Figure 28 Problems to solve, such as transforming bureaucratic traits to agile traits

Ample examples exist of misguided strategies impeding and even crushing companies. Dig deep enough and rest assured that every company has a horror story about some misguided strategy that is based upon looking backwards while planning forward. The eventual outcome is that these plans almost always fail during their execution.

One classic story is a short-lived company named Osborne Computer. In the Wild West environment of the PC's introduction in the early 1980s, Adam Osborne produced the first portable computer called the Osborne One. Flushed with success and while still producing the Osborne One in quantity, the company couldn't wait to boast of its new and improved version. Osborne then made the strategic and now classic blunder of announcing, with appropriate fanfare, the new Osborne Two model. Predictably for most, potential Osborne One customers naturally decided to wait and buy the new and improved Osborne Two. This quickly drove the company out of business before the large inventory of Osborne Ones could be sold. From start to finish, this whole process lasted only thirty months and destroyed one of the most promising new companies in Silicon Valley. This fiasco is now actually referred to as, "*The Osborne Effect*"[liv] and is the reason Apple and others never preannounce new products.

Benefits of a strong DNS and consequences of a weak DNS
It is not only Osborne. Below are some other fun facts about agile organizations:

- Fortyseven percent of the pre-2000 leaders (ranked in the top twenty percent of hi-tech industry) lost their leadership positions during the 2000-2002 recession
- New leaders emerged after the recession. They were the agile firms that quickly reacted to economic and industry shifts, cutting costs quickly and smartly. *Former* industry leaders lost their placement by not cutting costs as selectively, delaying important product improvements and marketing investments
- Decisive management moved early, which led to improvement in competitive standing. New, post-recession leaders were thirty percent more likely to make acquisitions in the heart of the recession and their deals were thirty seven percent larger than the post-recession laggards

40. Tool Twelve: STA+R Training Analysis

Note: The STA+R Analysis tool can be used for many other applications than those described below, but since we ourselves have used it with great success in training, we have chosen to focus on this area as our example in this book.

The Systematic Training Audit and Recommendations tool is a powerful auditing process that provides a clear, measurable handle for what a department or function delivers in value, compared to best practices, plus it suggests recommendations.

We have already seen that your internal training department should not be part of your company's core product *unless* your core product is training. Regardless of whether you make ball bearings, planes, books or software, you are probably very good at that and only marginally good at planning, executing and improving your training. Education is a craft that is now readily available from many external sources and is offered on an enormous variety of delivery platforms.

In today's uncertain business environment, combined with the shorter life-cycles of new products and services, training, *especially product specific training*, has now become a dangerous bottleneck. The current mind set that clouds the effectiveness of this type of training is that; *you cannot develop or start training until what you want to sell is developed and ready for market.* How can it any longer be acceptable to develop and distribute training for a year (only after the product is complete), when the product cycle you are training for may only survive for one or two? Even so, common sense still screams that you have to develop the product or service first, in order to *even know* what you need to train. Only then can you train. Isn't that right?

Right or wrong has now become a moot point. Waiting for the training until afterwards is no longer an option. Development and production cycles are getting squeezed to shorter and shorter lengths, forcing new solutions. Current business practices now demand that your training cycle be quickened or your edge will be lost. This situation is not helped by the usual coziness of an internal training department nestled snugly, deep within HR. In this configuration, training remains more of an administrative function than the marketing tool it is now absolutely needs to be.

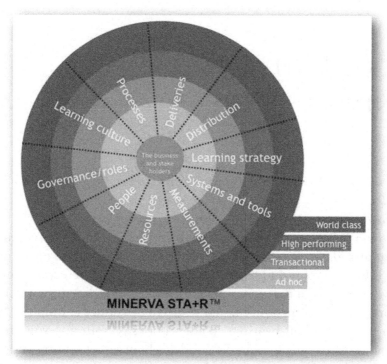

Figure 29 STA+R diagram

What to do?

To facilitate getting a handle on this training challenge, we would like to offer you a peek into a unique process we have developed called *Systematic Training Audit and Recommendations* or **STA+R** for short. It is a fairly complex process and one of our most effective tools, yet the fundamental components we list below can help you to get clearer head start on your challenge and how to tackle it.

First of all, it is important to distinguish the different types of training that are currently offered in the corporate sphere. This may help to highlight some forms that your current program may not yet address.

- **Introductory training:** This is offered internally for new company employees in order to ramp them up as quickly as possible. It provides

rules, guidelines, tips and tricks to get going quickly. Good introductory training also provides tips on how to avoid making predictable, costly mistakes.
- **General basic internal training**. Once you are in and settled, the next step is to get efficient. This is used to get everyone on the same page in your organization. It then goes into depth as to what is now expected of you. Written and unwritten cultural issues should be included to help familiarize everyone and to help dispel persistent myths and rumors. How to use the internal network, the dos and don'ts of security, the company mail and other communication systems are addressed.
- **Compliance training**. These training programs are broader in nature and provide information needed for dealing with global rules and universal standards.
- **Open, generic programs.** These are generic content programs to get you up and running on specific software or equipment used in your office. The most common would be training for standard software packages such as Oracle, Word, Adobe, etc.
- **Company specific training**. These courses are specific, not generic in their format. They are tailored or specially developed to support and promote efficiency on products and services, specifically designed or customized for use by for instance, your sales force or back office.
- **Customer specific programs** These connect your customers with your products, services or company. They are designed to not only make your customers' lives easier, but should also encourage them to cooperate and collaborate more with you. Executed correctly, this training will help you create and maintain your customers' loyalty. Done with excellence, what your customers experience will then naturally ripple out via their word of mouth while it handily and cheaply boosts your marketing message.

With the exception of open, generic, *off the shelf* training and possibly compliance training (usually offered by the governing body of those standards), each one of these areas can be developed into an important key to your company's success. It is essentially an avenue of growing importance for communication and marketing. It is a direct avenue that goes straight into your customers' thoughts and actions. Think of how easily training can become a bottleneck if it is not fresh and of the highest quality. Think of the damage possible if it becomes some corporate bureaucrat's political claim to fame? With all the other issues we have talked about on your plate, how can you handle this effectively also?

If you are looking for increased agility, you will probably need some sort of process, function, or reliable group with which to outsource. Before you can tackle this question internally or even think of outsourcing this too, you need to familiarize yourself with what to look for. Below are our suggestions.

Systematic Training Audit and Recommendations
This is done most effectively as a project consisting of interviews, workshops, coaching and analysis. A neutral third party is highly recommended to perform the process.

1. **Clarify company goals and objectives:**
   Is this beginning to sound familiar? Obviously, before you start out on any trip you need to decide where you are going. Sit down with those responsible and *define your goal in a specific and measurable way*. Describe what each program is meant to achieve. Those responsible can often include many other representatives *outside of your Training* or HR department.

2. **Discovery:**
   This is where you roll up your sleeves and look at the nuts and bolts of each program. You uncover the input and follow its development all the way to the results produced. You play the role of detective to discover differences and gaps between the amounts of *calories* invested in training compared to those returned. This can be done by gathering relevant data and conducting appropriate interviews to provide a subjective feel.

3. **Current state analysis:**
   Now it is time to get to work and create an effective gap analysis between what is actually happening, the results being produced and then *compare it to the best practices* within your industry. This is a rather complex task but even so, a relatively rough analysis can be created quickly even by you and your internal group. Google is an incredible source of information. Results from Google taken with a grain of salt and mixed with the experience of those responsible can produce a fairly accurate assessment.

4. **Recommendations:**
   Then it is time to present your findings. The purpose is to repair any imbalances or weaknesses uncovered. From all you have read so far, the size and scope of the role your marketing department can *and should* play a drastically bigger roll in this development process. The current compared to optimal effect of marketing should become fairly apparent. Keep in mind that the best "AHA" experience usually starts as an "*OH NO!*", or "*Is THAT why*" experience. This is

progress too, as before this you were not even aware of what you were missing. This step ends when everyone is in agreement and an action plan is drawn up.

5. **Implementation and follow up:**
   Then it is time for the responsible people to act and begin hitting the specified milestones in your Action Plan. The progress made here should also be easy to graphically depict and display in your *Dynamic Navigational Center or DNC (see the next tool)*. The same rules and need for simple displays of output apply for this project as all others in your DNC Pilothouse.

If this process sounds a bit challenging, that is probably because it is. The program that we created is complex on many different levels and has taken years to refine. Why?

Because creating and maintaining a world-class training offering, encompassing all the different categories of training necessary to compete globally, requires a lot of time, energy and money. Just some of the areas that need to be addressed are your learning culture, strategies, distribution and measurements. The key to get even slightly better results is following these steps. *To get world-class results will require the help of a specialist.*

Indeed, getting a good grip on just these areas *internally first*, will give you more control of the situation and a powerful and agile leg up on your competition. It is absolutely worthwhile doing. Once done, you will probably want to sharpen your edge further, possibly on a regular basis. This is especially true if you are serious about mastering the path of training agility.

41. Tool Thirteen: Setting up your virtual or physical DNC

This is not a tool so much as it is graphically clear, simple and measurable evidence that your plan to master agility is being implemented. This is the undeniable proof that your plan is working or needs to be acted upon immediately.

One of, if not *the* most powerful part of becoming and remaining agile is constantly practicing with the tools and methods described here. The more you use them the more agile you will become. Not using them will also have consequences. If you are now beginning to see the value in applying these tools, then what's the best way to continue? By keeping a simple, graphical representation of your progress in your crew's face.

This is done by building your own *Dynamic Navigational Center*, pilothouse or **DNC** for short. This is a great way to visibly keep these powerful tools from collecting dust. Just as on a ship, the DNC is your command center. What you observe in your DNC is the real-time graphical depiction of all your agility projects and initiatives important for your success as The Skipper. All the current, relevant information you need to run an agile organization should be clearly found here. This information will give you a clear view not only on your past results, but in ALL directions especially for what lies ahead.

It is from this physical room where you, as the responsible captain, and your crew will guide your ship towards its destination. Just as with a car or our beloved sailing yacht, the vast majority of instruments and tools located here are focused upon the present situation and often go further looking forward. Looking forward makes just as much practical sense when steering a company as it does when steering a ship.

Normally, a typical corporate dashboard configuration will contain anywhere between sixty to eightyfive percent historical (yes, backward looking) indicators. They measure your wake, but say little or nothing about the iceberg, storm or smooth sailing dead ahead. How could you, as Captain, honestly expect to maintain control of a large sailing ship or company if you are looking backwards sixty to eightyfive percent of the time? You are fooling yourself and endangering your crew and your customers if you naiively believe you are in control.

Key Performance Indicators (KPIs) fall neatly into this very common trap. Just like an athlete's statistics, KPIs measure what *has been,* instead of looking forward towards what could be. Again, looking back *is very human,* as looking back is quantifiable history and we should naturally learn from the past. Add to this that the information from the horizon can often be anywhere from overwhelming to scary. Therefore, both you and your crew have no doubt created a slew of unconscious habits, justifications and reasons *not* to monitor it. Today's CEO is still constantly bombarded with internal politics, corporate politeness and energy draining bureaucracy. All of these and more are designed to maintain a safe, comfortable, blind and unwavering course of *business as usual.* The reality is that they chew up enormous amounts of company time, energy and money without making any forward progress. In short, your very own DNC Pilothouse will directly eliminate all the *corporate bullshit* that can and will thwart the ultimate success of your enterprise.

Therefore, placing the results of your *Dynamic Navigational System,* in an easily understood format, where those directly responsible can see them, will be a constant and *in-your-face* reminder of your collective commitment to mastering business agility. By making these tools and their results visible and then updating them in real time, you directly transform agile management tools into a *Dynamic Navigational Center* or as we call it, your *Pilothouse.* Below are the steps to setting one up in your headquarters.

- **Step One**: Choose which tools you want to use from the selection of DNS tools in this book *or other forward-looking tools* that you find effective.
- **Step Two**: Find a small, secure, empty room as close to management and the CEO's office as possible. Go ahead and actually rename it *The Pilothouse.*
- **Step Three**: Populate your pilothouse with visual and graphical displays or charts that clearly and simply depict the output from those tools. The simpler and easier these visualizations are to read and understand, the harder it will be to avoid or downplay their raw, graphical truth.
- **Step Four**: Find a reliable, committed, up-and-coming junior manager from each relevant department. These will be from Marketing, Sales, Finance, Production and HR and will vary depending upon the tools selected.

Charge each of these designated champions with consistently updating the information provided, in the desired and agreed upon format. Take the necessary steps to make sure they understand the importance of delivering unedited or non-massaged data. Until everyone understands and is committed to this new way of working, the possibility of interception and tampering with the input to mask or hide a real or perceived problem needs to be expected and guarded against.

- **Step Five**: Place a conference table in your pilothouse and begin holding formal and informal meetings there *as often as possible*. This will greatly encourage other decision makers to have more and more meetings there too. Now all participants will have instant access to the latest information. All will be able to see how the situation looks historically, here and now, as well as going forward, *from their perspectives*. Providing this information will automatically force your team to become more agile. How? *Your managers will no longer be able to waste precious time* hiding behind, "*I'll get back to you with that information*," because it is now clearly and sometimes annoyingly in front of everyones' noses.

What is the value gained from your Pilothouse?

- **You are now the skipper** of your organization's future, not just its historian. You now have control of your ship's helm, *not just its logbook*. You and your crew now have all the current, graphical information necessary to effectively run the ship, spread clearly out before you.

    Starting now, you and your crew will be able to directly *respond* to threats and opportunities, *in real time*. Remember, responsible means the *ability to respond* and now you *can respond* directly, here and now.
- **In your face information**. No longer is there anywhere to hide for those responsible. The information on the charts that surround you tells the simple, unedited, non-political and current truth. Either the person responsible for the data can interpret it, explain it and present a plan to fix or improve it, or it is high time to replace him/her with someone who burns for this type of agile leadership.
- **An increased level of responsibility**. Having an ambitious person from each department responsible for regularly updating the displayed information will light a real fire under their manager in charge to act upon it, NOW! No leader likes to look inadequate, especially in front of a subordinate charged with providing reliable information. This will usually encourage even laggards to either shape up or wash out quickly. It will also strengthen your bench.

- **Meeting times will diminish**, as most opinions especially all HPPO's will be neutralized. Clear, simple and easy to understand information will negate the need for endless discussion, justification, positioning and politics. Precious minutes will be used instead of hours to decide, act and start measuring anew. The time saved will be massive and cumulative, as decisions and course changes can now be taken in real-time. Already at the next meeting changes in the charts will support the change or call for even more corrective measures.
- **The transformational effect** upon the agility of your crew should quickly become visible. Decision makers will have to practice and master thinking on their feet. They will learn to make changes directly and to be directly responsible for their actions and consequences. So when you look at the information and realize, for example, that:
    - The competition is eating our lunch
    - Sales margins are rapidly decreasing
    - Training costs are increasing while customer satisfaction is decreasing.

  Then you can go directly to the source, call on those responsible for direct answers, get briefed on what steps are planned and what date and time you can expect the problems to be corrected. Then leave and follow up *at the appointed time.*
- **Confidence in Management will increase** as visible decisions and actions will replace rumors and speculation. People can comfortably and efficiently focus on their tasks rather than the latest water cooler chatter.

Also, when all agree that the charts depict smooth sailing ahead, the second in command can calmly replace the skipper, who can then practice mastering the art of a well-deserved break.

An effective tip: *The DNC can also be operated as a project.* This will make the changes easier to swallow for the obvious or covert bureaucrats in your management team. Reactions to this decision and resistance (often from the usual suspects) to it will also send an early flag up to monitor those whose behaviors seem to inhibit agility rather than promote it.

This tool is also particularly effective and adds value in mergers and major transformations, as all mission critical projects are now monitored and managed from your DNC *in real time.*

An important final note is to make sure to have a secure lock on the door. This is not only the intelligence of your operation, but is literally its heart. The CEO and management can actively help increase security by frequently using this room.

42. E-Learning and Blended Learning and LMS

We have saved the best for last when it comes to one of the biggest forces of change currently rushing through company after company. All you need to know and find out is already available at your fingertips, with help of your smartphone. Even today, most users expect an individualized learning experience on demand, whenever needed, 24/7.

Using simple e-learning/online techniques and then blending them together with traditional, live *face-to-face* courses or workshop training has been confirmed to produce *drastically better results* and massively boost the agility within organizations. This will also create a side effect of increased customer loyalty, while you also profit from and enjoy massive cost reductions! Today's workforce now expects the same, seamless online experience, when it comes to training as they enjoy in most other parts of their lives..

Therefore, to truly become a learning organization, you need to take into account how people really learn. From our research we now understand that people gain knowledge according to the generally accepted 70-20-10 rule.

- 10 % is the average gain by formal learning. Today, formal learning can be done effectively by using a powerful combination of tailor made courses and universal *off-the-shelf* courses.
- 20 % is the average gain realized when colleagues and peers share knowledge. This can now be accomplished by utilizing a modern *Learning Management System* or LMS enhanced with social learning capabilities.
- 70 % is the remainder that occurs when learners search for knowledge on demand and solve a specific problem or challenge when the need is

identified. This is Kinesthetic learning. It is what people typically do when they are searching for more knowledge on for example Google, social media networks etc.

A modern and competitive company must be able to provide access to and support for all of these different learning styles within this growing, online arena. Here is where a modern Learning Management System is utilized to become the backbone for boosting your capacity for on-demand learning.

In his book, *The Fifth Discipline,* Author Peter Senge defined a learning organization as, "*An organization that constantly increases its capacity for success.*" Your chances for success will increase and your own effective learning organization will develop when you have addressed all these parameters and effectively implemented them throughout your organization.

The good news is that the task of learning and developing your employees has never been easier to accomplish! With all the modern techniques and methods available and since your future success depends upon staying current and agile, what are you waiting for?

Conclusion

The Governing Institutions, the Corporations and private individuals who choose not adapt to this new era of colossal transformation we are now entering will vanish or be left on the sideline as bystanders. At best, they will end up being forced to be reactive to all the new and exciting challenges and exponential growth caused by these new developments.

Think ahead just a few years from now. Some of us may then have children graduating from college. Some may be just starting a family, while still others will be heading into retirement. Regardless, all of us will be living in a world where we have either fought to solve the incredible challenges outlined in this book, or failed trying. Although newer challenges will still be bombarding us, we will have no option but to keep trying. This process is called *life*.

You have now been introduced to the wonders of metaphorical sailing in the treacherous and sometimes towering seas that are now building in today's business climate. We have used a sleek sailboat as our metaphor for your management group with you as El Capitan (the Skipper) or CEO.

It should now be painfully obvious that these seas are getting progressively, even exponentially rougher and more uncertain. There is no sign yet of any measurable change in this process. Our collective sin has been that we have been much too complacent with regards to honing our ability to get consciously agile. We now need to practice the art of looking forward more and master *acting decisively* instead of just relaxing into continued *business as usual*.

We will need a new and enhanced toolbox of skills and tools to confidently move into this turbulent weather system and this new era of *colossal transformation*. Explosive growth and new developments are making all product and service cycles increasingly shorter. Massive megatrends set against the background of an unpredictable and volatile economic, environmental and geopolitical storm squalls are *even now* generating the environment for a major perfect storm. This increasingly turbulent and uncertain environment will force corporations and institutions that wish to survive and thrive to become extremely vigilant, more trustworthy and most of all, very agile! In our opinion, corporate agility will be so vital going forward that if leaders disregard incorporating it into their every action, it will be equal to *abdicating their role as responsible leaders.*

For a good sailor, agility is second nature. For leaders of organizations, this quality has been and remains a struggle to take on. The problem is not so much in identifying the problem or taking a decision; *it is usually in its execution!* The tools for seeing the icebergs around us are getting more accurate, but ironically getting individuals in our organization to act, change or adjust direction is becoming increasingly *more difficult.* Up to now, we have enjoyed longer cycles, less competition and a more forgiving environment. Once upon a time the answer was to put finance and accounting in charge of squeezing every last penny out of one reorganization after another. Look around, is there anything still left to squeeze?

The answer going forward is *even now* proving to be the opposite of dumping the challenging and exciting task of leadership on your accountants, legal and other *masters of administration.* It is also not to prioritize actions that try to meet the increasingly disconnected or selfish demands from insulated, often isolated boards and investors. Tomorrow's successful leaders have to actively and consciously keep their hand firmly on the tiller and relearn the ability to execute change quickly and decisively.
Choosing to master agility, you will ultimately have to face all of the largest inhibitors of change and growth. One of the primary bottlenecks that encompass all four of these inhibitors is the decision and process of *doing or making it yourself.* This critical question pops up in virtually all of those following four areas:

- Systems and processes,
- Organizational structure,
- IT
- Company culture

You will need special tools and ability to responsibly master them to help you navigate all the internal challenges you are bound to face.

Furthermore, your agility challenge is seldom just in decision-making. That process was streamlined to a point *beyond efficiency* long ago. Rather, we see the *execution, implementation and adjustment of agile change* as the BIG issue here and now. In order to be effective, this has to be done with clearer forward vision and accurate, up to the minute information about all current variables, issues and situations. *Relying mostly on past performance will crush you!* Practicing "*The older I get, the better I was,*" is now a recipe for disaster. Going forward, the responsible CEO also needs a conscious, well-trained and agile crew. Your crew must be armed with simple and effective tools to rapidly execute course changes or adjustments that you, El Capitan, have ordered, usually based upon their accurate input.

Yes, your challenge to run a well-organized ship has increased, *but there is absolutely no need for despair*. Rather, there are many things you can do *immediately* to mitigate the biggest inhibitors of change, while mastering your ability to become agile. To review, the *worst inhibiting culprits* once again are; *Processes, IT systems, Organization* and *Culture*, all of which can be handled to encourage more agility instead of choking it off. In these pages we have mentioned a few of our favorite effective tools that have proven time and again to be helpful. In the end, all of these tools and suggestions, listed in section four have one objective in common. That objective is to *keep your customers happy and satisfied enough to buy more, while eagerly spreading the word about your products and services.* Continue with *business as usual* and expect your customers to move to more agile and competitive alternatives.

We sincerely hope this book has been a valuable read and that you have been inspired to join us on the path of *mastering corporate agility*. With any luck, you also see a possibility to use this as a handbook. Then you can practice using these tools to inspire your crew into action in real life. Let's move forward together in a joint quest of making your organization or institution more responsive to the changes and challenges that lie ahead. We also hope that you now have a heightened awareness of the uncertainty that lies before us all, but now feel as excited about the future as we do. You are also invited to participate and contribute to this conversation about agility by visiting our blog at www.masteringagilityblog.com.

Again, if you think the past thirty years of development have been fantastic, just wait for the next thirty!

They will be yielding COLOSSAL TRANSFORMATION in all areas of well-being, human interaction and enterprise; only now *you* will be successfully navigating this uncertainty, together with us, on the path of mastering agility in all we do.

Welcome aboard and prepare to cast off!

Index

Airbnb 18, 25
Amazon 11, 20, 30,
    39, 87, 100, 266
Asian Infrastructure
    Investment Bank 94
Baltic Dry Index 90
Bernays, Edward 47
Big Data 28, 30,
    31, 32, 34, 141, 230
Bill Gates 37
Bitcoin 25, 28,
    35, 88
Bitgold 25, 27, 88
Black Swan 65, 66, 103
Blockchain 26, 28
Blog 173, 228,
    311
Bonner, Bill 66, 85
Bretton Woods Agreement 16
Budget Process 44, 123
Business agility 146, 148,
    204, 280, 304, 321
Business as usual 10, 25,
    68, 73, 77, 87, 90, 94, 101, 103, 116, 132,
    144, 155, 160, 191, 223, 231, 245, 281,
    285, 290, 304, 322
Cars, Andy 289
Celente, Gerald 68, 124

Charles Darwin 8
Chopra, Deepak 135, 196
Climate change 36, 97, 106
Colony Collapse Disorder 105
Collard, Patrick 159, 197, 203
Commodification 11, 67, 231
Consciously agile 146, 152,
    160, 309
Convergence 6, 8, 11, 13
Creative Destruction 18, 37, 39,
    87, 143, 146
Customer capture 22,
    71, 84, 149
David Pogue 7
Davidson, James Dale 215
Decide 70, 143, 209,
    300
DevOps 18, 265, 266
Disintermediation 21, 27
Dislocation 20, 76, 79,
    81, 88, 123, 129
Disruptive technologies 25, 35
Earth Day 55, 97
E-commerce 22
EDX 26, 32
Empowered 111, 195, 227
Entitlement 46, 53, 116,
    120, 127, 201, 281

Entrepreneur..................................80, 119, 135, 145, 187, 203, 221, 279, 283
Facebook.......................................7, 30, 33, 113, 201, 286
Farage, Nigel.................................132
Fifth Discipline, The......................58, 308
Financial dislocation.....................76, 79, 81
Financial Repression 74
Fiverr 11, 26, 272, 277
Fractional Reserve Banking..........28, 87
Franklin, Benjamin.......................115
Future of Life Institute 7
Gary North....................................34
Globalization 12, 34, 57, 122, 129, 141, 293
Gold standard...............................15
Great Recession............................17, 72, 80, 86, 129, 190, 208
Greenspan, Alan 65, 80
Gutenberg......................................34
Hill, Napoleon...............................212
Holocene Extinction 105
Hot money.................................... 17, 74, 80, 89
HPPO 202, 242, 291, 306
In Search of Excellence.................ix, 237
Incorporate....................................26, 167, 173, 218, 256
Industrial Age................................15, 23, 119, 164, 188
Inhibitors of change 177, 190, 195, 220, 280, 287, 310
Internet of Things..........................29, 43
Irrational exuberance....................65, 80
Ives, Charles..................................132
Joseph Schumpeter 37, 146

Keynes, John Maynard....................72, 75, 148
Khan Academy 34
Kondratieff....................................63
Legacy..46, 79, 121, 163, 179, 187, 197, 297, 280, 285
Lewis, Michael 11, 128
Lipton, Bruce, Dr..........................132
LinkedIn 33, 34
Linux 7
Main Stream Media 22, 50, 132
Malthus, Thomas 45
Mark Twain 97
Market Pricing Mechanism.........89
Martin Armstrong 9, 63, 85, 131
Matt Callen 39
Max Tegmark...............................7
McKinsey......................................25, 46, 98, 151, 177, 237, 239, 261, 263, 277
Megatrends...................................3, 37, 45, 57, 118, 139, 147, 164, 224, 309
Mercedes.......................................10, 23
Mergers and Acquisitions............81, 84, 274, 286
Misinformation 35
Mixed-message 49, 191
Morgan, J.P 75, 134, 202, 212
Moore's Law 19, 42
Nader, Ralph................................68
Nassim Taleb................................65
Natural news................................94
Navigation....................................145
Negative Interest Rate Policy.....75
Neil Armstrong............................18
NINJA loans................................76
Nissan 10, 126
Normal distribution....................186

Open sourcing 7
O'Reilly, Bill 215
Outsource 12, 195, 272, 275, 299
Overcapacity 16, 64, 66, 70
Pareto's Law...................................119
Perfect storm 36, 61, 65, 139, 146, 164, 225, 309
Permission marketing....................22
Perot, Ross 127
Plaza Accord 80
Praxis 47, 49
Precarious 53, 77, 120, 122, 129, 146, 168, 188, 190, 264, 273, 282
Princeton Economics 9, 48, 85, 131
Quantitative Easing........................27, 47, 49
R&D....................................26, 47, 84, 87, 140, 170, 189, 254, 257, 266
Red Hat 7, 18, 266
Reframing 116
Relational business........................81
Research and Development..........18, 19, 87, 257, 258, 265
Respond 22, 54, 56, 58, 70, 115, 141, 145, 152, 153, 199, 217, 219, 225, 251, 288, 305, 321
Rockefeller......................................8
Senge, Peter...................................28, 308
Sheeple..............................50, 111, 113, 204
Siljerud, Peter..................................6
Singularity......................................4, 5, 7
social media 30, 48, 50, 83, 125, 200, 308
Sperry Univac 8, 42
Standing, Guy......................20, 119, 121, 205
TBTF 8, 11, 74, 146, 149, 150, 202, 229
The Precariat..............................20, 121, 122, 205
Titanic 133, 151, 152, 285
Too Big To Fail 8, 73, 133, 146
Toyota..10, 86, 289
Transactional business................81, 82, 169, 208
Transform 152, 164, 200, 204, 209, 220, 227, 229, 258, 265, 295, 304, 309, 311
Tyson, Mike..................................132
UBER..18, 25, 30, 65, 80, 116, 272
Vernor Vinge 5, 8
Virtuous circle 111
Volatility Index 76
Waterman, ...ix, xvi, 237
Wave cycles....................................9
World-class information 32, 34
Yen-Carry-Trade............................75
Zero Interest Rate Policy............79
Zombie 111, 114, 145, 204

Sources

i. http://futurewise.se

ii. Scientificamerican.com/october2015/Pogue

iii. 40 Years, 20 Million Ideas: The Toyota Suggestion System, Yuzo Yasuda, Productivity Pr (November 1990)

iv. "The Reckoning", by David Halberstam William Morrow & Co; 1st edition (September 1986)

v. http://www.cnbc.com/2015/10/26/toyota-at-top-in-global-vehicle-sales-for-first-9-months.html

vi. http://www.totallymsp.com/thoughts-on-technology-trends/

vii. http://www.mckinsey.com/insights/business_technology/disruptive_technologies

viii. http://reinvent.money

ix. http://www.edx.org

x. https://www.khanacademy.org

xi. http://www.garynorth.com/public/14327.cfm

xii. http://amazingsellingmachine.com

xiii. https://upload.wikimedia.org/wikipedia/commons/9/93/Moores_law_%281970-2011%29.PNG

xiv. http://www.econlib.org/library/Malthus/malPop.html

xv. http://www.mckinsey.com/insights/urbanization/urban_world_the_shifting_global_business_landscape

xvi. https://iamlegionnaire.wordpress.com/2015/03/25/select-quotes-from-edward-bernayss-propaganda/

xvii. http://www.discoverpraxis.com

xviii. http://money.usnews.com/money/retirement/articles/2013/05/13/the-baby-boomer-retirement-crunch-begins

xix. https://books.google.se/books?id=6NRDqtmcLZ8C&redir_esc=y

xx. http://news.yahoo.com/baby-boomer-retirement-crunch-begins-154056264.html

xxi. Photo from https://pixabay.com/en/hurricanes-kilo-ignacio-jimena-927042/

xxii. http://bonnerandpartners.com/category/parent/

xxiii. http://trendsresearch.com

xxiv. http://momentummachines.com

xxv. http://www.zerohedge.com/news/2015-11-10/dear-striking-fast-food-workers-meet-machine-just-put-all-you-out-job

xxvi. http://www.bloomberg.com/quote/BDIY:IND

xxvii. https://research.stlouisfed.org/fred2/series/M2V

xxviii. http://www.shadowstats.com

xxix. http://www.mnn.com

xxx. http://edition.cnn.com/2015/09/17/world/oceans-report/

xxxi. http://science.nationalgeographic.com/science/prehistoric-world/mass-extinction/

xxxii. Taken from a Speech from Oren Lyons, Tribal Council member of the Onondaga Tribe.

xxxiii. http://www.medicinenet.com/script/main/art.asp?articlekey=20909

xxxiv. Guy Standing, The Precariat, 2010

xxxv. http://www.futuretech.ox.ac.uk/oms-working-paper-future-employment-how-susceptible-are-jobs-computerisation-dr-carl-benedikt-frey-m

xxxvi. GENESIS RESEARCH REPORT OCT 2014
FAST FORWARD 2030 The Future of Work and the Workplace
http://www.cbre.com/Research-Reports/Future-of-Work

xxxvii. http://www.greatplacetowork.com/publications-and-events/blogs-and-news/2883-the-global-workplace-of-2030#sthash.sXcOW0sS.dpbs

xxxviii. http://trendsresearch.com

xxxix. http://www.lobbyists.info/About_Us.aspx

xl. https://www.brucelipton.com/books/biology-of-belief

xli. https://www.youtube.com/watch?v=hV-05TLiiLU

xlii. http://www.mckinsey.com/Insights/Organization/Agility_it_rhymes_with_stability?cid=other-eml-alt-mip-mck-oth-1512

xliii. CEB in the Harvard Business Review, July-August 2015 page 20

xliv. Taken from Sensational Presentation Skills by Kurt Larsson xlv. http://tompeters.com/docs/Structure_Is_Not_Organization.pdf

xlvi. Fortune, November 1, 2015, Every aspect of your business is about to change, p103

xlvii. "Make Overhead Cuts That Last," by John L. Neuman, Harvard Business Review, May 1975

xlviii. http://www.mckinsey.com/insights/innovation/disrupting_beliefs_a_new_approach_to_business-model_innovation?utm_content=buffer88d51&utm_medium=social&utm_source=facebook.com&utm_campaign=buffer

xlix. https://en.wikipedia.org/wiki/Entrepreneurship

l. http://techcrunch.com/2013/12/20/backed-by-steve-blank-more-startup-genome-founders-launch-next-gen-benchmarking-tool-for-startups/

li. https://www.cbinsights.com/blog/biggest-startup-failures/

lii. https://en.wikipedia.org/wiki/Business_Model_Canvas

liii. The word pretotype was coined by Alberto Savoia, formerly Innovation agitator at Google

liv. http://www.technologizer.com/2011/04/01/osborne-computer/

43. About the Authors

Something clicked when a former director from one of the world's most recognized consulting firms compared notes with an executive coach whose focus has been on the growing importance of conscious communication when doing collaborative business. Coming from opposing sides of both business and life, they absolutely agreed upon one thing; *future success depends upon your ability to sense and respond with agility to the colossal and quickening change that lies ahead.*

At their first meeting, they quickly realized that they were both addressing the same challenge; helping organizations and their leaders become more prepared for future shocks and opportunities through:

- Greater awareness of what lies ahead
- Improved tools, systems, processes for quicker results
- Increased flexibility to effectively and consciously implement and adjust for change
- More efficient communication to get key players quickly on board

The more they get to know each other, the more they realize their totally different backgrounds and diverse experiences powerfully compliment their different ways they choose to walk the path of agility, which they have now both chosen to master.

This book you now hold is the first result of this timely and exciting partnership. "Mastering Agility" contains both powerful and proven tools to increase your business agility, add value and cut costs; plus simple and effective tips to be more conscious of each application and its consequences.

Reading this compilation of their experiences and suggestions will help you develop a working knowledge what agility means, powerful tools and methods to comprehensively implement it, as well as a painfully clear understanding of the consequences should you choose to continue doing *business as usual*. The choice is yours; continue to use tools and processes that have their roots in the agricultural society or successfully navigate the danger and opportunity ahead. Agility in everything!

About The Authors:

Hans Amell, is a Harvard trained Swede who has lived in the U.S.A. since 1987. He is a McKinsey alumni, and former executive officer in leading global corporations such as Dun and Bradstreet Group, Cognizant Corp, Ericsson and others. He is called upon to execute major change in corporations and institutions via board memberships or via his company, Catalyst Acquisition Group. Mr. Amell is also the founding partner in the Minerva Group. He is a leading player in the cutting edge of agile consulting services with his *Dynamic Navigational System* products and in the application of efficient blended learning solutions for large organizations through Minerva. He was also the lead founder and Executive Chairman of Intrepid Learning Systems and created Gartner Custom Research after acquiring the GCR unit from Gartner. His passion is creating and applying agility within organizations that understand the need for quicker implementation of change, but very wisely recognize they will need assistance to accomplish this.

Kurt Larsson is an American who has been living in Sweden since the late 1980s. He has sold everything from Automobile tires in Houston, Texas to retail banking delivery systems in over twenty countries. He has driven his own educational consulting company, Expanding Understanding, for more than twenty years. His niche is transforming *consultative* business teams into *collaborative* ones. To do this he specializes in effective selling, leadership and customer service practices, focused on more conscious and efficient use of human communication and body language. His skills work perfectly in line with transforming management, sales and customer service teams from a transactional to a collaborative business model *where attracting customer loyalty is the prime goal.* He has now become an active member on both Catalyst's and Minerva's Board of directors.

For more information about the authors or to come in contact with them, you are welcome to contact us via our webpage located at www.minervagroup.com and follow our blog at www.masteringagilityblog.com.

Contact information:
Hans Amell: hamell@catalystacquisition.com,   Tel: US, +1 973 903 0100

Kurt Larsson: klarsson@catalystacquisition.com   Tel: Sweden, +46 708 736 375

We have neither asked for nor received any promotional money from any of the companies or people mentioned in this book. We offer them up only as examples we consider to bring home the point we are trying to make.

Made in the USA
Middletown, DE
07 February 2020